# the IWA in CANADA

# the IWA in CANADA

## the LIFE and TIMES of an INDUSTRIAL UNION

by Andrew Neufeld *and* Andrew Parnaby

Foreword by MARK LEIER

IWA Canada / New Star Books
Vancouver
2000

IWA Canada
500 – 1285 W. Pender St.
Vancouver, BC
V6E 4B2

New Star Books Ltd.
107 – 3477 Commercial Street
Vancouver, BC V5N 4E8
*www.NewStarBooks.com*

Co-ordinated by Norman Garcia

Edited by Audrey McClellan

Produced by Working Design  39

Scans by Broadway Printers  2

Printed and bound in Canada by Transcontinental Printing and Graphics

1  2  3  4  5   04  03  02  01  00

Canadian Cataloguing in Publication Data

Neufeld, Andrew, 1961 –
    The IWA in Canada

    Copublished by: IWA Canada.
    Includes bibliographical references.
    ISBN 0-921586-80-9

    1. IWA Canada – History. I. Parnaby, Andy, 1970 – II. IWA Canada. III. Title.
    HD6528.L92192 2000        331.88'13498'0971        C00-910978-1

*This book is dedicated to the pioneers who built this union;*
*to the activists whose faith and guts helped it grow;*
*and to all those who died in the service of the union or on the job.*

# Contents

# Foreword

There's a reason people often don't like the history we're taught in schools and find on the bestsellers' lists. Most of it is a cheery myth about wise politicians and far-sighted business leaders who built Canada and gave the rest of us jobs, homes, and the good life. It's not an accident that it is presented that way. History is a political weapon, and it is easy to see who is served by that tale.

What is worse, that version purposely leaves out the most exciting and valuable lesson history has to teach us: that the past was created through struggle and conflict. If we remember that, we understand that the present and the future are up for grabs. There was nothing inevitable or preordained about the past. That means that what working people do now matters. It will change things. That is a lesson some would like us to forget.

That's why this book is so important. It recaptures and retells the struggles of the IWA to create a better future. In it are the stories of the organizing drives, the strikes, the politics, and the personalities that shaped the union, the industry, and the nation. That is the grand narrative of the union, one that is intertwined with the history of Canada. It celebrates the successes and underscores the lessons of the failures.

At the same time, this book tells the stories that did not make the headlines: the history of small or distant locals, the day-to-day experiences, the hopes and fears of those IWA members who do not appear on television or in photographs of the union executive officers. These stories are just as significant, for they show that the union is about individuals and how their daily lives make up and influence the so-called big events that are recorded for posterity.

This book is important for what it tells us. It is also important for the challenges it leaves for others to take up. The authors have done a remarkable job of putting together a history of the union and many of its members. But they haven't told us the whole story, for that is too big and too complicated to be put between the covers of a single book. For every episode told here, hundreds of others remain to be written. This book opens the way for other members and other locals to tell their stories in greater number and detail, to add their history to our understanding of the past.

Nor can a single book provide the final word on the past. How crucial was the 1946 strike? What was the role of the Communist Party? What should have been done during Operation Solidarity? How should the union have responded to technological change and the needs of the environment? For the first time there is a popular account that addresses these questions. Yet while the authors have provided a balanced account, many readers will disagree with them, for there are no single, simple answers. That is the nature of history, and this book will encourage others to reinterpret the past. As they take up the debates, our understanding of the past will grow.

Finally, this is not the complete chronicle of this union because the IWA is still making history. The union continues to change itself and to change Canada. Its original slogan, "one union in wood," so powerful and encompassing in the early years, is now too small to hold the new vision of the IWA. The story does not end with the conclusion of this book.

How will the rest of the story unfold? That is up to the members of the IWA and other working people in Canada. In this book they have a powerful tool for regaining our past and for claiming our future.

*Mark Leier*
*Department of History*
*Simon Fraser University*

# Acknowledgements

IT IS OUR PLEASURE to recognize publicly the many people who made this book possible. Thanks to Dave Haggard, David Tones, and the rest of the IWA's officers for their recognition of the importance of the union's history and their unswerving determination to see that history shared. Thanks, too, to the IWA's Kim Pollock for his careful reading of the text and his written contributions. The support staff at the IWA's national and eastern Canada offices provided important technical and administrative assistance on a day-to-day basis. Of course this project would not have been possible without the efforts and generous contributions of countless rank-and-file members, officials, and staff, past and present, who built the union and left us their history and their example. We have tried to honour their experiences – and have used their voices in this book wherever possible.

Professor Mark Leier of Simon Fraser University has provided us with support and inspiration for many years now. George Brandak and his staff at UBC Special Collections provided invaluable assistance. Thanks to George Gidora of the Communist Party of Canada for sharing historic photos and granting us access to the Ernie Dalskog Collection. Sean Griffin and Dan Keeton shared the *Pacific Tribune* collection of photos, which filled large gaps in the 1970s and 80s. Thanks to Dale Fuller of the Hospital Employees' Union, Geoff Meggs, and the IWA's Aaron Mireau for their assistance. Thanks to Audrey McClellan for her calming influence and fine editing work, and to Kris Klaasen, Antonia Banyard, and the rest of the staff at Working Design for bringing their considerable talents to bear on the design and layout of the book.

Special mention of two individuals is in order. We are indebted to former IWA staff member Clay Perry who, decades ago, understood the importance of seeking out pioneer unionists and preserving their stories. Looking at the mounds of transcripts, documents, tapes, and photos that he amassed during his time with the IWA makes one thing perfectly clear: much of the heavy lifting was done for us.

Just as Clay helped lay the foundation for this book, Norman Garcia, current editor of the *Lumber Worker*, helped construct it. Put simply, there is no one we wish to acknowledge more than Norman. His tireless work as researcher, photo and graphics guy, and critic was pivotal to the making of this book, and we are indebted to him for the good spirit, humour, and occasional stogey that he brought to this project. Of particular importance to us was his unwavering insistence on the importance of the locals, the local stories, and the rank-and-file members. *Muchas gracias.*

And finally, thanks from Andy Neufeld to Debby Meyer for her support and patience throughout this project. Andy Parnaby wishes to acknowledge Jill Perry for her ongoing help and the Parnaby clan for just being there.

# the IWA in CANADA

CHAPTER ONE

# *Radical Roots*

# Radical Roots

THE WORKING MEN AND WOMEN who attended the International Woodworkers of America's founding convention in Tacoma, Washington, in 1937 shared a simple, but compelling idea. Only by organizing all workers "from the stump to the finished product" could they tip the balance of power on the job, which had shifted so decisively in the boss's favour with the onset of the Great Depression.

This commitment to forging one big union of all woodworkers – a bold and controversial step – linked the IWA to a radical heritage that ran deep into the North American working-class past. No doubt many of the delegates at the IWA's inaugural meeting understood this fact, as many were veterans of the labour movement and had cut their political teeth in such organizations as the Industrial Workers of the World and the Lumber Workers Industrial Union, to name but two. Like the IWA, these earlier unions had posed a fundamental challenge to the mainstream labour movement – dominated since the late nineteenth century by the American Federation of Labor (AFL) and its Canadian counterpart, the Trades and Labor Congress (TLC) – which embraced a craft model, as opposed to an industrial model of union organization. Chartered by the AFL-TLC, craft unions organized more "respectable" skilled workers, such as plumbers and masons, into exclusive organizations. While various craft unions were active among the lumber industry's skilled trades, for the most part they wanted little to do with the rough, unskilled, and largely immigrant "timber beasts."

The IWA, then, was the latest in a long line of organizations that sought to break the stranglehold of the craft unions and organize the unorganized. While few of these pioneer industrial unions survived the early decades of the century, their struggles for a more inclusive, democratic, and militant labour movement and a better life for all working people – regardless of "race, color, religious or political affiliation" – provided the foundation upon which the IWA was built.

## Loggers in a Dangerous Time

From the late nineteenth to the early twentieth century, the Canadian economy underwent a significant transformation. Small shops, once the home to skilled tradesmen, slowly gave way to larger, more complex corporations.

Workplaces expanded in size and sophistication, drawing more and more men and women into urban areas to work for wages, and machines of all kinds revolutionized the world of work. At the same time, the industrial frontier, once bounded by the resource-rich St. Lawrence River and Great Lakes region, shifted westward as capitalists looked to northern Ontario, the Prairies, and British Columbia for new investment opportunities, new markets, and new ways to make a buck.

The lumber industry, like the economy as a whole, changed too as entrepreneurs like Frederick Weyerhaeuser rushed to exploit northern Ontario's untapped pine and spruce and the massive, lush stands of Douglas fir on the Pacific Coast. "I followed the pine trees that were disappearing in Minnesota and came to Canada in 1902," an American businessman working in Ontario remarked. "The greatest forest region in the world, unquestionably, is the Pacific slope of North America," gushed *Harbour and Shipping*, a Vancouver-based business publication. "In its forests are the timber giants of the earth, world famous, oldest in years, largest in size, yielding the best and clearest timber available and in the largest dimensions." By the early decades of the century, Ontario and BC were the country's top lumber producers ahead of Quebec and the Maritimes, regions that had dominated the lumber trade since colonial times.

As the organization of the lumber industry changed, so too did the origins of the people who worked in the woods. In the early years, when the industry was centred in the northeastern corner of the continent, the Canadian lumberjacks – or "Canucks" as the Americans called them – came primarily from rural areas in the Maritimes, Quebec, and southern Ontario, supplementing their work on the farm with work in the woods to make ends meet. But as the 1900s began, the federal government, committed to a policy of settling the new western provinces, set about bringing millions of immigrants to Canada. Drawn primarily from the British Isles and continental Europe, many of the new arrivals worked in the mines, on the railways, and in the factories of the burgeoning industrial economy, while countless others, especially those from Scandinavia, headed for logging camps and mills in the north and west. There they joined the streams of French-Canadian workers that pooled in northern Ontario, as well as the First Nations and Asian workers who could be found in the ranks of BC's handloggers and mill hands.

"Quite a few had left wives and families in Finland, came over here, and worked all those years in this country, and sent monthly remittances to their people in Finland and never went back, never saw their families again," recalled Fred Niemi, a veteran Finnish logger from Ontario, in Donald McKay's *The Lumberjacks*. "Worked here, died here, and their families never

*As the organization of the lumber industry changed, so too did the origins of the people who worked in the woods.*

IN THE LAND
OF GIANT TREES

Near Fred Band's
sawmill, in Port
Alberni, BC, circa
1910.

IWA LOCAL 1-85 ARCHIVES

came over. Sometimes they'd sing songs in a homesick vein, sing and hum to themselves to release their feelings." After several decades of massive immigration, the face of logging, both literally and metaphorically, had changed immensely. As one logger remarked, "It looked like the goddamn United Nations out there."

But as culturally diverse as woodworkers were, on the job they faced the common concerns associated with being working-class men in that era: finding work, poor living and working conditions, and technological change. Like

## Getting the Wood Out the Hard Way

THE PRECISE METHODS and tools used to "get the wood out" varied with local conditions and the preferences of both bosses and workers. In general, though, early fallers worked in pairs or in groups of three and used cross-cut saws, axes, and wedges to, in the words of logger-poet Peter Trower, "[gnaw] the big ones down the hard way."

Once on the ground, the trees were bucked, or cut, into appropriate lengths by a single man with a cross-cut saw and skidded out of the woods by teams of oxen or horses along the "skid road" – a pathway made of roughly hewn logs laid side by side like railway ties. The bucked logs were roped or chained together, and a skidding crew, armed with

RIVER DRIVE, BULL RIVER, BC

**Drawn from the ranks of the winter crews, the river drivers used long poles to poke and prod the logs downstream, some working from the river banks, others on the water in narrow boats.**
BC ARCHIVES F-0972

iron bars, peavies, and other tools, assisted the teamster in pulling the logs to the loading area.

As Jack Aye, a pioneer logger and mill worker from the BC Interior, observed in Ken Drushka's *Tie Hackers to Timber Haulers*: "A mill in those days, to get that much lumber, had to have a big crew in the bush, a lot of men and a lot of horses…There would probably be about sixty horses out in the woods with them, and every time you put a team of horses out there you had to put a man with them, to drive them."

The final stage in this arduous process involved moving the logs from the loading area, or landing, to the sawmill. Depending on the region, this was accomplished in many ways. In northern Ontario and parts of the BC Interior, for example, workers stacked the logs on massive sleighs that hauled each load to nearby rivers or streams in preparation for the annual log drive in the spring. In coastal regions, where rivers were scarce or too shallow for the massive logs, logging railroads were used to accomplish this final task. ☐

LAMB'S LUMBER
CAMP, 1926

By World War I,
massive immigration
had changed the face
of logging in Canada;
the crew of this
lumber operation near
Menzies Bay, like most
in BC, was largely
Scandinavian.

BC ARCHIVES D-04834

the "Canucks" of earlier decades, woodworkers in northern Ontario, parts of Saskatchewan, and the Interior of British Columbia were drawn from the ranks of unemployed labourers on a seasonal basis – the need for men peaking in the fall and winter when the demand for labour was at its highest. In contrast, on the Pacific Coast, with its temperate climate, large trees, and heavily capitalized industry, loggers were able to ply their trade on a more or less full-time basis. Indeed, unlike many of their Interior counterparts who were tied to a Prairie farm, these men considered Vancouver their home base, migrating to the waterfront district of the city whenever camps shut down – due to fire, poor weather, and market fluctuations – or when they needed a holiday from the hardships of work.

"Of course loggers in those days could go back and forth fairly easily," Jack Gillbanks, logger, union activist, and IWAer, recounted. "I worked up in [a] camp for nine months I think it was, which was quite a long time for that. And then I went down to Vancouver…Down on Cordova and Carrall, that's where you'd meet everybody. And we used to get into all kinds of discussions. Chew the rag and soap boxing on the corners. There was lots of that going on." These distinctive patterns of employment, rooted in the uneven development of the lumber industry, played an important role in shaping patterns of unionization in the woods. Support for industrial unionism emerged first amongst the full-time, professional loggers on the Coast, not the farmer-loggers of the Interior.

At the turn of the century, logging operations in both eastern and western Canada, as in other regions of North America, were dependent on the strength and skill of loggers, the brute force of horses and oxen, and the rushing water of rivers and streams to "cut and get out." While the more "respectable" elements of the working class, and society generally, often viewed the work that "rough" loggers did with skepticism, if not outright disdain, timber beasts themselves understood that mastering the arts and mysteries of the job required equal amounts of brains and brawn – talents that underpinned their ability to influence the timing and pacing of work and, as a result, were vital to an operation's success. "The faller is the most important man in the woods…as one tree broken by a good faller would mean a loss greater than two or three days' wages," remarked one employer.

But loggers' status on the job started to change in the late nineteenth and early twentieth century. At that time, lumber operators, like employers in other sectors of the economy, experimented with new labour-saving machinery, new ways of handling their "human resources," and new methods of organizing the labour process to boost both productivity and profit, a practice that persists to this day. This process of technological change in the woods was marked by distinct regional patterns. Faced with smaller trees and abundant rivers to transport cut logs, few operators in northern Ontario, Saskatchewan, or the Interior of BC found it necessary or economical to invest in the mechanization of logging. In contrast, in the early 1890s, British Columbia's Pacific Coast operators started to introduce steam-powered donkey engines to the skidding process and invested in logging railways to move cut logs to the mill. Donkey engines enabled logging operators to move logs over greater distances at a faster rate of speed – pulling the log from the forest floor with brute force.

"The 'donkey' surged against its moorings; its massive spread began to rear and pitch as if striving to bury its nose in the earth. There was a startling uproar in the forest, wholly beyond seeing distance mind you," an anonymous writer observed in 1906, highlighting just how impressive, if not frightening, the new ground-lead system really was. "In a moment a log came hurtling out of the underbrush nearly 1000 feet away. It burst into sight as if it had wings, smashing and tearing its own pathway…It is an awesome sight to see a log six feet through and 40 feet long bounding toward you as if the devil were in it."

The changes brought about by the use of the ground-lead system of yarding were superseded in the early twentieth century by the widespread adoption of a more sophisticated – and more efficient – system of "overhead" logging on the Pacific Coast, a development analyzed in depth by historian Richard Rajala. Although the precise nature of overhead logging systems varied widely, the basic form, as the name implies, was a complex arrangement of cables and rigging used to lift logs off the ground and transport them to the landing area. Originally employed in parts of the Great Lakes region and in the swamps of the southern United States at the turn of the century, these "flying machines" allowed Pacific Coast operators to harvest trees on terrain too rough for the ground-lead system. But as many loggers knew well, by eliminating the need for animal power, speeding up the pace of work, and redefining what it meant to be a logger, the widespread use of this new technology had a profound impact on workers themselves: eliminating some skilled positions such as the teamster, while creating new ones like the high rigger.

It also made an already hazardous job even deadlier. "One place I was working, three guys got killed in four days," Waddy Weeks, a long-time Vancouver Island logger, recounted in *The Lumberjacks*:

> There was a Chinaman got killed, a faller got killed, and an old guy who was slinging riggin' on a donkey. The first one killed was the Chinaman. He was cutting wood for the steam engine when a line hit him on top of the head. You get a break in a skyline, 1000 feet long and it strung up there like a fiddle string, and when that breaks, Lord God, something goes. That thing just wipes everything right out, a big steel line like that. Woosh! You could hear the thing starting to go and guys were off at a bloody gallop.

UP THE TREE

**A high rigger swings a bull block around the spar tree at a high-lead show.**
PHOTO COURTESY
GEORGE McKNIGHT

FLYING MACHINE
More intricate high-lead systems were eventually developed, like this one at Lake Logging, near Lake Cowichan. They made it possible to log on ground that was too rough to work with a ground-lead system.

Well, the next day old Charlie, a big old Finn, was standing in the bight of a cable and when the donkey started up it got him. That man weighed 240 pounds and it up-ended him 20 feet away and busted his neck. Never knew what hit him, killed him instantly…[T]here was three of them in four days. There was this guy from Ontario and he said, "Oh my God, is this the way they work out here? I'm gettin' the hell out of here." We always used to knock off, you know, go home for the afternoon, if anybody got killed. It was always the custom. One a day was enough, they'd say, let's get the hell out of here.

In places like Lake Cowichan on Vancouver Island – where in the early 1900s logging was done within earshot of the company town – it was not uncommon for residents to hear the bell of the ambulance as it sped to the scene of an accident. "Sometimes the people in the houses knew when an accident had happened," Myrtle Bergren, historian, union activist, and wife of IWA founder Hjalmar Bergren, recalled. "They might hear from the logging close by, after the donkey machines came, the seven long piping blasts on the steam which meant a man had been maimed or killed, and the skin rose in gooseflesh on those who heard, and the word spread, and dread clutched the hearts of women until they knew." For the women of Lake Cowichan, as for the wives of woodworkers across the country, the loss of a husband or son to injury or death was not just an emotional loss, as painful as that was, but a financial one as well. At a time when few jobs were open to working-class women and no social safety net existed, it was all but impossible for a woman to replace her husband's lost income. The loss of a male breadwinner, then, left families struggling day in and day out to make ends meet, a reality that laid bare just how precarious life on and off the job was for working people.

At the same time that the world of work – especially on the Pacific Coast – was undergoing a significant transformation, loggers faced other challenges as well. Company managers and foremen treated workers brutally. They hired their employees at the lowest possible rate, pushed them ruthlessly on the job when market conditions were favourable, and chopped their wages or fired them when lumber prices plummeted. Bosses did not suffer opposition gladly – sending workers "down the road" at the first sign of trouble. Given the instability of the lumber economy, few operators deemed it necessary to invest in the long-term health or security of their workers; it was an approach to labour relations that was easily justified by the popular image of loggers as tough, resilient, working stiffs. "They know when they go to work that they must put up with the most primitive kind of camp accommodation," Thomas Shaughnessy, president of the Canadian Pacific Railway, once remarked. "[I]t is only

*At a time when few jobs were open to working-class women and no social safety net existed, it was all but impossible for a woman to replace her husband's lost income.*

13

prejudicial to the cause of immigration to import men who come here expecting to get high wages, a feather bed, and a bath tub."

This appalling lack of concern was reflected in the condition of the logging camps. In all regions of the country they were condemned by workers, unions, and health inspectors for their unsanitary conditions, poor sleeping arrangements, rotten grub, and lack of facilities. "We are dealing with an industry still determined by pioneer conditions of life," a US commission investigating labour unrest in the woods concluded in 1918. Like thousands of loggers across the continent, Neil Gainey lived and worked in these pioneer conditions. Born in 1890, Gainey started his life in the woods at the age of 14, working as a timekeeper for a small outfit on the shores of Georgian Bay, Ontario. In his late teens, Gainey, like other men of his age and class, tramped west looking for work, eventually settling in British Columbia after stints in Montana, Idaho, and Washington. "See when wages were around two and a half, three dollars a day, you had to be a pretty good lumberjack to earn three dollars a day and those were the good old days you work ten hours. Six days a week anyhow," Gainey recalled later. "And if they want to work you seven, there was nothing you could do about it." But meagre earnings and long hours were not the only problems. "We wanted showers in the camps, that was one of our demands. But people in town, business people, would make fun of that. I remember one guy I talked to, he said, 'Showers in camps! I've never in my life seen a clean logger!' So I said, 'Of course you haven't, you asshole, we don't have showers!!'" Gainey's rage – still in his voice decades after he retired – was directed at both the lack of facilities in the camps and, more importantly, the "business people" who refused to treat him, and others like him, as an equal.

In this context of economic boom and bust, technological change, and poor living and working conditions, many loggers fought back. Individually they demonstrated their opposition to exploitative foremen by quitting their jobs and tramping from camp to camp looking for a better deal. While employers often cited this behaviour as an example of workers' "bad attitude," for loggers themselves, "taking off down the road" was about resistance. "I cannot make any more here, I made $21 clear for March after paying for board, doctor $1.00 [and] compensation 30¢," 19-year-old Ivan K. wrote from Comox on Vancouver Island to his mother, Anna, in Vancouver in 1921. "The Campbell River Company is only 14 miles from us and I might go over there as soon as it is open. The pay is more there." Others took matters on the job into their own hands. "In one case [Rough-house Pete] had a feud with a camp cook," Al Parkin, IWA member and editor of the *BC Lumber Worker*, recalled in *Men of the Forest*:

*While employers often cited this behaviour as an example of workers' 'bad attitude,' for loggers themselves, 'taking off down the road' was about resistance.*

Now these were the days when there was no union, and there was only one way of expressing disapproval to the boss or anybody else, and that was by individual action. So he walked into the cookhouse one night, sat down, and looked at the usual stew…and decided that he had enough of it.

So he just simply got up and started down from one end of the table to the other, kicking all the food off as he went along. A lot of it landed in the laps of the poor devils – fellow workmen and so on – you know, hot potatoes and gravy and so on.

By the early years of the twentieth century, many sought out collective solutions as well. Among the most militant organizations to emerge was the Industrial Workers of the World.

## 'The Working Class and Employing Class Have Nothing in Common'

Fellow workers!…We are here to confederate the workers of this country into a working class movement that shall have for its purpose the emancipation of the working class from the slave bondage of capitalism…The aims and objects of this organization should be to put the working class in possession of the economic power, the means of life, in control of the machinery or production and distribution, without regard to capitalist masters.

ROUGHING IT IN
THE BUSH, 1920s

An employee of the Victoria Lumber and Manufacturing Company takes time out on Sunday for a shave and a haircut.

IWA LOCAL 1-80 ARCHIVES

With these fiery words, William "Big Bill" Haywood, secretary of the Western Federation of Miners, welcomed more than 200 delegates to the founding convention of the Industrial Workers of the World held in Chicago on 27 June 1905. Drawn from the ranks of a wide range of socialists and labour radicals, the IWW, or "the Wobblies," emerged at a time when sweeping economic and technological change, coupled with employers' time-honoured use of the speed-up and piece-rate system, reduced workers' power both on and off the job. At a time when the Trades and Labor Congress and the American Feder-

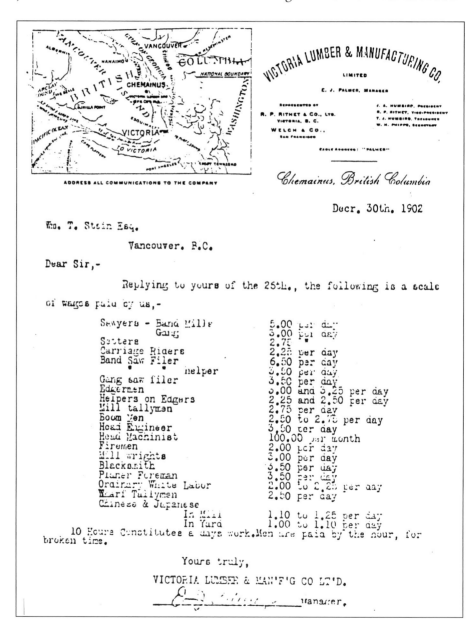

**UNEVEN SCALES**

In the early years, white workers monopolized the more lucrative positions of sawyer and saw filer, while Japanese and Chinese workers were usually confined to the unskilled position of general labourer – and even in this poorly paid job classification, they were paid less than "ordinary white labor."

IWA ARCHIVES

ation of Labor, dubbed by some critics as the American *Separation* of Labor, showed little interest in organizing workers on the margins of society, the Wobblies crafted a democratic, highly decentralized form of union organization that suited the lives of its core constituency well: the unskilled, the migratory, and the foreign born – those who did not fit into the established craft union structure.

On a day-to-day basis, the IWW, unlike its more conservative rivals, charged low membership fees and permitted any member to be an organizer. As well, in many towns and cities Wobbly halls served as a mail drop, dorm, hiring hall, and social centre – services important to workers who tramped from place to place looking for work and, perhaps more importantly, to forging solidarity. On the job, the organization refused to sign contracts with employers, rejected electoral politics, and believed in spontaneous strikes – "miniature revolutions" – and sabotage. "Everything is founded on the job, everything comes from conditions on the job which is the environment and life of toiling slaves," one Wobbly opined. By confronting the power of the boss directly and organizing all workers – regardless of "color, creed, or religion" – into one big industrial union, the Wobblies hoped to bring about a general strike wave that could topple the entire oppressive system. Known to labour historians and workers alike as "syndicalism," to Big Bill Haywood the Wobbly way was just "socialism with its working clothes on."

This mix of revolution and reform found its most receptive audience amongst the so-called blanket stiffs, single men who worked their way from northern Ontario to British Columbia and across the Pacific Northwest with their possessions rolled into blankets and carried on their backs. By the early decades of the twentieth century, approximately 50,000 blanket stiffs crisscrossed the country, labouring in the construction, transportation, and primary resource sectors of the burgeoning industrial economy.

Like the "Wops" and "Bohunks" who blasted rock, pounded spikes, and laid track, woodworkers also joined the Wobblies to protest the deadly working conditions, poor wages, and lack of security that marked their work-a-day world. In northern Ontario the IWW established a branch in Sault Ste. Marie around 1910 and, about the same time, organized sleigh drivers in the Algoma district; individual Wobblies also played a crucial role in sustaining radical labour politics in the north after the IWW withered as an organization during World War I. "[T]he plan of the IWW was to organize the lumber industrey Makeing [sic] Port Arthur their base," an Ontario Provincial Police officer wrote. According to Peter Campbell, a historian of Canadian labour radicalism, the activists who piqued the OPP's interest – Finnish Americans who fled

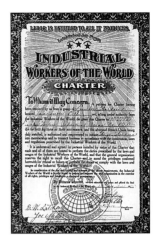

**IWW CHARTER**
The IWW charter proclaims that labour is entitled to all it produces.
IWA ARCHIVES

compulsory military service and government assaults on labour radicals in the US – were part of a wider immigrant Finnish community with a tradition of class politics.

In British Columbia the IWW was at its strongest in the woods during the years leading up to World War I, its activism amongst the timber beasts running alongside campaigns in other industries like the hardrock mines of the Boundary area. Fragmentary evidence suggests that the Wobblies led union drives amongst loggers in several regions of the province including Vancouver Island, the Lower Mainland, and the Kootenays. And even when not active in the province, Wobbly agitation in the woods of northern California, Oregon, Washington, and Idaho often spilled over the border; in 1907, 1912, 1913, and 1917 strikes in the US for the eight-hour day and better camp conditions shut down or reduced production on both sides of the line.

## Breaking Down Racial Barriers

LIKE THE IWW, radicals in the Lumber Workers Industrial Union and the One Big Union were critical of the anti-Asian policies of the mainstream labour movement and Canadian society more generally. To break down barriers between workers of different races, OBU organizers often attended political meetings held at the local "Hindoo" temple in Vancouver; as well, the union opened an office in the heart of the city's Chinatown to attract Asian workers to the cause and made attempts to bring Native workers into the union fold as well.

"You say I don't want the oriental into the union, his eyes are slant; you don't want the Hindu, why not [?][A]s they are not to blame for the place where they were born; I can't help I was born across the water. You people have got to help them," H. Allman, a delegate and member of the BC Loggers' Union (later the Lumber Workers Industrial Union), told the Western Labor Conference in 1919. "The master class wants them in order to whip the white slave, beat him down to a lower standard, and therefore you must take in the oriental if you are to do away with the club the master has over you and you are going to uphold your own standard of living." His remarks were greeted with applause.

Asian workers themselves were also active. In New Westminster, BC, for example, the Chinese Nationalist League endorsed a motion to support the burgeoning Lumber Workers Industrial Union. At the same time, approximately 200 Japanese Canadians at the Swanson Bay sawmill near Ocean Falls, BC, formed the "Nihonjin Rodo Kumiai" or "Labour Union" and went on strike in 1919, demanding the abolition of separate wage rates for white and Asian workers. By 1924 the Labour Union, renamed the Japanese Camp and Mill Workers' Union, had about 1,600 members and published a daily newspaper; two years later the organization was admitted to the Vancouver Trades and Labour Council. But as historians Audrey Kobayashi and Peter Jackson have noted, "There was never any discussion of integration of its members with white sawmill workers" – not until the emergence of the communist-led Lumber Workers Industrial Union of Canada in the 1930s.

Although small in numbers, the IWW had a reputation for militancy – and its impact went far beyond those who actually signed a Wobbly card. When boss loggers in BC met to discuss the state of the industry, they spoke often of "difficulties between camps in labour matters" – including direct action on the job, work stoppages, and quickie strikes, to this day known to loggers as a "wobble" – committed by card-carrying members of the IWW and those inspired by their spontaneous calls to strike, strike, strike. An unknown labour radical, likely a member of the Communist Party of Canada, writing for a party publication in the late 1920s, described the activities of a fictitious Wobbly organizer in Ontario this way:

> Two or three days after…[he] had sized up the situation and lined up his men the proposition would be put up in the bunk house at night. Clean beds, better food – STRIKE – the one word with a magnetic and instinctive appeal against exploitation and filth. "We'll nail the Preamble [of the IWW Constitution] to the wall Boys." "Ah ban tank its goddam high time," said the Big Swede and none contradicted him…
>
> "All right boys, roll out!" [bawled the camp boss the next morning]. "Yust a meenut," says the Big Swede, "Ah ban tank ve strike from the yob this morning." "Strike! Hell, you can't pull that stuff here, if you won't work you'd better pack your kit down the hill." (Down the hill meaning anywhere from six to sixty miles, thru mountain road, portage, and frozen lake) "Yah," rumbled the Big Swede, rolling a cigarette, "Ah ban tank we stay right here."
>
> Sensing that his immediate world of authority and logs had stripped its gears and would no longer rotate…the Camp boss got down to business. "What's your trouble?" "Plenty," says the Big Swede. "[V]e like dem goddam beds yanked out wit spring beds and someting like clean mattresses put in…Ve like to mak a dry-room so the Yacks are not steamed to a pulp in the bunkhouse and choked by stinkin socks hanging around mit the stove. And nother ting, ve like beter you feed the pigs separate by us. There is just a little goddam too much vat the company has got that the Yacks and the pigs are yust the same, and by yimminy ve gon to change that idee."

Intended to be a humourous sketch of camp life, this account of the "Big Swede" captures both the potent power of a camp foreman and how Wobbly-inspired activism fulfilled some of the most elemental needs of workers – the desire for a clean bed, edible food, proper amenities, and to be treated with more respect than a "goddam" pig.

But by the mid to late 1910s, the Wobblies had all but disappeared from

**GREATEST THING ON EARTH**

The IWW called for "one big union" of all workers and the "abolition of the wage system."
IWA ARCHIVES

**SINGING SOLIDARITY**

The IWW songbook encouraged workers to "fan the flames of discontent."
IWA ARCHIVES

**GETTING TO WORK**

Packed in a "crummy" like sardines, loggers risked their lives just getting to work.

IWA ARCHIVES

the woods of British Columbia and Ontario. The reasons for this downfall were many. On the eve of the Great War a severe economic slump, coupled with the end of the railway building boom, weakened the organization considerably, a condition made worse by the union's own internal divisions. What was more, both government and employers in the US and Canada fought the IWW with great – and sometimes deadly – force. "[T]he time has now arrived to prosecute and imprison [the IWW] on every possible occasion," the BC attorney-general told the superintendent of police in 1911. Neil Gainey was an IWW organizer during this period, operating mostly out of Idaho, eastern Washington, and parts of BC; his recollections illustrate the viciousness of this opposition and – graphically – one reason why the IWW faltered:

> They [employers] used to hire gunmen whenever we camped, to keep [union] delegates out, to keep the organizers out of there. And I think one day there was a camp delegate, you see, and they'd be working on the job and organizing at the same time. Once the gunmen found them there they'd chase them right out of town. A lot of them got more than chased too. There was a lot of guys disappeared there...
>
> [I]n the First World War the union got pretty busted up. They railroaded the guys out of there and put them in jail. If they couldn't do anything else, they bagged them anyhow and put them on the streets with a ball and chain. But in the States it was worse than Canada. I understand there was a strike, the first thing they did was build a big bullpen...

They'd have these gunmen…there guarding that thing and they'd have them all herded into the big bullpen. A big crowd. They'd keep them there for months…And then they'd frame [the organizers and] start to pass out criminal sentences…[Y]ou could pretty nearly convict a man under anything there, for doing anything.

The IWW emerged at a time when woodworkers, like many working people, faced poor working conditions, staggering class inequality, and a labour movement unwilling to organize those on the margins. Although the Wobblies never established a permanent presence in the woods, its vision of industrial union-ism persisted. Many of those who preached the Wobbly creed or were simply enticed by its defiant temperament ("Fire your boss!") later channelled their political energies into organizations like the Lumber Workers Industrial Union and the One Big Union, unions that gathered steam as workers across Canada were swept up in the turmoil of World War I and a national labour revolt.

## From World War to Class War

From 1917 to 1920, Canada, like other industrialized countries, was rocked by unprecedented levels of class conflict. The climax of this labour revolt took place in 1919, when a massive strike wave rolled across the country. That year,

GENERAL STRIKE

**The Winnipeg General Strike of 1919 marked the climax of the national labour revolt that followed World War I.**

MANITOBA ARCHIVES N-2762

21

*'The realization
is growing that
there is a class
war, a war in
which there is
no discharge.'*

about 150,000 workers participated in 428 separate confrontations, including local battles, wider general strikes that shut down entire industries and cities – the largest and most well-known taking place in Winnipeg – and sympathy strikes held in solidarity with the men and women on the picket lines in the Manitoba capital. In total, the equivalent of 3,401,843 days of work were lost to industrial strife. "[T]he realization is growing that there is a class war, a war in which there is no discharge," William Yates, a member of the Amalgamated Association of Street and Electric Railway Employees in New Westminster, BC, remarked in 1919.

From coast to coast, workers in nearly all sectors of the economy – from telephone operators and waitresses to miners and loggers – confronted both employers and the government for higher wages, better working conditions, and union recognition; others called for a radical reconstruction of society and the creation of a "new democracy" based on production for use, not for profit. "Let the workingman, the one who produced, have control and then we shall see the light of a new dawn," exclaimed Resina Asals, a member of the Regina Women's Labor League. Surveying the situation in the eye of the storm in Winnipeg, the commissioner of the Royal North-West Mounted Police, A.B. Perry, remarked: "At the foundation of this agitation is [a] general restlessness and dissatisfaction. The greater number of labour men, and probably the community as a whole[,] are in an uncertain, apprehensive, nervous and irritable temper."

The causes of this restlessness and dissatisfaction were many. With the out-

## State Repression of Labour and the Left

THE FEDERAL GOVERNMENT learned its lessons from World War I and the national labour revolt that followed. It merged the western-based Royal North-West Mounted Police and the old eastern-oriented Dominion Police in 1920 to create a single national police force – the Royal Canadian Mounted Police – to better keep an eye on labour radicals and other subversives across the country. While both forces had experience operating labour spies, the creation of the RCMP was evidence of Ottawa's desire to place matters of internal security on a more comprehensive footing. To this end, a Criminal Investigation Branch (CIB) was created to supervise and co-ordinate the activities of secret agents on a national basis. The role of the CIB was supported by a new Central Registry, an elaborate file system that contained records of individuals, publications, and organizations thought to be subversive. The information gathered by the CIB and archived by the Central Registry was passed along to the prime minister, cabinet, and other senior government officials by the newly created Liaison and Intelligence Officer. By the early 1920s, then, the government was able to keep tabs on union activists with ease – and it did so with great zeal. By 1977 this registry contained nearly 700,000 files and a name index of 1.3 million Canadians, including many members of the IWA. □

break of war in Europe in 1914, the depression of the pre-war years gave way to a robust wartime economy, and workers, who just years before faced widespread unemployment and meagre wages, found themselves once more in demand. But this initial wave of enthusiasm for the war eventually dissipated. On the homefront, manufacturers continued to make enormous profits while inflation pushed the cost of living up – making it extremely hard for workers and their families to make ends meet. In its bid to mobilize the country for war, the federal government suspended civil liberties and imposed conscription over the heated opposition of workers across the country. "There were two major views on the War, that of the exploiter and that of the exploited," stated Alphonse Verville, former president of the Trades and Labor Congress and member of parliament for Montreal-Hochelaga. Overseas, the success of the 1917 Russian Revolution inspired Canadian workers who were already battling the government's recruitment policies and debating the possibilities of reconstructing a society so deeply defined by class inequality.

In the labour movement itself, significant changes, years in the making, also fuelled the fires of working-class opposition. Militant workers, most notably in the west, were becoming increasingly dissatisfied with the moderate, eastern-based leadership of the Trades and Labor Congress. Led by the Socialist Party of Canada (SPC), several hundred delegates – loggers and mill workers among them – attended the Western Labor Conference in Calgary in March 1919 to lay bare a more radical agenda for the labour movement and create a rival umbrella organization called the One Big Union (OBU). The prominence of the Socialist Party at this historic event reflected a wider resurgence of left-wing forces across the country – the rising tide of working-class activism pushing more moderate political ideologies to the sidelines.

Founded in 1904, the party emerged at the same time as the IWW, and like the Wobblies, the SPC stood for revolution, not reform. Unlike its syndicalist rival, however, its opinion of trade unions was decidedly mixed: at best, they were easily co-opted by the piecemeal reforms offered up by capitalist politicians; at worst, they stood in the way of a more radical agenda. While not all SPCers endorsed this hard-line position – it drew most of its support from union strongholds in the mining districts – both radicals and moderates alike believed that the best way to eliminate "wage slavery" was to take control of the government, not in a violent revolution but by electing SPC members to the legislature. It was a position that the IWW, with its emphasis on workplace activism, rejected out of hand. After a period of decline prior to the war, the party re-emerged during the heady days of the labour revolt and, with a new willingness to combine economic and political struggles, played a decisive role in bringing workers into the militant fray. Loggers were in the thick of things.

**'LABOUR PRODUCES ALL WEALTH'**

The One Big Union drew most of its support from transport and metal trades workers, miners, and loggers – the so-called vital trades which, according to an OBU leader, "were the keystones of the industries in any particular centre."
IWA ARCHIVES

## Solidarity and Fragmentation

As the labour revolt gathered momentum, the socialist-led British Columbia Federation of Labour, the provincial rival of the Trades and Labor Congress, initiated an aggressive campaign amongst the province's loggers in 1918. Spurred on by the general militancy of the times and the day-to-day grievances that had plagued the industry for decades, loggers greeted this campaign with great enthusiasm, flocking to the BC Fed's new organization – the BC Loggers' Union, later renamed the Lumber Workers Industrial Union (LWIU) – in droves. Working-class journalists at the time estimated that by the autumn of 1919 about 11,000 woodworkers representing 70 percent of the province's total workforce in the woods had signed up. The core of the new union's support came from the coastal loggers – those who worked in the woods more or less full time and bore the brunt of the technological and managerial revolution that was transforming the lumber industry. Like workers across the country, they showed their anger, frustration, and heightened sense of possibility by going on strike. According to reports of the federal and provincial departments of labour, between 1919 and 1920, loggers in BC walked off the job on 81 separate occasions.

At the helm of the LWIU was Ernest Winch, a one-time mason, longshoreman, president of the Vancouver Trades and Labour Council, and member of the Socialist Party of Canada. Under his leadership, the union affiliated with the One Big Union and, from its base in BC's Lower Mainland, spread to other parts of the province and the country. As labour historian Gordon Hak has shown, the LWIU spearheaded several strikes amongst sawmill workers, loggers, teamsters, and tie-hackers in and around Prince George, BC, from 1919 to 1922, securing modest gains in wages and working conditions. "OWING TO THE MANY THREATS HAVING BEEN MADE BY PARTIES OF BOLSHEVEKI INCLINATIONS TO EITHER BURN OR DESTROY OUR MILLS AND LUMBER THE COMPANY HAVE CONSIDERED IT NECESSARY TO PLACE ARMED GUARDS TO PROTECT THEIR PROPERTY," read a sign posted at a local sawmill in 1919. Significantly, many of the rank-and-file members of the LWIU in the Prince George district were not members of the Socialist Party of Canada, but were attached to the vision and temperament of the Wobblies – an orientation to labour politics that flowed from their experiences as workers on the railroad.

**LABOUR LEADER**
**Ernie Winch**
**of the LWIU.**
IWA ARCHIVES

Against this backdrop of activity in BC, Winch and other Socialist Party activists left the west for northern Ontario, hoping to reproduce the union's organizational success in pine-tree country. "Are you willing to assist in winning…[better] conditions? Or are you willing to drift along in the same old rut that your grandfather did, ignorant of the fact that the world has changed?" a union leaflet asked provocatively, referring to the gains made in British Columbia. While evidence of union membership in northern Ontario is hard to come by, one historian estimates that by 1919-1920 about 3,000 to 4,000 bushworkers had signed an LWIU card – though only a fraction of these workers paid dues. Here, too, many of the new members were drawn from the ranks of the radical Finnish community and were ardent supporters of the Wobblies. Drawing on this political inheritance, workers engaged in educational and cultural events, camp meetings, and sporadic walkouts; others published labour newspapers and petitioned the government for better camps and inspectors to enforce health and safety regulations.

At the peak of its power in 1920, the Lumber Workers Industrial Union claimed a membership of 14,000 to 16,000 workers, representing about 40 percent of the total membership of its parent organization, the One Big Union. It had offices in Prince George, Prince Rupert, Cranbrook, Edmonton, Prince Albert, The Pas, Sudbury, Timmins, and Cobalt and published a newspaper called *The Camp Worker*. But the LWIU's spectacular rise was followed by an equally impressive collapse. On a broad level, the union's fortunes followed the trajectory of the national labour revolt in general and the One Big Union in particular. In Winnipeg, for example, the six-week stand-off in 1919 was crushed by the combined power of the employers and the government.

SIGN ME UP

BC Loggers' Union membership booklet (above) and dues receipt (below) from 1919.

IWA ARCHIVES

Mounties clashed with strikers, labour halls were ransacked, workers were deported, and the leaders of the strike and the One Big Union were arrested, prosecuted, and jailed for advocating revolution. Such coercion was not limited to Winnipeg; indeed, it was part of a wider counterattack that took place across the country against what one industry spokesperson called "this disease on the body politic" – the One Big Union and its affiliated unions.

In the lumber industry, employers came out swinging. In the fall of 1919 the BC Loggers Association, an industry organization that included nearly all of the big coastal logging operators, established a hiring hall in Vancouver and refused to hire anyone not vetted by association officials; this was followed by an aggressive open-shop drive and consolidation of the industry blacklist. When unemployment levels started to increase between 1920 and 1922, employers once again assumed a dominant position. The power that workers possessed in the context of low unemployment and the robust wartime economy had disappeared. "It is the foreman's day, and, being human, he has not forgotten his trials of the last two years, and may be excused for exercising considerable severity in dealing with the labourers," a forestry student from the University of Toronto visiting northern Ontario remarked.

"Exercising considerable severity" was but one dimension of this attempt to place class relations on a more secure footing. Like employers in other sectors of the economy, throughout the 1920s boss loggers supplemented their more coercive actions – the industry blacklist and open-shop drive, for example – with measures designed to reduce labour turnover and, in the process, cultivate good will on the job. "Oust the Bolshevists and Make the Camps Clean," an employers' organization concluded, underscoring the political dimensions of this move to "industrial democracy." To this end, employers in the Pacific Northwest experimented with joint employer-employee grievance committees, established company picnics, and encouraged workers to join company sports teams. But most importantly, they set about making the camps more hospitable and, in specific locales, creating permanent and semi-permanent logging communities, complete with schools, libraries, and company-sponsored stores. No doubt these changes improved the day-to-day lives of loggers and their families and, on a wider plain, were indicative of just how spooked employers really were. But as the above quotations indicate, in this new "industrial democracy" there was no room for unions – of any kind.

The decline of the Lumber Workers Industrial Union was the result of internal factors as well. Significantly, it was unable to extend its reach to mill workers – though it was not for lack of trying. In BC, mill workers in the Lower Mainland battled with employers on many occasions from 1917 to

BIG HARVEST

The big trees were harvested by rough-and-ready crews, like this one at a Bloedel, Stewart, and Welch camp in 1926.

*When the LWIU started to organize in areas not linked to the lumber industry, OBU leaders moved to curtail its power and influence.*

1919, but in most cases were defeated decisively. Thus, when the LWIU started to gather steam, mill workers – understandably – had no appetite for further struggle. But even without them, the LWIU was the largest player in the One Big Union, a fact that troubled the leadership of the umbrella organization. As a result, when the LWIU started to organize in areas not linked to the lumber industry, OBU leaders moved to curtail its power and influence, provoking a bitter disagreement over the relationship between the union centre and its affiliated members that culminated in the departure of the loggers' union in 1920. To make matters worse, the LWIU itself splintered as political differences between socialists and Wobblies fractured both the eastern and western wings of the organization. Weakened, demoralized, and internally divided – and facing an employer and government offensive – by the mid-1920s the LWIU had all but disappeared.

## À La Prochâine

In the 1920s, things looked bleak for organized labour. The push for industrial unionism was beaten back; across the country, membership in the mainstream labour movement declined sharply; workplace battles were being lost left and right; and workers' expanded sense of possibility – the wellspring of the labour revolt – was starting to constrict. The giant, it appeared, had been tamed.

But even amidst labour's great silence of the 1920s, radical voices could still be heard. In northern Ontario, Finnish Wobblies maintained a visible presence in many towns, including Kapuskasing, Sault Ste. Marie, and Sudbury. Perhaps the most important development during this time was the founding of the Communist Party of Canada (CPC) in 1921, an organization that attracted former members of the Wobblies, Socialist Party of Canada, One Big Union, and ethnic organizations such as the Ukrainian Labor Farmer Temple Association and the Finnish Organization of Canada. Inspired by Russia's Bolshevik revolution, the CPC was committed to industrial unionism, parliamentary procedures, and a radical reconstruction of society. Like its Russian counterpart, the CPC embraced the notion that a well-trained leadership cadre was necessary to ensure that the party stayed on the path to revolution and avoided the internal divisions that plagued other radical organizations. The party did allow for debate over policy and strategy, but once a decision was made, members were expected to adhere to its particular "line" on an issue. Shortly after it was founded, the CPC affiliated with the Communist International, the centre of gravity for the global communist movement, headed by the Communist Party of the Soviet Union. The international body was responsible for establishing the broad parameters within which national communist organizations operated.

Throughout the 1920s, Communist Party activists were, in the words of the Russian revolutionary V.I. Lenin, "boring from within" the mainstream labour movement and challenging the more conservative craft union leadership. Signs of this new movement could be found outside the ranks of the Trades and Labor Congress as well; in northern Ontario, local Communists founded the Lumber Workers Industrial Union of Canada in 1924 – the words "of Canada" meant to distinguish it from the defunct OBU-affiliated Lumber Workers Industrial Union. Drawing on many tricks of the trade pioneered by the Wobblies, the union recruited pulp cutters in the Algoma and Lakehead regions, and by 1926 had orchestrated a successful walkout for higher wages that involved about 700 men. There were signs of organizational life in BC as well. "I worked in that camp there [Buckley Bay] and that's where I first came in contact with organization. The old fellow, well, he wasn't as old as all that but he slept alongside me, you know, and he was a donkey puncher and he was a delegate for the old Lumber Workers Industrial Union, you see," Jack Gillbanks told IWA historian Clay Perry years later:

> [H]e used to talk to me quite a lot, give me stuff to read and all that. And I thought it was alright. I could see the conditions in the bunk, for instance, the bunkhouses, although by that time they had done away

ORGANIZING IN NORTHERN ONTARIO

**The Lumber Workers Industrial Union of Canada gathers in Port Arthur (now Thunder Bay) in 1928 to plot strategy.**

PROGRESS BOOKS

with the double decker [bunks], you know. You could see through the walls, and floors were all torn up with caulk shoes, and the likes of that… He was a Marxist. He was no anarchist about him. No. And, you see, we organized the boys in the camp.

Although these pockets of agitation were a far cry from the groundswell of support that once existed for the One Big Union, the very existence of the Lumber Workers Industrial Union of Canada spoke to the influence that com-

## Rosvall and Voutilainen

FEW ORGANIZATIONAL campaigns in northern Ontario during the 1920s matched the effectiveness of the 1926 pulp cutters' strike. But at Shabaqua in 1929, another effort was made to further improve wages and working conditions in the region. Although this initiative was short and ended in failure, it has received great attention from historians because of two men: Viljo Rosvall and Jon Voutilainen, organizers with the Lumber Workers Industrial Union of Canada.

In an attempt to drum up support for the union drive, the men planned to organize about 100 men, stationed at Onion Lake, who were working for Pigeon Timber, a modest show under the direction of Leonard Maki, a Finnish lay preacher known for his strident opposition to unions. After setting out on foot in mid-November, the two men were never heard from again. Five months later, a union search party discovered their bodies in a river flowing out of the lake. A coroner's inquest was held and it ruled – after eight minutes of deliberation – that the two men died of "accidental drowning," despite evidence that one of them had been struck on the head and had his clothes torn. Understandably, many in the union suspected foul play. As one LWIU member wrote to the Canadian Labor Defense League, a communist-run legal aid organization:

> [U]ndoubtly you have heard about the 'disappearance' of the organisers in the Lumber Workers Industrial Union. These men left for an organising tour on Nov 18th and have not been heard of since…
>
> These men, who are experienced bushmen…had to go through a district where the boss of the camp threatened that if any organisers came around he would shoot them. The last heard of these men is when they were seen near the camp of the boss who made the above threat.

munists were having amongst some loggers and the labour movement more generally. With the onset of the Great Depression in 1929 and the eruption of another nationwide labour revolt, many woodworkers would find themselves in the ranks of the "reds," challenging, as did the IWW and the LWIU, both the mainstream labour movement and the power of the ruling class. Yes, indeed, there would be a next time.

They were walking on the other side of the lake and were called across by…Maki's men (Maki is the boss of the camp) to come over and warm themselves by the fire[.] They stayed a little while and proceeded, according to the story told by these men, to walk on the ice (Onion Lake)[.] According to Maki he and his men followed about half an hour later…

The theory that they have been lost in the ice which is given by Maki is foolish for sleighs haul provisions with 5 or 6 men walking with the sleighs. The men could not have been lost for they are experienced bushmen and one of the men[,] Voutilainen[,] has his own trapping camp in this district. Without a doubt these men met with foul play here.

HAILED AS MARTYRS
**Rosvall and Voutilainen were buried on 28 April 1930 in Port Arthur. The funeral procession drew over 5,000 mourners.**
THUNDER BAY FINNISH HISTORICAL SOCIETY

On 28 April 1930 a funeral was held for the two men in Port Arthur. An estimated 5,000 people – reds, Wobblies, and others – walked in the funeral procession as a band belonging to the Finnish Organization of Canada played "The International," a communist anthem, and Chopin's "Funeral March." To many at the grave side, the two organizers were casualties of the class war, martyrs to the cause of working people – a sentiment that many still hold today.

CHAPTER TWO

# Emergence of the IWA

# CHAPTER TWO

# Emergence of the IWA

**IMMIGRANT LOGGER**

Ernie Dalskog, member of the Communist Party of Canada and pioneer IWA member.

IWA ARCHIVES

PREVIOUS SPREAD

Once described as a well-read man with an "enquiring, reflective, and energetic intelligence," Norwegian-born logger Arne Johnson was an organizer with the LWIU and IWA in the 1930s.

UBC SPECIAL COLLECTIONS BC 1974-1

IN THE SPRING OF 1930, Ernie Dalskog was working for Stella Lake Logging in Elk Bay, British Columbia. It was his second season with this particular outfit, cutting the massive fir stumps left behind by the horse-based logging that took place there 30 years before. Sitting in the bunkhouse one night after a day "working off and on with the high riggers," Dalskog struck up a conversation with three loggers who had just arrived from Vancouver. He was amazed by what he heard. "All three of them had the same tale of woe from Vancouver and the panic that was hitting from the [19]29 [stock market] crash," Dalskog remembered years later. "This one guy…he was really panic-stricken about it. The other two guys took it very philosophically."

For someone who had spent many years labouring in resource-based industries – Dalskog worked on the family farm in Finland and later in the woods in northern Ontario and in the mines on Vancouver Island – the roller-coaster ride of a capitalist economy was nothing new. But what made the visitors' revelations so startling was both the severity and the suddenness of the crisis: "It was beginning to have its effect on the employment situation although it hadn't yet hit too hard in the logging industry." But it would. And when Dalskog left the Elk Bay camp in the summer of 1930 in search of a "better deal" elsewhere on the Coast, he discovered just how bad things had become: wages were falling rapidly – if they were paid at all – and opportunities for employment were scarce. "Then [in 1931] there were no jobs," he observed. "That's when the riots began." Little did the 26-year-old logger know at the time that he was on the front end of an economic crisis that would last the better part of ten years.

With little hope of finding steady work, Dalskog headed for Vancouver, joining thousands of unemployed workers from across the country who preferred to weather the economic storm in the relative comfort of the city's hospitable, if rainy, climate. It was there, amidst the ranks of the unemployed, that Dalskog first became "conscious that there was an organization in the lumber" – the communist-led Lumber Workers Industrial Union of Canada. He signed a union card in 1931 and two years later joined the Communist Party of

Canada, becoming active in all facets of party life. "That made me think. It's true. We are now getting involved in languages of a different kind than the ordinary worker ever heard before, when we start talking about class struggle and the issues of unemployment and so on, socialism," Dalskog recalled. "A lot of these people had come from the farming country in Finland, Sweden, and Denmark and other countries. They're not used to it and they think that it's goofy what we are preaching, what we are agreeing to. By this time, there's quite a lot of street struggles, organizational work and so on."

Throughout the Depression, the burden of "organizational work and so on" in the mass production and resource sectors of the economy fell primarily to communist and communist-inspired activists. Indeed, it was the dogged determination of "reds" like Dalskog, coupled with the militancy of Depression-weary rank-and-file woodworkers, that sustained the promise of industrial unionism in the woods and mills at a time when the options for working people looked so grim.

## From Boom to Bust

For Canadian workers, as for workers throughout the industrialized world, the Great Depression brought the modest period of economic growth that fol-lowed World War I to an abrupt halt. While the working class had certainly weathered cycles of boom and bust before, this period of "bust" was unlike anything anyone had seen. Myriad factors produced this traumatic turn of

BREADLINES

During the Depression, unemployed workers, like these men lining up outside the First United Church in Vancouver, survived on a mix of relief cheques, food rations, and charity. As the economic crisis worsened, many were forced into government-run work camps.

PHOTO COURTESY
SEAN GRIFFIN

In June of 1938, unemployed workers and their supporters held a demonstration at the Powell Street Grounds following the "Post Office Riot" in Vancouver.

BC ARCHIVES C-07965

## 'Work and Living Wages!'

AS CATASTROPHIC as the economic and social crisis of the 1930s was, most politicians did little to assist those in need. Trapped in an ideology that viewed unemployment as a personal and moral failing, rather than a condition caused by the instability of the economic system itself, Liberals and Conservatives alike vowed, in the words of Conservative Prime Minister R.B. Bennett, not to "put a premium on idleness." In their opinion it was a worker's family, friends, church, and local charity that formed the first line of defence against unemployment, the government only stepping in after all other resources were tapped out.

The relief "benefits" that were available were pathetic, a hodgepodge of ration cheques and make-work projects administered by all levels of government. Eligibility requirements were punitive and levels of support painfully low as the government wanted to ensure that no workers lost their work ethic by becoming dependent on handouts. "If we dont [sic] get work and wages, and 'living wages' to, we are going to tell the Canadian government they have a 'murderer' in the house at Ottawa," an angry, anonymous, unemployed worker wrote to the prime minister in 1934. "You said a rich uncle left you your wealth, bah. We know better. We are not trying to scare you, but we are tired, of relief camps and going hungry and cold. No homes, or anything else."

Perhaps the most stunning example of the government's unwillingness to confront the worsening crisis was the plight of single unemployed men – many loggers and mill workers among them – who were taken off the relief rolls and sent to work camps in isolated regions of the country. Initially run by the provinces, most of the camps were later taken over by the Department of National Defense, the "inmates" receiving a steady diet of poor food, meagre wages for backbreaking work, and military discipline. "What was a slave [?] Everyone knows that a slave had no social rights. Now I ask my fellow workers: What have we got to-day? Have we any rights. The answer I get from [the] facts is: No," an unemployed woodworker wrote from a camp in BC. "We just get enough to keep us from starving completely…But the time will come when our glass of bitter misery will be filled up, and we'll take more. The workers will break the chains of this modern and civilized slavery."

Many of those who wanted to "take more" joined the ranks of the Communist Party of Canada (CPC), which was active across the country organizing unemployed workers in both the cities and the relief camps. The Single Unemployed Workers Association and the Relief Camp Workers Union (both under the direction of the Workers Unity League, the CPC's trade union arm) undertook propaganda campaigns, provoked spontaneous protests, and co-ordinated wider strikes and demonstrations amongst the unemployed for "work and living wages."

In most cities and towns, demonstrations by the unemployed were met, in the words of Prime Minister Bennett, with the "iron heel" of police brutality. In Vancouver, where the movement was particularly vibrant, police and demonstrators clashed in the streets on an almost daily basis. Ernie Dalskog recalled one incident:

I was all by myself, walking on Water Street [in Vancouver]. I was going to see what was going on down at the dock. I'd been down there and had been chased off by a squad of city and RCMP police. I was coming down by myself but there was a gang of about five or six [demonstrators] about 100 feet ahead of me. They saw the squad of police over on the north side of the street, so they cut into the alley way. I just kept on walking 'cause I didn't think they'd mistake me for part of the gang that had run away, but instead of chasing the gang, they stopped to take care of me first. By God, they started hitting me with their billy clubs over the head…Of course, when they came, I grabbed my hat and scrunched it up.

I held it over my head and tried to protect my head as much as possible, but they kept beating me. There was an old lady coming up the street and she saw them. She started poking them with her umbrella – bawled the Jesus out of them. By this time I was just about passing out, on my knees and not fully conscious, but she chased them off. The last guy to leave, [a] provincial police [officer], was going to have the last swing at me. She grabbed him and boy did she tell him off. She was a woman who used to hang around the beer parlours. They used to call her "Beer Parlour Queen." She helped me up and started walking with me. There was a restaurant…where I used to eat. The woman who run the place came from the Old Country, where I was from…They took me into the back of the kitchen, put some cold compresses on my head and made me lie down.

One of the largest protests took place in April 1935 when 1,500 relief camp workers in British Columbia went on strike, congregating in Vancouver to demand, among other things, abolition of the camps, better relief, and a system of unemployment insurance. The protests culminated in the On-to-Ottawa Trek, a march of unemployed men who set out from the Pacific Coast – "riding the rails" – en route to Ottawa to meet with Prime Minister Bennett. But they never made it to the nation's capital. In Regina the trekkers were hauled off the trains and held by police at the local exhibition grounds while a delegation was permitted to meet with the prime minister to discuss the issues facing the nation's unemployed workers. The talks went nowhere. Shortly after, the Mounties, tear-gas canisters and clubs in hand, moved to crush the cross-country trek, provoking a bloody confrontation – known as the Regina Riot – that left one police officer dead and many Trekkers injured.

Although the demonstrators never made it to Ottawa, the debacle in Regina contributed to the defeat of Prime Minister Bennett in the 1935 federal election and the eventual closure of the despised relief camps. Unemployed protests and clashes with police continued throughout the late 1930s – veterans of the On-to-Ottawa Trek and others occupied the main post office, art gallery, and a hotel in Vancouver in 1938. The agitation over unemployment only lifted with the onset of war in Europe in 1939.

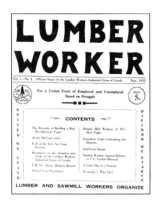

HOT OFF THE PRESS

**Published in September 1932, the first issue of the *Lumber Worker*, printed in Sudbury, called for a "United Front of Employed and Unemployed Based on Struggle."**

COMMUNIST PARTY OF CANADA ARCHIVES

events, but at its core it was caused by overproduction and underconsumption: by the late 1920s, both domestic and international markets for consumer goods were saturated and, as a result, the economy simply collapsed. In the wake of Wall Street's "Black Thursday" – merely a symptom of this underlying structural problem – Canada's gross domestic product and level of foreign investment nosedived. "The machinery of capitalist production had slowed to a walk," one working-class journalist wrote. For working people, the upshot was massive under- and unemployment; by 1933, the year the Depression hit rock bottom, about 32 percent of all wage earners were unemployed. The industrialized world, it appeared, was starving in the midst of plenty.

When the economic storm hit the lumber industry, it did so with a vengeance. In British Columbia, for example, total lumber production dropped by almost 30 percent, from a peak of three billion board feet in 1929 to less than two billion board feet in 1931, and exports to the United States, the province's principal export market, contracted sharply after Washington slapped an import duty on all BC lumber. But the collapse of the lumber industry was not confined to British Columbia. Across the Pacific Northwest, on the coast and east of the Cascade mountains, and in Ontario, thousands of loggers and sawmill workers swelled the ranks of the under- and unemployed. They joined tens of thousands of working people forced to endure the humiliation of enforced idleness, meagre government assistance, and, in the case of single men, hard labour in provincial and federal work camps. Woodworkers who were fortunate enough to hold on to their jobs faced bosses determined to cut costs by slashing wages and letting conditions deteriorate. "I can let you know that I am working – we are working pretty hard in this weather. (It is raining everyday)," one anonymous logger wrote from Squamish, BC, in 1931. "Board is fair, but the bed is no good. Taking everything all round, there is nothing good here…Some of the slaves that work in this camp do not realize or do not want to realize, that this is a disgrace [to] any man with common sense."

For those who realized just how disgraceful things really were – on relief and on the job – the palette of left-wing politics had many political shades. And for some workers, especially in the mass production and resource sectors of the economy, red was the colour of choice.

## Inside/Outside

Against this backdrop of economic calamity, the Communist International, the guiding organization of the worldwide communist movement, set about charting a new political course. Capitalism was on the brink of an acute economic and political crisis, the Moscow-based leadership told its affiliated

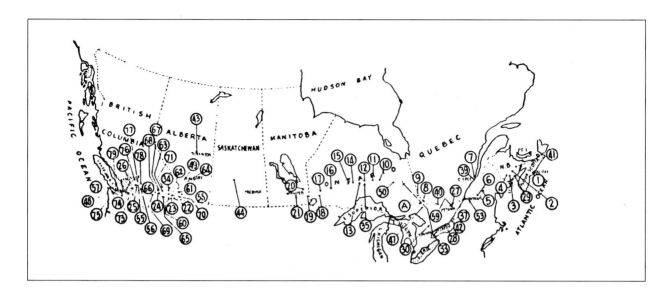

organizations, and only by creating independent, revolutionary unions and waging an unyielding campaign against "the capitalist class and the capitalist state" could it finally be laid to rest. To this new militant end, the Communist Party of Canada created the Workers Unity League (WUL), its national centre for "red" unionism, in 1930. With the establishment of its new trade union arm, the Communist Party's relationship with the mainstream labour movement changed dramatically. No longer would activists "bore from within" the ranks of the AFL-TLC, as they had during the 1920s; rather, they would chart an independent path and work to expose the conservatism of the craft unionists, the "labor fakirs" who kept Canadian workers from achieving their true revolutionary potential.

While the international and national executives of the Communist Party discussed the official trade union policy, at the grassroots level several of the "boys" – including Glen Lamont, Jack Gillbanks, Jack Brown, Andy Hogarth, and Arne Johnson – were meeting in a rooming house in downtown Vancouver across from Woodward's department store to discuss the revitalization of the Lumber Workers Industrial Union in British Columbia. "Things was kind of tough then, you know, and lots of unemployed there," Gillbanks recalled years later. "A few of us that would discuss these questions, well, we thought that there should be a little more done in going out and organizing, you see." While bushworkers in Ontario were able to keep a tiny membership together in the camps after the collapse of the One Big Union, in BC, save for the remnants of the Wobblies, there was no union presence in the camps and mills at all. Indeed, so bad was the BC situation, that before anyone could do anything, they had to send "back east" for pamphlets, union cards, and other union material.

TARGETING THE JOBLESS

**Through its affiliated organizations, the Workers Unity League organized unemployed workers in the relief camps to protest the camp conditions, levels of relief, and the absence of unemployment insurance.**

GRAPHIC COURTESY
SEAN GRIFFIN

Looking back on these tough times, Arne Johnson, a member of the Communist Party and future IWAer, recalled the "surprise mixed with pity" that he encountered on Vancouver's skidroad as he canvassed for the LWIU. "I remember distributing leaflets advertising the [upcoming] convention," he said. "In our visits to all the rooming houses and hotels down around the skidroad we met up with some who were in favour of doing something, some who were afraid to be seen talking with us, and others who felt sorry for us attempting to do such an 'impossible' job as try and organize the loggers." According to Jack Gillbanks, things were just as "impossible" out in the bush and in the mills: "We never had much literature, we had to do the talking ourselves. So you had to be a pretty good convincer to talk with them because, you know, there was so much anti-union propaganda going on and hopelessness. Didn't think it could ever be done…The sawmill bosses and all that, they were on us, you know, so we couldn't spend much time there."

In the fall of 1929 a handful of loggers – many of whom had deep roots in the left-wing union movement – attended the founding convention of the Lumber Workers Industrial Union in Vancouver. With Andy Hogarth in the chair and Glen Lamont acting as secretary (and an RCMP operative close by!), the group got down to business, sketching out a program dedicated to waging a struggle "based on the camp and mill" for better wages and working conditions, unemployment insurance, and "the unity of the employed and unemployed against war and fascism." That the new LWIU was affiliated with the communist-led Workers Unity League was clear; on the reverse side of its membership cards was printed a simple but compelling phrase: "Workers of the World Unite!"

> *'You had to be a pretty good convincer to talk with them because, you know, there was so much anti-union propaganda going on and hopelessness.'*

## 'The boys aren't dumb'

Two years later, the LWIU fought its first significant strike at Fraser Mills, BC, against the Canadian Western Lumber Company. The company's operations were massive. In addition to its huge sawmill, reputed to be the biggest in the British Empire, the company also operated a plywood plant, shingle mill, and planer mill – all on the same site. Clustered around the mill site was Fraser Mills, a company-controlled "shanty-town" populated by East Indian, Chinese, and Japanese workers, and the community of Maillardville, populated by French Canadians. Throughout the 1910s and 20s, labour relations at the mill were relatively peaceful as management's attempt to cultivate harmony on the job by helping workers to buy lots and houses, workers' common dependence on the mill for their livelihood, and the buoyant post-war economy bevelled the hard edges of class difference. But with the onset of the Depression,

when wages were slashed and working conditions became worse, whatever good will existed quickly evaporated. Ironically, it was the dense web of family and friends at the core of this diverse working-class community – the very relationships that the company hoped to cultivate – that formed the basis of the workers' solidarity.

Throughout September of 1931, the fledgling Lumber Workers Industrial Union held several meetings at Fraser Mills. At the top of the workers' list of demands was a ten-cent hourly wage increase to offset the loss of real income over the past few years, recognition of a union-led negotiating committee, abolition of the scrip system employed at the company stores, and renovation of the living quarters used by Asian workers. During this short period of mobilization, about half of the employees signed LWIU cards. In mid-September, after several failed attempts by the newly formed strike committee to negotiate a settlement with company president Henry Mackin, the workers went on strike. Government and employers alike decried the presence of "agitators and Communists," but as the president of the LWIU told a meeting of the New Westminister Trades and Labour Council, the basis of the strike was not communism but "bread and butter." By this time, the circles of resistance had widened further as more than 70 percent of the mill workers swelled the union's ranks.

The strike lasted for nearly three months. During this period, the strike committee, led by a 27-year-old shingle weaver at Fraser Mills named Harold

**BLOCKING THE RAILS**
Members of the LWIU block the entrance to the mill site during their battle with Canadian Western Lumber in 1931.
IWA ARCHIVES

Pritchett, was expanded to include workers from different departments of the mill and all nationalities; it also received the backing of local unions, moderate and left-wing alike, that endorsed resolutions calling for the elimination of "the vermin infested…shacks" and "Chinese and Japanese [labour] bosses" who routinely skimmed "25¢ on each [Asian worker's] cheque." The tactical manoeuvres of the committee were bolstered by the activism of strikers and their families. A 24-hour picket line, periodically supported by the communist-led National Unemployed Workers Association, was maintained and clashes with the police were common. As well, a cook house for strikers, staffed by local women and children, was created, and social events – including boxing and wrestling – were scheduled to boost solidarity. "I was booked to wrestle Maillardville['s] strongest man, Doudouin Proulx," Leo Canuel, a mill worker and picket captain at Fraser Mills, recalled. "But at the last minute he was taken from the card and replaced by Albert Paquette, longshoreman, top bully and rough-and-tumble fighter. This fight lasted 40 minutes officially. He won, but I got out of the ring and he stayed on his back in the centre of the ring. I got all the applause."

But as Leo Canuel no doubt knew at the time, securing a victory at Fraser Mills required a campaign that was capable of shutting down other operations that provided wood for the Canadian Western Lumber Company. This the young union had great difficulty pulling off. In the end, it *was* the closure of a CWLC subsidiary that forced the company to soften its position, but it came at

# Father Teck and the Model Ts

DURING THE Fraser Mills strike, Canadian Western Lumber attempted to break the workers' solidarity by playing on the racial, ethnic, and religious differences in the workforce and wider community. Early in the confrontation the company convinced the local parish priest, Father Teck, to assist it in getting the French Canadian men back to work. From the pulpit Teck criticized the "communists" and the spirit of "radical revenge" that their presence had brought to the company town; later he withheld absolution, telling the strikers that they

ANTI-LABOUR CRUSADER Father Teck.
VANCOUVER PUBLIC LIBRARY

could not receive God's forgiveness until they broke ranks and went back to work.

Although Father Teck's move created friction amongst the rank and file, no one scabbed. Undeterred by this flagrant attempt to split the union's ranks, LWIU leaders used their Model Ts to shuttle French Canadian workers to and from a neighbouring church, where a more sympathetic priest had agreed to perform religious services. "Father Teck is a good priest," one striker remarked. "We do what he tells us – on Sunday." □

the behest of declining market conditions, not a sympathy strike. Nevertheless, with the prospect of other branches of the company's far-flung lumber empire closing down, Mackin made an offer that included a pay hike, a new wage rate for shingle workers, a guarantee to meet with a workers' committee, and a promise not to discriminate against union workers. The offer, first tendered in early October, was accepted in late November, the workers originally voting it down to protest the company's earlier attempt to pressure the men back to work.

Although the LWIU was unable to secure a closed shop, these modest gains stand out as impressive accomplishments at a time when few in the labour movement believed that working people were willing, let alone able, to fight back. No doubt the presence of a skilled and committed union leadership played an important role in this regard, providing – in the words of one IWA veteran – "the experienced forces, the organization, the material that it takes." But as historian Jeanne Myers has noted, ultimately the conflict was won by the rank and file themselves, on the ground, where "[t]he network born of residential, familial, and class bonds sustained communal survival during the long strike." Many paid a heavy price for their beliefs: homes were lost when payments could not be made; jobs were lost when the boss fired men, including Harold Pritchett, thought to be active in the union. "Mrs. Taboue was hit by a police stick. Bollock Coutier had head injury…Some died from the hard times caused by the strike, and worries," Canuel recounted. "In this struggle, many good men and women were involved, now forgotten."

In other parts of the country other "good men and women" were involved in campaigns headed by the Workers Unity League and its affiliated unions. But victories were few and far between. Plagued by internal party divisions, lack of resources and skilled organizers, and a knack for alienating moderate workers with absurd revolutionary rhetoric, the League's first two years of operation were a complete disaster. "What in the hell is the need of trying to persist and subjecting yourself to unlimited hardships in the face of Goddamn driveling shit like this?" Communist Party member and future IWAer J.M. Clarke wrote to the leader of the Workers Unity League from his post on the Prairies. "Words, words, words; oceans of empty verbosity; miles of trollop; reams of junk; hours of scatter-brained blah that in no way indicates the slightest understanding of conditions as they actually exist in the country among the rank and file of the workers." Clarke was not the only one who felt this way. Indeed, at a Communist Party convention in 1931, members vowed to abandon "leftist slogan[s]" and fight, instead, for workers' "immediate economic demands." The objective was still to create industrial unions independent of the mainstream labour movement, but given such poor results, the WUL was

CUT THE CRAP

**One-time member of the One Big Union, J.M. Clarke – "a sandy-haired Scot with a gift for strong words" – was one of many rank-and-file communists who criticized the WUL's knack for alienating workers with extreme rhetoric and absurd "leftist sloganeering."**

NATIONAL ARCHIVES OF CANADA PA-124397

now officially committed to a somewhat more practical line. It was, after all, an approach that rank-and-file activists and workers had been committed to for some time. "The boys aren't dumb," an IWA organizer in the 1930s remarked, underscoring the gap between the official Communist Party position and the day-to-day reality of union work.

By the mid-1930s, the revamped Workers Unity League had emerged as a formidable force. It led between 75 and 90 percent of strikes in a wide range of industries between 1932 and 1935 and claimed a membership of approximately 40,000 – and it was particularly active in the woods. Fallers on Vancouver Island struck successfully for better living and working conditions

## 'The Most Hated Outfit on the Coast'

IN THE WAKE of the Fraser Mills confrontation and several smaller skirmishes at Barnet, Fraser, Timberland, and Sterling Mills, the LWIU's organizational work ground to a halt. But things started to pick up again in 1933 when Arne Johnson, Hjalmar Bergren, Eric Graf, Ted Gunerud, and other organizers undertook a union drive amongst the fallers on Vancouver Island who plied their trade for Bloedel, Stewart, and Welch – a firm that Johnson considered "the most hated outfit on the coast."

After several months of agitation, 33 delegates from various camps up and down the Island met in Vancouver on Christmas Eve and adopted a tough program: a wage hike of 50 percent, recognition of camp committees, Sundays off, and

overtime provisions. Within weeks, the BC Loggers Association went on the offensive, and shortly after refusing to grant any wage increases it fired 40 fallers for union activities on 26 January 1934. This prompted approximately 500 men to walk off the job and set up a picket camp at Campbell River. Within a few weeks the ranks of the strikers swelled to about 2,500 men from 20 different camps, donations started to pour in from supporters, and strike bulletins, printed on a mimeograph machine, were issued. The company, still smarting from the Depression, attempted to re-open its Great Central Lake operation near Port Alberni with replacement workers. As Ernie Dalskog recalled, the union responded by marching across the Island to prevent the scabs from reaching their destination.

[Later] we got called to come up to Great Central Lake to [keep scabs out. From there] we walked the rest of the way to Campbell River to the picket camp. To avoid letting them know where the hell we were striking at

in 1934. In northern Ontario a revitalized LWIU, which included Bruce Magnuson and Carl and Martin Palmgren, orchestrated a wave of protests that involved bushworkers from Port Arthur, Fort Frances, Hearst, Kapuskasing, Iroquois Falls, and Chapleau between 1933 and 1934. Years later, Magnuson recalled the "merciless brutality" of these "rough strikes": "[T]he next morning about 4 a.m., after boozing all night, several of the local constables surprised hundreds of workers [who were] sleeping in two halls adjacent to the previous day's skirmish [with the scabs] by driving the workers out of the halls into the streets in 25 degrees below zero temperature, attacking them with their billies as they fled." After 2,100 pulp cutters walked off the job for a month in June

we hiked into the bush – we couldn't get up to Great Central Lake because the only way was railroad to the Great Central Lake mill and then by boat to the Lake and so we hiked into the bush over the mountain and up into the Lake. Ted Gunerud organized that.

I don't know how many there were of us altogether, but we must have been 100 anyway in the truck, maybe more...There were a lot of people from Port Alberni that came and joined the march. At least 300 in the parade. But we were quite a bunch and we got there and they couldn't spot us. They had planes flying all over the place looking for us.

[The purpose of the hike] was to try and scare the scabs. They've already brought scabs in there...We couldn't get in there. I guess [Bloedel, Stewart, and Welch] figured the Lake was [their] reserve. Well, it sort of became a futile thing because we got out. But, oh, they were scared. They had police up there and a couple of machine guns. There was no way we could force them out. There was a cop for every man they had there.

After two months, the provincial Department of Labour intervened and recommended a wage increase across the board – higher rates for the skilled workers, a smaller increase for the unskilled – camp committees, and an informal agreement to give the men Sundays off. The union rejected the proposed settlement on the grounds that all classes of work should receive the same wage increase. As a consequence, the strike continued and the Loggers Association, which was prepared to endorse the government-brokered deal, withdrew its final offer and waited. After 96 days on strike, the fallers started to drift back to work. "We realize that an organized return to work would [be] preferable to hanging on while camps filled up with scabs leaving a large number of Union members outside holding the bag," a strike bulletin read.

In the end, the fallers did secure a wage increase, though it was substantially less than their original demand. More important than this monetary gain, however, was the new sense of possibility that percolated amongst both union organizers and rank-and-file workers. "The union had permanently established itself on the BC Coast," IWA historian Clay Perry concluded, "permanently established confidence among the loggers in their ability to fight back. Perhaps most importantly, they had developed a cadre of dedicated, capable, trusted union leaders."

REACHING OUT

Like the industrial union movement, the CCF challenged the ugly, anti-immigrant sentiment – captured here in a 1935 Liberal Party election ad – that pervaded much of Canadian society.

IWA ARCHIVES

FACING PAGE

Fallers participating in the 1934 strike against Bloedel, Stewart, and Welch congregate at a picket camp in Campbell River on Vancouver Island.

IWA ARCHIVES

1935, the union secured a small wage increase and recognition of camp committees. More importantly, Clay Perry observed, "it put forest industry unionism, at least among the pulp cutters, on a firm footing, the basis of unionism in northern Ontario to this day" – a conclusion just as applicable to the Pacific Coast as it is to the Canadian Shield.

## The Parliamentary Road to Socialism

The Communist Party of Canada was not the only organization challenging the political and economic status quo in the 1930s. In 1932, representatives from various western-based farmer, labour, and socialist groups met in Calgary to debate the politics and possibilities of a non-communist, social democratic movement dedicated to a "far-reaching reconstruction of our economic and political institutions." The new organization was called the "Co-operative Commonwealth Federation (Farmer Labour Socialist)" – the final three words indicating the delegates' diverse, left-wing political backgrounds. A year later in Regina, delegates gathered again, this time at the CCF's first national convention, to adopt a political program entitled, aptly, the "Regina Manifesto."

"The CCF is a federation of organizations whose purpose is the establishment in Canada of a Co-operative Commonwealth in which the principle regulating production, distribution, and exchange will be supplying of human needs and not the making of profits," read the manifesto's preamble. "Social and economic transformation can be brought about by political action, through the election of a government inspired by [this] ideal…and supported by a majority of the people." To this end, the CCF demanded public ownership of power, transportation, and communication companies and the creation of agricultural co-ops, socialized medical care, unemployment insurance, and a progressive income tax system. It was a government-centred vision of reform that reflected in part the influence of the League for Social Reconstruction, a group of university-based intellectuals from Toronto and Montreal that believed in socialism. At the helm of this new left-wing organization was a former Methodist minister, social activist, and labour Member of Parliament from Winnipeg, J.S. Woodsworth.

To many Depression-weary Canadians, this kinder, gentler path to economic and political salvation was attractive, especially at a time when the Communist Party, the other left-wing alternative, was opposed to working with moderate organizations and was tacking left and right in tandem with the shifting policy of the Communist International. In the wake of the Regina meeting, the CCF secured official opposition status in both British Columbia and Saskatchewan and sent seven members to the federal parliament in 1935 –

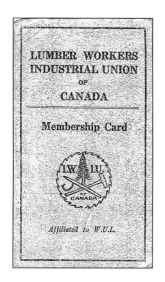

PAYING THEIR DUES

An LWIU membership card (top) and dues stamps (bottom). In 1934, the union took up a special assessment to organize workers in Quebec.

IWA ARCHIVES

success that both rattled business leaders and pushed established political parties to pursue more left-wing policies. But despite its breakthrough at the polls, the CCF remained on the margins of the trade union movement in these early years – a status that flowed from its youth, emphasis on political as opposed to economic struggle, and its rivalry with the Communist Party. In the latter half of the decade, however, as the new social democratic party became more established and both the CPC and the labour movement underwent a significant realignment, it would emerge as a player in the push for industrial unionism.

## The Coming of the CIO

For woodworkers in Canada, as for workers across North America, 1935 was an important year. In the depths of the Depression, two decisions were made – one in Moscow, the other in Washington, DC – that fundamentally reshaped the labour movement on both sides of the border. Overseas at its Seventh Party Congress, the Communist International called upon its comrades to abandon its policy of building independent, revolutionary unions and instead to build broad alliances with progressive working-class allies; the enemy of labour radicals was no longer the conservative elements within the ranks of the labour movement or the CCF, but – more importantly – the rise of fascism in Europe and around the world. As a result of this shift in political direction, the Workers Unity League and its affiliated unions, including the red-led Lumber Workers Industrial Union, were disbanded, and skilled communist organizers, once infamous for their unwavering criticism of the AFL-TLC, swelled the ranks of the craft unions. For members of the LWIU in British Columbia and Ontario, this new political orientation meant working alongside the United Brotherhood of Carpenters and Joiners (UBCJ) – no easy task for unionists long committed to a more inclusive agenda and long resentful of the carpenters' unwillingness to organize those men thought to be too "uncarpenterlike." Thus, shortly after Moscow's announcement, the responsibility for organizing the woodworkers was turned over to a new organization: the AFL-TLC–affiliated, Brotherhood-approved Lumber and Sawmill Workers Union – "Lumber and Saw."

While communists set about courting their newfound allies, in Washington, DC, on the heels of the annual convention of the AFL, a group of disgruntled union leaders met to discuss somewhat similar issues: the mainstream labour movement's neglect of unskilled workers in the mass production and primary resource sectors of the North American economy. For proponents of a more progressive labour movement, like United Mine Workers of America president John L. Lewis, the convention had been a complete disaster; resolu-

"Bush Strikers" at Port Arthur, Ont., July 1935

ACTIVISM IN
NORTHERN ONTARIO
Bushworkers gather in
front of the Hoito
Restaurant in Port
Arthur (Thunder Bay)
during their 1935
battle for better wages
and recognition of
camp committees.
IWA ARCHIVES

tion after resolution that endorsed industrial unionism was defeated by delegates who were skeptical of the left-wing politics associated with such unskilled "riffraff" and "rubbish" as auto, rubber, and woodworkers. Lewis was so infuriated by this turn of events that he crossed the floor of the convention and punched William "Big Bill" Hutcheson, head of the carpenters' union and one of the staunchest defenders of a more exclusive union movement, on the jaw. It was in this environment of intransigence and infighting that Lewis and a small caucus of like-minded unionists created a committee within the AFL dedicated to "organizing the unorganized." It was called the Committee for Industrial Organizations: the CIO (later renamed the Congress of Industrial Organizations).

Spurred on by President Roosevelt's "New Deal" for labour – legislation enacted in 1935 that gave working people the right to organize and bargain collectively – and the political acumen of rank-and-file activists from the disbanded communist-led unions, the CIO spearheaded an organizational boom in the United States not witnessed since the heroic struggles of 1919. Throughout the 1930s, the organization's name possessed a near magical quality that resonated with unorganized workers in a way that specific bargaining positions or political pronouncements did not. "The onrush of the unorganized millions demanding organization has swept over the barricade the [AFL] sought to build," working-class journalist Len Caux observed at the time. "A labor movement has already been built such as few of the debaters…believed possible in so short a time." This organizing fever was exemplified by the dramatic sit-down strikes in the auto industry, pitched battles that, in the words of the *BC Lumber Worker*, "shook the world." Indeed, by 1937, just two years after it was founded, nearly four million workers had voted to "Go! Go! CIO!"

The emergence of the CIO as a powerful rival of the AFL resulted in heightened pressure from rank-and-file woodworkers to take Lumber and Saw out of the mainstream labour movement and form an independent industrial union. Indeed, woodworkers on the West Coast had not forgotten the alleged "sell-out" of the great Northwest lumber strike of 1935 by Abe Muir, executive member of the carpenters' union, or the indignity of being seated as non-voting second-class delegates at the carpenters' 1936 annual convention. Not surprisingly, then, when the AFL suspended the CIO for its unsanctioned organizational activities, the tenuous alliance between the West Coast wing of Lumber and Saw and the carpenters' union disintegrated. (In contrast, in northern Ontario, Lumber and Saw members decided to stay with the Brotherhood, arguing that, unlike out west, its members had to work more closely with pulp mill unions organized by the AFL and therefore should remain tied to the carpenters.) In the fall of 1936, delegates from the ten West Coast Lumber and Saw district councils gathered in Portland, Oregon, to form the Federation of Woodworkers and to protest the treatment of the CIO. Harold Pritchett, leader of the BC delegates, was elected president of the new federation. The creation of "one union in wood" was not far off.

## 'It Shook the World'

*Len Caux,*
*BC Lumber Worker, 13 October 1937*

THE 1935 CONVENTION of the American Federation of Labor was the scene of a debate that shook the labor movement and stirred the whole country. From the moment…[a] report [was introduced] calling for an aggressive campaign of industrial organization in the mass production industries, to be followed shortly after by John L. Lewis pounding home argument after argument before a packed and almost breathless audience, the floodgates of ora-

FOUNDED CIO
**John L. Lewis.**
CANADIAN PRESS

tory opened. All day long and far into the night for the rest of the convention, the delegates wrestled with the greatest issue to confront an AF of L gathering for decades. Against the swelling demand for industrial organization, the craft standpatters fought with all the emotion and venom of a bureaucracy at bay.

"The unorganized millions in the mass-production industries must and can be organized." "They never have and never will, industrial unionism won't work, and the craft approach is all we will permit." That was what the two sides of the argument boiled down to. The craftists had their way at that conven-

## 'From the Stump to the Finished Product'

On 17 July 1937, representatives from the Federation of Woodworkers were meeting in Tacoma, Washington, to discuss the politics and possibilities associated with "organizing the unorganized." As Pritchett recalled years later, topping the agenda was one key question: "whether we should stay in the Carpenters [as] B-class members with no voice or vote or any other benefits, or whether we should consider approaching the CIO for affiliation and set up our own autonomous international." In advance of the convention, a rank-and-file referendum on this very question was held – a campaign in which Pritchett worked hard to drum up support. "It necessitated that we should conduct a real campaign and I was the person, the only one on the payroll, which was $50 a week," he recalled.

> [T]he plywood workers[,] realizing how tremendous this job was, how big it was, put down the down payment on a brand new Plymouth car for me with the understanding that I would meet the payments and we bought the car in Aberdeen [Washington] with the business agent and officers of the plywood local of Aberdeen present.
>
> So that gave me a big lift because heretofore I've been travelling by, all up and down the Coast by bus, and it was out of the question to fly…So

*By 1937, just two years after it was founded, nearly four million workers had voted to 'Go! Go! CIO!'*

tion, through the block votes of an unconsulted membership, but they lost the argument. The chuckles of triumph have long since died in the throats of the men who thought thus to build a barricade against industrial organization. For in the two years that have followed, every one of the arguments of the industrial unionists has been proved again and again, up to the hilt. The onrush of the unorganized millions demanding organization has swept over the barricade the craftists sought to build. Industrial organization has met the test. And a labor movement has already been built such as few of the debaters of 1935 believed possible in so short a time.

The argument of 1935 is dead and ended beyond hope of resurrection. Two years of labor history have made a laughing stock of the petulant and pettifogging claims of the craftists. The CIO that gathers its four millions of members in the mass production industries is living proof that its founders were right and the other side wrong… [T]he CIO represents a new labor movement, with many new leaders who have won their spurs in the organizing campaigns of the past two years. It is perhaps not without significance that the youthful CIO will set its face to the rising sun in the east, at a time when the remnants of the AF of L are rallied…by aging leaders whose gaze is fixed on the setting sun of their lost opportunity.

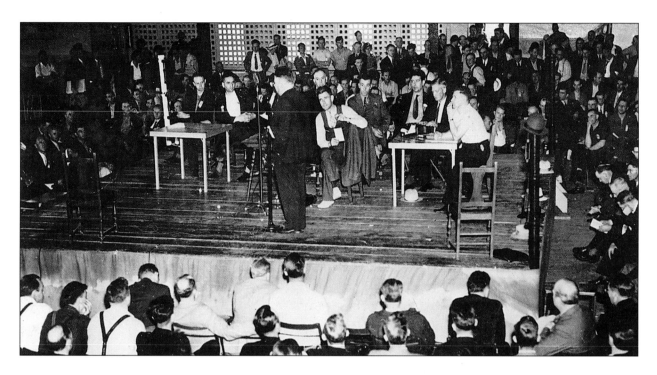

**FOUNDING CONVENTION**

With the backing of the vast majority of rank-and-file woodworkers, delegates to the IWA's inaugural meeting voted to affiliate with the CIO. Harold Pritchett, the IWA's first president, is seated in the middle of the stage – a boxing ring – wearing a vest and white shoes.

IWA ARCHIVES

with my new Plymouth I started out and I covered all of the District Councils and as many local unions as possible. And I must say that when I entered [a local meeting]…I had the warmest reception…In fact, they went overboard to give me a standing ovation every time.

In the end, all that agitating (and driving) paid off. To the delight of Pritchett and the vast majority of delegates, the results of the referendum – tabulated and announced at the convention – were decisive: 16,754 woodworkers, representing 76 percent of the rank-and-file workers who cast a ballot, voted in favour of flying the CIO flag. With the winds of political change at their back, the convention ratified the results by an equally impressive margin (385 to 71) and – on the final day of the meeting – voted to rename the Federation of Woodworkers. The new union was christened the International Woodworkers of America. "We've gone CIO boys, we've gone CIO. The Carpenters and Joiners have always tried to corner all our dough. But we'll stick together, for rank-and-file control," a quartet from an Oregon local sang enthusiastically. "Our Federation is stronger, and we are Carpenters no longer. We've gone CIO!"

But not all of the district councils were singing from the same songbook. Representatives from the Puget Sound District Council in Washington, for example, were wary of affiliating with the CIO so quickly and later withdrew from the IWA altogether after the convention endorsed the referendum results. Equally controversial was Pritchett's bid to become the first president of the new international union, a move that was opposed by Al Hartung and Don Helmick, leaders from the Columbia River District Council (CRDC) in Portland, Oregon. Not only did the two men want the leadership for themselves, but, more importantly, they objected to the new union being run by a suspected member of the Communist Party of Canada. "In Tacoma, I had the experience of being called into a room by one of the leading officers of [the] Columbia River District," Pritchett remembered:

> [T]hey asked me if I could find [vice-presidential running mate] Mick Orton [because they had] a very important question they'd like to discuss. I said, "Sure." So I located VP O.M. Orton and we went to the room and there must have been 50 people in the room, a special room, big enough to hold them. And that was a hostile group and they proceeded to put me and Brother Orton on the spot in a number of very important questions that were coming up in the convention. The hostility was so great that I felt that there may be an attempt to use physical violence.
>
> However, my wife and O.M. Orton's wife were outside listening and knocked on the door, and when they opened the door, the meeting subsided and we left with our wives. But that was a real experience, even, you could say, a terrifying experience because we were in the process of building a new union and this kind of thing, unless it was by provocateurs, was very unethical to say the least.

Despite this strenuous and openly hostile opposition, Pritchett and his left-wing slate emerged victorious, the delegates' overwhelming endorsement of his leadership later approved by a separate rank-and-file referendum.

This opposition from the CRDC – a sign of the divisive internal struggles to come – paled in comparison to the battles that awaited the young International out in the field. Indeed, like the organizational campaigns waged by other industrial unions in other sectors of the economy, the IWA's move to unionize the lumber industry was met with fierce resistance by the combined might of employers, local governments, community organizations, and, not surprisingly, the United Brotherhood of Carpenters and Joiners and the AFL. "Let me tell you this – and this is no threat," Frank Duffy, general-secretary of the carpenters' union barked. "Go on out of the Brotherhood, and we will give you the sweetest fight you ever had in your lives." It was not long after the IWA's founding convention that its rivals made good on their promise to fight for the allegiance of the region's woodworkers.

While battles raged in states throughout the Pacific Northwest, it was in Portland, where the workers in seven of the city's eleven major sawmills voted to affiliate with the IWA, that the AFL mounted a massive, and often violent,

THE PRESIDENT
Harold Pritchett attended the 1937 convention, which was originally set to run for two days. It ended up stretching over four days and saw the birth of a new union.
IWA ARCHIVES

*It was not long after the IWA's founding convention that its rivals made good on their promise to fight for the allegiance of the region's woodworkers.*

product boycott to stem the organizational tide. Local Teamsters, who refused to haul "tainted" lumber, overturned trucks driven by IWA men and their sympathizers; sailors loyal to the AFL used their boats to clog streams that carried raw logs to the mills; a pro-CIO factory was set ablaze; and men on both sides of the battle were beaten up. At the same time, IWA supporters and their families were subjected to intense scrutiny from the Portland Red Squad, the American Legion Subversive Activities Committee, and the US Congress, organizations that feared the rise of the IWA was tantamount to a communist takeover. "With one hand, we could win against the employers with our economic strength," one IWAer said at the time, "but we have no weapons to fight those foes aided by the local and state authorities."

No weapons except one. With the assistance of the National Labor Relations Board, a cornerstone of Roosevelt's New Deal, the IWA successfully retained control over six mills, but not before the dispute had thrown hundreds of men out of work. At the first constitutional convention of the IWA, Pritchett railed against the "starvation policies" of the AFL in Oregon. It was not rank-and-file workers who were to blame for this ugly battle, Pritchett maintained, but conservative union leaders. In fact, he continued, the membership of both organizations shared "common problems…namely food, clothing, and shelter; or, in the words of President Roosevelt, 'the right of every man and woman to work who is willing and able.'" In this regard, added Vice-President Mickey Orton, it was crucial for the IWA to deliver the "economic security" of a "new deal" to all wage earners. By the late 1930s, with a membership in the US fast approaching 100,000, it was clear that the IWA was capable of doing just that.

## Raw Deal

While the Oregon and Washington district councils forged ahead, the push to unionize British Columbia's estimated 25,000 woodworkers was at a virtual standstill – and the obstacles facing the IWA were many. Arne Johnson, president of one of the Vancouver-area locals, certainly understood the dangerous, and often frustrating, nature of organizing at this time – in 1937 he was convicted of trespassing on company property and assaulting a camp manager who attempted to prevent him from distributing the *BC Lumber Worker*. This state of affairs was complicated further by the transient and seasonal nature of logging employment. As Hjalmar Bergren, president of one of the largest locals on Vancouver Island, remarked: "[A]s soon as [the workers] leave the district, that is [the] last you hear from them." The itinerancy of woodworkers was rooted in the earlier days of the industry, when they often moved from camp

FACING PAGE

Loggers at Industrial Timber Mills Caycuse Division Camp 6, shown here in 1937, were among the first men to join the IWA's newly formed Local 1-80 based in Lake Cowichan on Vancouver Island.

IWA LOCAL 1-80 ARCHIVES

to camp looking for "the best deal" or went on strike where and when it was needed. What was more, it was also difficult to sustain union organizers. "You couldn't spend very much time doing organization work on the Island here at that point because you had to live," Jack Gillbanks observed. "[A] union could not pay anybody salt and therefore you would have to go to work, you see, and keep your trap shut about organization for a while." Although the launch of the famous "Loggers' Navy" provided the BC Coast District Council with an effective means of contacting men in isolated northern areas, without a sustained union presence in the bush, its success in the early years, like that of organizers on land, was limited.

But perhaps the largest obstacle to an organizational breakthrough in British Columbia and in Canada generally was the fundamentally different political environment that existed north of the border. In the US, President Roosevelt's "New Deal" for labour, more commonly known as the Wagner Act, provided working people with the right to organize and bargain collectively, identified unfair labour practices, and created the National Labor Relations Board to bring about collective agreements. In BC, no comparable legislation existed. In 1937 the province's Liberal government, under pressure from the labour movement, the communists, and the CCF, did pass the Industrial Conciliation and Arbitration Act, but unlike American legislation, the BC government's "New Deal" failed to grant working people the unconditional right to organize a union, let alone the right to bargain collectively. "We have a labour act which is so drafted in the interest of the employer in conjunction with the government to make the work of organization a hundred times more difficult," local IWA leader Hans Peterson remarked, highlighting the connection between the law and class struggle. Having witnessed the meteoric rise of the CIO, and the pitched battles between the carpenters' union and the IWA south of the border, the BC government was not interested in empowering working people. Its agenda was far more coercive: to stem the tide of militant industrial unionism that was washing over much of North America.

Key to the IWA's success, then, was bringing the existing provincial law in line with its American counterpart. By 1938, the IWA would have a chance to do just that as the struggle for workers' rights shifted from the legislature to the workplace when Local 163 of the IWA, headquartered at Blubber Bay, Texada Island, found itself in a bitter confrontation with the Pacific Lime Company.

## Contested Terrain

Blubber Bay was a company town. It was small, isolated, and dominated by a single employer, the Pacific Lime Company. At the centre of the company's

*The BC government was not interested in empowering working people. Its agenda was far more coercive.*

FACING PAGE

A crew poses with its steam-powered locomotive on a wooden trestle near Industrial Timber Mills Camp 6.

IWA LOCAL 1-80 ARCHIVES
W.H. GOLD COLLECTION

operations was a massive open-pit lime mine, known to workers as the "glory hole," and a modest sawmill that produced lumber for local markets. For three decades, labour relations at Blubber Bay had been relatively peaceful, but that changed in July 1937 when a group of workers led by Jack Hole, Bob Gardner, and Stan Abercrombie organized nearly all of the 150 employees – both white and Chinese – under the banner of the fledgling woodworkers union to protest poor working conditions and wage reductions instituted by a new company manager. Not surprisingly, after three decades of labour peace, the company was in no mood to negotiate with organized workers, let alone a union with a membership of "Orientals" and ties to "Communistic elements." Fearful that the company was going to bust the union, Local 163 asked the Department of Labour to intervene to bring about a collective agreement in accordance with the yet-to-be-tested Industrial Conciliation and Arbitration Act. At stake, then, were not simply the work-related grievances as they pertained to Blubber Bay, but the legal definition of the new labour legislation itself and, by extension, the organizational future of the IWA in British Columbia.

Over the course of the winter and spring of 1938, government-sponsored conciliation and arbitration proceedings failed to give the IWA an exclusive seat at the bargaining table, offering instead a committee consisting of union, non-union, and company officials. Rank-and-file workers in Blubber Bay and the IWA executive were incensed. In a stern letter to Minister of Labour George S. Pearson, executive board member Frank Lundstrum demanded that working people be given "not only the right to organize, but [the] freedom to organize." In the minister's opinion, however, there was nothing wrong with the board's decision to prevent the unionization of Pacific Lime; indeed, it was in keeping with both the letter and intent of the new law. Not surprisingly, the board's recommendations were rejected by an overwhelming majority of the workers, ushering in a bitter and often violent 11-month dispute that was remembered by one CCFer as a "fight waged against the most brutal police and company tyrants known in BC."

The Pacific Lime Company responded swiftly to the union's challenge and evicted Chinese and white workers and their families from their company-owned houses. "I was afraid to open the door, but asked [the company manager] to leave the eviction notice at the door," Elizabeth Maylor, a long-time resident in Blubber Bay and mother of one of the strikers, recalled. "This he refused to do, but raised his voice in a threatening fashion [insisting] that I open my door …I again refused." Other tactics designed to undermine the strikers' actions included requiring some children who wanted to attend school to present a pass signed by the company manager, monitoring phone calls placed by union officials in the company-owned telegraph office, and keeping union activity

## 'We're Having a Meeting'

*Syd Thompson*

I DON'T THINK there were more than 200 people living in Winfield [Alberta] that year [1937], and there were 20 bootleggers in the town. I got plunked into the middle of this mess by Doc Savage, CIO organizer for Alberta. He said, "OK, you go into the bush there in Winfield."

The first place I went to, Savage had been there before me. There was a drunken Irishman runnin' this bloody camp. The secretary of the union was a little fella who wore glasses. He was a preacher's son, and he looked it; meek and mild, you know. When we went into this camp, I had the garage owner drive me, and I paid him for it. He provided a taxi service.

I didn't go near the office. I picked one bunkhouse and then I went around to all the other bunkhouses and said, "We're having a meeting." So they all came into the bunkhouse and I started talking. I just nicely got started and the door flew open and there he was, the bloody boss. He starts screaming and hollering, "Get out! Get out!" I said, "The law gives me the right! If you want me out of here, fella, you're going to have to call the police. I ain't moving."

And, Jesus, that stumped him – and he got out. He got his sleigh, he didn't have a goddamn vehicle. He had to get to a telephone. He was madder than a bastard. That organized the whole camp. The secretary was busy all night signing them up.

ALBERTA BOUND

The first large-scale gathering of IWA supporters in Alberta took place in Edson, located between Edmonton and Jasper National Park, in 1938. Doc Savage and Syd Thompson were two of the early organizers in that province.

PHOTO COURTESY DOC SAVAGE

After a while I laid down on a bunk to have a rest, and about 11 o'clock the door flew open again. Here he was with the RCMP. There was a constable there by the name of Pook. We called him "puke" and he was monstrous, and with his buffalo robe on, ugly as a bear. He said, "What's going on here?" The secretary was there peeking over his glasses. I jumped out of bed and said, "We're organizing the place!" He grabbed me by the scruff of the neck and the ass of my pants and out the door I flew – out in the snow bank! I'm standing there waiting for the secretary to come flying out after me, but he'd cooled off by then.

The garage owner who drove us down was his personal friend. They used to drink together, and I'll be an SOB if he didn't charge him for providing a taxi without a licence. That's how I got started in that country. The organization fell apart in the spring because the bushworkers were all temporary, all winter workers. □

HARD DAY'S WORK

Chinese workers, pictured here in the late 1920s, labour in Pacific Lime's open-pit lime mine located on the northern tip of Texada Island.

BC ARCHIVES H-01414

under surveillance. Pacific Lime was aided in this endeavour by the BC Provincial Police, which escorted scabs to the mine and helped enforce the company blacklist by recruiting unemployed workers from the provincial welfare rolls.

In the face of such staggering intimidation, the IWA mobilized too. The union established a picket camp on one of the few plots of land not owned by the company; pickets singing "Hold the Fort!" paced back and forth on the government wharf when steamships arrived with replacement workers; and the Ladies' Auxiliary canvassed the province for cash and food. In Vancouver, unionists searched the loggers' district and Chinatown for support picketers, and the local and district executives of the IWA increased their efforts to secure alliances with social democratic allies in the trade union movement and the provincial legislature, including CCF MLAs Colin Cameron and Harold Winch. "[The strike] stirred the whole trade union movement into action and roused public opinion to the need for legislative protection of…trade union activity," one IWAer recalled.

Over the course of the strike, the strained relationship between the company, police, union, and non-union forces often erupted into outright confrontation. The worst encounter took place at Blubber Bay on 17 September 1938 when a riot erupted after a steamship arrived loaded with passengers looking for work at Pacific Lime. When the dust and tear gas finally settled, 23 union members were charged with unlawful assembly and rioting; 15 of them were later committed to trial. The morning after the riot, with rumours swirling in trade union circles that the police action had been "premeditated and prearranged," 40 members of the Pulp and Sulphite Workers Union – an organization with roots in a local CCF club – rushed to Blubber Bay from Powell River to offer comfort and support for the strikers. "Our men are not going to put up with any more police violence," union representative Stubby Hanson told the commanding officer, Sergeant Sutherland. "If it continues, 400 of us will be back and we won't fool with you bastards." It was a sentiment echoed later in the week when 60 seine boats clogged the Blubber Bay harbour to protest the police actions.

But such moments of working-class solidarity were not enough to sustain the strike. The mass arrests of key activists that followed the melee and the trials of the "Blubber Bay 15" drained the union of scarce human and financial resources. The riot of 17 September, then, marked the beginning of the end of the IWA's first organizational campaign in BC. After several months of judicial proceedings, 12 of the 15 strikers were convicted of unlawful assembly and rioting. The Crown easily persuaded the jury that to jail the unionists – cast as

*Over the course of the strike, the strained relationship between the company, police, union, and non-union forces often erupted into outright confrontation.*

## 'That Sadistic Cop'

UNION MEMBER ROBERT GARDNER certainly understood the level of police hatred in Blubber Bay. In the wake of the dockside clashes of 17 September, he was arrested for being a member of an unlawful assembly. While in custody in Blubber Bay, he was beaten badly by Officer Williamson of the BC Provincial Police. The police officer was later convicted of the assault and sentenced to six months at hard labour.

In a separate trial, Gardner was convicted for his role in the riot and sentenced to four months in prison.

"Have you seen Bob? Expected a letter from him last night but did not get one, hope he isn't sick worse than he was," Gardner's wife wrote to IWA lawyer John Stanton. "Bobby is taking it pretty hard, he is very melancholy. [H]ope I can snap him out of it before I have to be in town. Bob spoiled us all and now it is hard on us to have to be here without him."

While serving his sentence, Gardner – still weak from the injuries sustained at the hands of what one Blubber Bay striker called "that sadistic cop" – contracted influenza and later died. Some consider Gardner one of the first martyrs of the IWA, along with Rosvall and Voutilainen.

members of "an imported, subversive, terrorist organization" in this legal drama – was to strike a blow for peace, order, and good government.

Like the union lawyers' attempt to exonerate the Blubber Bay 15, the campaign waged by CCF members of the legislature to bring about a judicial inquiry into police brutality at Blubber Bay was also unsuccessful. "What kind of police do you think you'd have if they were afraid of a judicial inquiry every time they acted?" Liberal Premier T.D. "Duff" Pattullo asked the legislature without a trace of irony in his voice. By the spring of 1939 the picket line in Blubber Bay was almost non-existent and donations from union allies had all but dried up. In May, with no new deal from the company, the IWA officially called the strike off.

## Down But Not Out

After eleven months of struggle against the combined opposition of the company and the provincial government, the IWA had little to show for its trouble. Union members and their allies were beaten and bruised, bank accounts were depleted, and, as a consequence, membership levels continued to

## 'Them Chinamen Were Solid'

*John McCuish*

THERE WAS A LOT OF militancy shown in that fight [at Blubber Bay]. For instance, you know the cops made a threat that they were goin' to burn the picket camp. Well, the Chinaman told me, ol' Lim Yim, he said, "They no burn our camp. We're ready for 'em." And every Chinaman there was armed with two sticks of powder and a fuse about that long on it. See that was the time that the…miners in Spain used the powder, and they got the idea from that. Well, the cops come up that night and I met them right at the gate at ol' man Woods' and I said, "Look, Officers, your lives [are] in your own hands if you go in there tonight."

"Well, we're not scared of you."

I said, "You don't need to be scared of me." But I said, "If you got any idea what these Chinamen are planning you'll get the hell out of here and stay out!"

"Well, what are they planning?"

"I'm not goin' to tell you, they'll tell you, and they'll tell you the hard way."

Well, they knew what they had the first day. Every Chinaman there, some of them had knives, machetes, and everything else. And they [the police] were scared of 'em. They weren't scared of us, they were scared of the Chinamen…I tell you what they lived on. These Chinamen went out on the docks and on the rocks they caught rock cod. They killed deer. There was quite a few pheasants on the island and they lived mostly on that.

It was nothing to see the Chinamen were smart, though. There was only three Chinamen beat up in all that strike, because when the Chinamen went someplace there were seven or eight of them and the cops never tackled them. But our boys would get wandering away…Them Chinamen were solid. I never seen such a bunch as solid as they were. □

drop, reaching an anemic 226 in 1939. While the debacle at Blubber Bay did push the ruling Liberals to amend some of the more glaring deficiencies of its Industrial Conciliation and Arbitration Act, employers were still not compelled to recognize, let alone bargain with, a bona fide trade union. "Well they…got nothing there [in Blubber Bay]. No. Nothing out of it. No. Except a lot of expense," Arne Johnson remembered. The union would have to wait till World War II – when the federal government took control of the industries deemed essential to the war effort and introduced more progressive labour legislation – to achieve its first large-scale breakthrough in BC. But even in the exceptional political and economic context created by the pressures of war, success only came through struggle.

'STRIKE ON
AT PACIFIC LIME CO.'

Sporting bilingual sandwich boards, IWA activists walked the streets of downtown Vancouver, including the city's Chinatown, to raise both awareness of the Blubber Bay strike and donations for Local 163.

PHOTO COURTESY
ALLAN LUNDGREN

*Breakthrough*

# Breakthrough

WITH THE OUTBREAK OF World War II, the economic and social crisis associated with the Depression evaporated, replaced by the challenges of assembling a fighting force, mobilizing the nation's economy, and cultivating public support for yet another European conflict. "So this is how salvation came to the neighbourhood," Canadian writer Gabrielle Roy wrote bitterly in 1945. "Salvation through war!" For workers on the home front, high levels of wartime production meant finally getting back to work as the war effort, in the words of *Nation: Canada Since Confederation*, "needed every foot of lumber that the British Columbia forests could yield, every fish that the Maritimes could produce, every ounce of ore that the mines of the Laurentian Shield could process." Coupled with the ever-increasing demand for healthy men and women to serve overseas, this sharp increase in economic activity resulted in a widespread labour shortage, a condition that bolstered workers' power on the job. As a result, working people once again went on the offensive, participating in a wave of militancy not seen since the national labour revolt of 1919. Between 1941 and 1943 about 425,000 workers downed tools in over 1,100 separate work stoppages.

Working people struck back at the ballot box too. The CCF, running on a program that promised jobs, security, and a good standard of living through government intervention, made substantial gains in British Columbia in 1941 (14 seats), Ontario in 1943 (34 seats), and Saskatchewan in 1944 where, under the leadership of Tommy Douglas, it formed the first elected socialist government in North America. With these election results it appeared that workers were asking a simple, yet far-reaching question: if the government was prepared to fight for democracy overseas, why not at home too?

Spooked by both the rising tide of labour activism and the CCF's electoral success, the federal government and many of its provincial counterparts answered this question by adopting more left-wing policies, including labour legislation more in line with President Roosevelt's Wagner Act. In Ottawa, the ruling Liberals under Prime Minister Mackenzie King approved Privy Council Order 1003 in 1944; this special wartime act granted Canadian workers in industries under federal jurisdiction the same rights that their American counterparts had enjoyed for nearly a decade. The government's objective was to bring workers into stable collective bargaining relationships

PREVIOUS SPREAD

**Members of the BC District Council hold court in Vancouver in 1943. Pictured from left to right around the table are Mark Mosher (third vice-president), Ernie Dalskog (second vice-president), Darshan Singh Sangha (board member), Winnefred Williams (office secretary), Bert Melsness (financial secretary), Harold Pritchett (president), Hjalmar Bergren (first vice-president), Nigel Morgan (International board member), Jack Lindsay (board member), and Percy Smith (board member).**

IWA ARCHIVES

so that the war effort could proceed unimpeded. As well, it hoped to avoid a repeat of the class conflict that rocked the country from coast to coast in the wake of the Great War. The new labour legislation did dampen worker militancy momentarily, but by 1945, with peace in Europe in the offing, strike activity soared again as workers struggled to hold on to the gains secured during the war. In Windsor, Ontario, for example, two weeks after the war ended, 10,000 auto workers walked off the assembly line at Ford for 100 days demanding union recognition. Inspired by this war-induced militancy, the potential of progressive labour legislation, and a deep sense of entitlement that flowed from a collective experience of toil and sacrifice, the IWA – like other CIO-affiliated unions – achieved massive organizational gains in the immediate post-war period and cemented its position as the sole representative of BC's woodworkers.

## A War On Two Fronts

Buoyed by the restlessness and combativeness of rank-and-file workers across the country, the BC Coast District Council, under the leadership of Harold Pritchett, Nigel Morgan, and Ernie Dalskog, initiated an organizational drive on the Queen Charlotte Islands in 1941. In the union's sights were four logging operations under contract to the federal government to supply wood for

EVERY FOOT
OF LUMBER

Industrial Timber Mills, located in Youbou, BC, on Vancouver Island, was but one of many operations across the country producing wood products for the war effort.

IWA LOCAL 1-80 ARCHIVES
W.H. GOLD COLLECTION

the manufacture of military aircraft. "Strange, isn't it, that when the war is over, that [the] boss will be among a new group of millionaires, while our living standards will still be at the bottom of the well," Morgan told delegates at the union's annual convention, highlighting the reasons behind the District Council's militant strategy. "To be silent in the face of such hypocrisy is a betrayal of those whose patriotism cannot be bought at a price. Patriotism is dear to us, who have to do the fighting, the bleeding, the dying, and the paying.

Executive and Shop Stewards, Local 1-118, I.W.A.
July 9, 1944. Victoria, B.C.

**MORE ENGLISH THAN THE ENGLISH?**

**The executive and shop stewards of Victoria's Local 1-118, pictured here in 1944, reflected the racial and cultural diversity of woodworkers on southern Vancouver Island.**
COMMUNIST PARTY OF CANADA ARCHIVES

## LOCAL 1-80 (INCLUDES 1-118)

# On the Island

WITH A HISTORY that stretches back to the BC Loggers' Union and the One Big Union, Local 1-80, located on the southern half of Vancouver Island, is one of the oldest locals in the IWA. During the early 1930s, Local 80 – which at that time was affiliated with the Lumber Workers Industrial Union of Canada and included pioneer unionists Bert Flatt, Owen and Edna Brown, and Hjalmar and Myrtle Bergren – fought several pivotal strikes, most importantly the 1934 campaign against Bloedel, Stewart, and Welch. This battle, which included several thousand loggers from across the island, convinced Lake Logging, a Bloedel rival, to sign a union contract, the first such deal in the province. In the wake of this victory, the Lake Cowichan-based local, like others in BC, moved through the ranks of Lumber and Saw and, with the birth of the IWA, received a charter

from District 1 in 1937, designating it Local 80. It was also at the forefront of activism during World War II and the immediate post-war period. In 1941 it signed a new collective agreement with Lake Logging that contained a closed-shop provision – the first of its kind in the Canadian lumber industry – and in 1946, after consolidating its gains in the Lake Cowichan area, it played a key role in the 37-day provincewide strike that secured voluntary dues check-off, wage increases, and a reduced work week. During the long economic boom that followed the war, Local 1-80 experienced tremendous growth in membership, peaking at about 6,000 in the early 1960s. Notable members of 1-80 include Joe Morris, president from 1948 to 1952, who went on to become president of District 1 from 1952 to 1962, president of the Canadian Labour Congress, and Canadian representative to the International Labor Organization.

Also on Vancouver Island was Local 1-118. Originally tied to the American Federation of Labor, the Victoria-based local, under the leadership of Al Slater and Al King, joined the IWA in

It is cheap to the profiteers. Organized labour cannot be silent; we must fight to protect our union standards."

John McCuish and Hjalmar Bergren were two of the organizers in the Queen Charlottes and toured the area at the helm of the Loggers' Navy. Speaking to historian and activist Myrtle Bergren in the 1960s, McCuish described one of the first meetings held with the buckers and fallers who cut the massive sitka spruce on the islands:

### MEN AT WORK

Members of Local 1-80, employed at Industrial Timber Mills Nitinat Camp 3 in 1943, take time out to smile for the camera.

IWA LOCAL 1-80 ARCHIVES
W.H. GOLD COLLECTION

1937. IWA pioneer Nigel Morgan was also involved with 1-118 in the early years. "He had a desk there which was the IWA desk on one side of the room and he had another desk which was the CCF desk on the other side of the room," Harold Pritchett recalled. Between 1938 and 1946, 1-118 extended its reach to the camps, mills, and factories over much of the southern portion of Vancouver Island. It played a significant role in the 1946 strike by rallying support in Victoria for the union cavalcade en route from up Island to the capital city. Throughout the 1950s and 60s, Local 1-118, like other IWA locals, grew steadily, solidifying its position amongst loggers, sawmill workers, and plywood workers in and around Jordan River, Sooke, and Victoria and pushing such critical issues as job safety and worker education to the fore. Between 1952 and 1975, its membership increased from 500 to approximately 2,300. But by the early 1980s

a string of closures – most notably Pacific Forest Products plywood plant and BC Forest Products sawmill, long strongholds for 1-118 – cut deeply into the local's support. Some jobs in the industry were saved when 1-118 and 1-357 (New Westminster) orchestrated an employee-buyout of Sooke Forest Products and Lamford Cedar in 1985, but the organizational writing was on the wall. In 1989, Local 1-118 was folded into Local 1-80.

Drawing on the collective experience of members from both the Victoria and Lake Cowichan organizations, Local 1-80 has been at the forefront of path-breaking initiatives within the IWA. In 1989 it formed the Woodworkers' Survival Task Force to raise public awareness of destructive logging practices. This task force was instrumental in pushing the BC government to introduce an export tax and other regulations to curb the shipping of raw logs out of the country. Two years later, as environmental concerns percolated throughout the province, Local 1-80 and a host of green organizations, including the Western Canada Wilderness Committee and the Sierra Club, signed the South Island Forest Accord, a short-lived attempt to bridge the gap between economic and ecological concerns. Today, Local 1-80's membership, like the economy of Vancouver Island, is changing: about one third of its 3,800 members are drawn from outside its traditional stronghold in the lumber industry.

CONTESTED LOYALTY?

Before they were designated a security risk and herded off to internment camps in the Interior by the Canadian government, these Japanese Canadian men worked for Hillcrest Lumber on Vancouver Island, falling trees for the war effort.

IWA LOCAL 1-80 ARCHIVES
W.H. GOLD COLLECTION

FACING PAGE

Hjalmar Bergren (right), a member of Local 1-80, was one of the IWA's leading organizers in the 1930s and 40s.

IWA LOCAL 1-80 ARCHIVES

The beginning of the IWA in British Columbia was one day in August when Bergren and I held a meeting on the raft camp at Allison's in the Queen Charlotte Islands. Thirty-six people were there. Not counting Hjalmar and myself.

That old bugger [Hjalmar] spoke to them. An agreement, and it was mis-spelt, mis-worded agreement. And the boys voted for it. It was [an]…agreement that Hjalmar [and I made up] and I got typed by a young girl in the Queen Charlottes. She didn't know how to spell words…Every logger that was in Moresby Islands agreed with that program we started. Bergie's trip to the Queen Charlottes was the turning point in the union…And do you know that Bergie said he didn't say a word more than he had to.

Despite this initial success, the push to organize the Charlottes was hampered by the high turnover rate of workers – logging on the islands was one of the toughest gigs going – and the BC Loggers Association's steadfast refusal to bargain with the men who, in Morgan's words, "did the killing work of production."

The campaign picked up steam in the spring of 1943 after the BC government, under pressure from the labour movement – including the IWA – and left-wing political parties, amended the province's labour legislation, granting

MAY DAY MARCHERS

IWAer John McCuish (far right, wearing hat) and long-time communist and journalist William "Ol' Bill" Bennett (middle, wearing cap) celebrate International Workers Day in Vancouver in the late 1930s.

IWA ARCHIVES

workers the clear-cut right to organize and bargain collectively. To Morgan, these legislative changes, coupled with Ottawa's desire to facilitate collective agreements in the name of the war effort, were "a green light for an all-out drive to organize the unorganized." Hjalmar Bergren agreed: "The idea became a material force, it became a mass movement. Nobody asked anybody for permission for this or that anymore. We would simply walk in, that's all…[I]f the crew was agreeable, well, we called a meeting." A win on the Queen Charlottes, then, would nail down these legal rights and pave the way for an industry-wide agreement, changing the face of labour-capital relations in the BC lumber industry.

Negotiations between the IWA and the logging companies took place over the spring and summer of 1943. Since the industry in question was vital to the war effort, bargaining was under the direction of a federal board of conciliation. In an attempt to undermine the legitimacy of the IWA, the island spruce operators, backed by 42 other Lower Coast companies, took aim at the leaders' links with communism. "Personally I feel that while soldiers are sleeping on the ground…it is not altogether up to the logger to insist on spring-filled mattresses at this time…I think unionism is a grand thing, but when it is worked

MORGAN'S FLOAT CAMP
Located in the Queen Charlotte Islands, this operation was home to dozens of workers who played a key role in the 1943 strike.
IWA ARCHIVES

to death, I think it is a pernicious thing," a company lawyer argued, simultaneously belittling the workers' demands for union recognition and calling into question their patriotism. "We will submit that this union is one which a Canadian company engaged in war work should not be asked to contract with," added another. "[It is] a political movement hiding behind the mask of a trade union." A sign posted at one of the camps was far more explicit: "Not All Saboteurs Are Japs."

In response, the union dismissed the companies' allegations as a "smoke screen" designed to deflect public attention away from the one crucial issue at hand: under federal *and* provincial law, workers possessed the right to organize a union of their own choosing and to bargain collectively with their employer. What was more, the union argued, whether the union leaders were members of a certain political party was simply irrelevant. As IWA lawyer John Stanton argued: "If it should be established as a matter of principle… that the political beliefs of union leaders alone constitute grounds for refusal by the companies to bargain collectively, then the whole principle of collective bargaining falls to the ground. It is obvious that the adoption of such a principle would lead to veritable witch-hunts." The conciliation board concurred and after several weeks of hearings handed down a decision in the union's favour. "The employers should enter into an agreement with the local union of the IWA for a period of one year," the board's final report stated. Pritchett and the IWA brass were elated, arguing in the daily papers, as they had before the board itself, that an agreement was "in the interests of industrial peace, harmony, and improved production."

Predictably, the logging firms refused to budge. "The operators will, of

SILENT AGITATORS

In the 1940s, the IWA represented a beacon of hope (top), guiding workers through the rough seas of class conflict. Out in the camps, IWA members demonstrated their union pride by posting placards (bottom) in their bunkhouses.

IWA ARCHIVES

course, comply with their legal bargaining obligations, but on the question of a signed agreement with these individuals, we have not changed our mind," a representative told the local media after the report was handed down. "Anyone who heard the sworn testimony regarding their past activities would hardly expect us to do so."

Rank-and-file workers were certainly familiar with the "past activities" of IWA activists, but in their opinion it was the reprehensible actions of employers who flatly refused to sign collective agreements, not the activities of those at the helm of the IWA, that deserved to be opposed. In this regard, after nearly three years of organizational work and negotiations, the workers on the Queen Charlottes became restless. On 6 October 1943, 90 men employed at the Kelley Logging Company staged a wildcat walkout to protest the company's intransigence; this action was followed by a legal strike on 8 October that involved 600 loggers from nine Queen Charlotte camps and lasted two weeks. "The strike…was quite unusual because at the time, all the left-wingers and all the progressive unions across Canada were solidly behind the war effort and committed to a 'no strike' policy. But here was a situation where it just had to happen," Al Parkin, then editor of the *Lumber Worker*, recounted. "[I]t had to happen because the workers wouldn't go for anything else. They just weren't content. Once the union began to gain its membership, they wanted to use it and there was no holding them back."

With important war-related production dropping, public opinion seemingly on the union's side ("The operators should sign," read a *Vancouver Province* editorial), and not a legal leg to stand on, the companies capitulated, signing an agreement that recognized the IWA as the workers' sole representative. The

# 'QCI On Strike This Morning'

*John McCuish*

THE QUEEN CHARLOTTE Island Strike started October 2, 1943. And it started at Skidanse Bay. They were promising us that they would come through with the agreement on the hours and overtime and all that. They were not living up to it. In fact they were getting tougher.

They were the best bunch on the Queen Charlotte Islands that time…"When are we going to strike, John?" [they asked]. And I said, "You name the date. You wire me, 'QCI Skidanse Bay on strike

this morning' and I will send a wire to the Morgan's camp and the Kelley camps and Pacific Mills."

Lorne LaFontaine was cooking there [at Pacific Mills]. And I said, "For Chrissake, fill that goddamn house full of food before the strike. Butter in tubs. Bacon on cooker. Flour, bacon, butter, sugar, etc. Lots of that." Boys organized a hunting crew. Two men were doing the hunting. They were bringing in a deer a day…There was a strike committee in every camp…Morgan about that time had 400 men. Kelley's had about 350. Pacific Mills about 250. We were propagandizing for this move for three years. □

'IT WAS A BEAUTIFUL
FEELING THEN'

IWA leaders converted
the union's 1943 strike
fund surplus into war
bonds and presented
them to the Federal
Government's National
War Finance Com-
mittee. Pictured here
are (second from left
to right) Nigel Morgan,
Bert Melsness,
Harold Pritchett,
Ernie Dalskog, and an
unidentified Finance
Committee official.

IWA ARCHIVES

deal also called for an eight-hour day and 48-hour week, seniority provisions, and other demands; in return, the union agreed not to call a strike during the life of the agreement. Both the IWA brass in BC and rank-and-file workers were extremely pleased with the results. "The agreement marks one of the biggest forward steps yet made in the lumber industry in the province," Nigel Morgan told the press after he signed off on the deal. Indeed it was. By December of 1943, the terms of the agreement were extended to cover approximately 8,000 union workers in the coastal mills and logging camps. The cornerstone of a master agreement on the Coast was finally in place. "It was a beautiful feeling amongst the workers then," John McCuish said.

## From Hot War to Cold War

As the negotiations between the IWA and the logging firms on the Queen Charlotte Islands illustrate, the union's ties to communism were controversial. But the questions related to Pritchett's and other IWAers' political sympathies were not raised just by employers who hoped to roll back the tide of militant industrial unionism, but, increasingly, by other political traditions within the labour movement itself. Indeed, during this period, the IWA, like other industrial unions, found itself immersed in a series of bitter internal scraps between communist and anti-communist factions tied to the CCF over the political direction of the new, burgeoning woodworkers' organization. To be sure, the house of labour had always been a raucous place, where debates between rivals were often passionate, but during the war years, and especially in the post-war period when the US and the Soviet Union were busy dividing the spoils of war

*'The communists had a very strong organization of disciplined activists, but they had not won the loyalty of the broad masses.'*

in Europe, these tensions took on a new, more intense form. On a broad level, the anti-communism of the 1940s and 50s was fuelled by an emerging Cold War mentality in North American society – a way of seeing and interpreting the world that rested on a widespread belief that entire groups or classes of people might be working on behalf of the Soviet Union to undermine the national interest. "In the Cold War," historian Reg Whitaker has concluded, "the ultimate ground upon which disloyalty was based was *ideological* – that is to say, the personal political beliefs of individual citizens." As one Montreal newspaper concluded, of particular concern were the "leftists [who] did not accept the basic political ideology of the Canadian people."

While no labour historian doubts the pivotal role that this emerging Cold War mentality played in framing the bitter debates within the labour movement, there is little agreement amongst writers as to the specific issues that divided the IWA into communist and anti-communist factions. Writers sympathetic to the CCF like Paul Phillips have placed emphasis on the communist leaders' shifting relationship with the mainstream labour movement and its flip-flop on the question of war in Europe. After the Soviet Union had signed a non-aggression pact with Germany, Pritchett and others linked to the Communist Party had come out strongly against the Allied cause; but after

## Taking The Pledge

*Harold Pritchett*

I'VE GOT TO make it very clear that the no-strike pledge adopted by the International Woodworkers of America was not only a district policy, it was IWA international policy, and it was CIO policy on top of all that, it was the policy of the Canadian Congress of Labour that everybody of any reasonable brains realized that with the drive of Hitler across Europe in which he destroyed trade unions, socialist parties, communist parties, even fraternal organizations and people were subjected to complete dictatorship including prison camps and millions murdered, that the trade union movement now must pledge to fight to defeat Hitler and nothing must stand in the way…

We had a strike in the Queen Charlotte Islands of the loggers who were working under bad conditions to produce the sitka spruce for the sitka bombers. And it lasted for a few days. Over a week. And we obtained a dollar a day increase for them because of the heavy timber, the side hills, the bugs, and the rain. They were entitled to a preference pay and they got it. Now, that was a spontaneous strike and nobody wanted to stop it. But we put it out to the bosses that if you continue to put those signs up that, "Not All Saboteurs Are Japs," then you're not going to get the kind of co-operation that we all want to win the war. So they were forced to pull the signs down.

Now, top leaders, right-wing leaders of the CCF…were opposed to the no-strike pledge only as it give them something to swing on. Not because of a principle question. So I fully supported the no-strike pledge and fought continuously and we did all we possibly could to win the war…As a matter of fact I had four sons in the armed services. Two of them overseas.

Hitler violated the pact and invaded the USSR, they pledged allegiance to the war effort and agreed not to strike during the duration of the conflict. Who, the anti-communists were asking, was pulling the strings? In this rendering of the past, the battles between anti-communists and communists appear not as a witch hunt – Canadian McCarthyism – but as a struggle to retain what CCF MLA and future IWAer Grant MacNeil called "self-government" in the union and to put forward a more pragmatic left-wing program. "The communists had a very strong organization of disciplined activists," Clay Perry has concluded. "But they had not won the loyalty of the 'broad masses' – ordinary, non-political working-class people who were turning in increasing numbers to the CCF."

Not surprisingly, writers who are less charitable to the CCF, like Bryan D. Palmer, have a different take on this bitter struggle. They point out that by the early 1940s, about one third of the membership of the Canadian Congress of Labour, the CIO's Canadian counterpart founded in 1940, was attached to unions with close ties to the Communist Party, including the IWA, the United Electrical, Radio, and Machine Workers, and the International Union of Mine, Mill, and Smelter Workers. Ridding the labour movement of those thought to be out of touch with the wishes of the rank and file or, at worst, mouthpieces for the Soviet Union was not going to be easy, but for those committed to "fighting the good fight" – the CCF and its allies – there was much to be gained. Indeed, by tapping the language of the red scare and ousting the communists, the industrial unions could be brought within the orbit of the new social democratic party, boosting its profile as a national political movement. Put simply, it was a power grab. What is more, they argue, the grassroots activists who were responsible, to a large degree, for the IWA's success possessed a significant capacity for independent initiative – acting as good trade unionists, not good Bolsheviks – and it was them, not just the "Party muckymucks" zigging and zagging in tandem with the Communist International, who paid the price for their beliefs, associations, and actions.

While there is little scholarly consensus on the question of motivation, both sides agree that the struggles between communists and anti-communists were both volatile and disruptive. Indeed, from the earliest days of the Federation of Woodworkers, communist (the "reds") and anti-communist members (the "whites") fought hard over questions of principles and politics. Throughout the 1930s and 1940s, the International executive of the IWA –

## LOCAL 2171 (INCLUDES 1-71 AND 1-217)

# Strength In Numbers

PRODUCED THROUGH a merger of Locals 1-71 (Loggers) and 1-217 (Vancouver) in 1998, Local 2171 represents 6,700 workers in a wide range of industries – including forestry, construction, transportation, and services – from Vancouver to the Alaska border.

With links to the Industrial Workers of the World, One Big Union, and the Lumber Workers Industrial Union, the Loggers' Local was one of the original organizations in the IWA, receiving its charter in 1937, the year the International was founded. The home of activists like John McCuish, Ernie Dalskog, and Harold Pritchett, Local 1-71 achieved its first large-scale breakthrough in 1943 on the Queen Charlotte Islands and was the driving force behind the 1946 25-40 Union Security strike. From the earliest days of the IWA, Local 1-71 used the famous *Laur Wayne, Loggers' Navy*, and later a series of boats called *Green Gold* to organize workers up and down the coast and, prior to the advent of the compulsory dues check-off, to collect members' dues. One of the largest locals in the union, 1-71, like other organizations in the IWA, was the site of an intense struggle between communist and anti-com-

**A WALK IN THE PARK**

**Members of the newly formed Loggers' Local strut their stuff en route to Stanley Park during Vancouver's annual May Day parade in 1938.**
PHOTO COURTESY ALLAN LUNDGREN

munist factions; when the International split in 1948, red bloc members absconded with the original charter. The founding document was returned to the IWA by Maurice Rush, former leader of the Communist Party of Canada, in 1997 at the local's 60th anniversary.

Like the Loggers' Local, Local 1-217 has deep roots in the labour movement. Originally located in New Westminster, BC – where a group of ply-

President Harold Pritchett, Vice-President Mickey Orton, and Executive Secretary Bertal McCarthy – were locked in an intense conflict with the so-called White Bloc centred around Oregon's Columbia River District Council, (CRDC) a powerful opposition group that was determined to make "membership in, or the support of, Communist, Nazi, or Fascist movements" grounds for expulsion. Pritchett and his allies on the International executive survived these early challenges mounted by the CRDC – in 1939 the rank and file returned them to power with a strong majority – only to be defeated in 1940 when the US immigration service, at the behest of lumber operators and conservative unionists on both sides of the line, refused the International president entry into the country because of his ties to communism. Unable to preside over the

wood and veneer workers held the original charter, granted in 1939 – the local moved to Vancouver in 1944 just as the IWA was gathering support throughout the province and the lumber industry in the Lower Mainland was growing. By the late 1950s it represented upwards of 7,400 workers in a wide range of sectors – such as plywood, milling, shake and shingle, and manufacturing – in workplaces in North Vancouver, the industrial areas of False Creek in Vancouver, and on the Fraser River. According to IWA historian Clay Perry, during its heyday Local 1-217, under president Syd Thompson, was "the home of opposition to conciliatory unionism [in the IWA]." Thompson, a former organizer for the Communist Party in Alberta, was elected president of the local in 1958, defeating incumbent Lloyd Whalen in a campaign that featured vicious anti-communist rhetoric and accusations that Harold Pritchett, who had left the union after the debacle of 1948, was orchestrating a takeover. Thompson held the position until 1980.

Throughout the 1960s, 70s, and 80s, Local 1-217 had its share of strikes – including a losing but hard-fought five-year battle for a 40-hour week at MacMillan Bloedel's Red Band plant in 1972 and a victory against contracting out in 1986 – and took stands against the war in Vietnam, nuclear

THAT'S *DOCTOR* SYD THOMPSON

**Syd Thompson went from "lousy jobs to relief camps to organizing in cold Alberta winters" to receiving an honorary doctorate from Simon Fraser University in 1978.**

IWA ARCHIVES

weapons in Canada, free trade, and discrimination against women in the workplace. Over the last two decades, however, the economy of the Lower Mainland changed substantially as mills and plants closed down or moved and industrial lands, most notably in preparation for Expo 86, were put to commercial and residential uses. The closure of the Eburne sawmill in 1998 was but the latest example of this industry-wide trend. Against this backdrop of change and declining membership, Local 1-217 merged with 1-71 to produce Local 2171. "There has been a conscious decision to merge now while the locals are still strong," Darrel Wong, president of 2171, remarked. "Strength is what the merger is all about."

union's business, Pritchett resigned and took up the leadership of the BC Coast District Council. Clearly, even before the "hot" war in Europe had ended, the Cold War had come home to the house of labour.

Anti-communists in Oregon were assisted by the leaders of the CIO itself. Once willing to tolerate reds within the movement, at least when they were busy building industrial unions, John L. Lewis had emerged in the late 1930s as a particularly passionate advocate of the need to expel anyone linked to communism – on either side of the border. To this end, Lewis appointed Adolph Germer, a former socialist, as director of organization in the IWA's International office to assist him in "oust[ing] Communists from control of an important union." Germer, once described by Pritchett as a "bitter old socialist who made a career out of going to jail with [prominent US radical] Eugene Debs," co-ordinated the activities of anti-communists, including the CRDC, United Brotherhood of Carpenters and Joiners, and various employers. "The rank and file of the woodworkers want none of the Communist Party interference, influence, or control. The CIO wants none of it," he told the *Seattle Post-Intelligencer* in 1940, shortly after taking his new position.

The ensuing battle between Germer and the IWA dominated union conventions, disrupted organizational campaigns from Washington State to

# 'Why Should You?'

*Green-chain Pete*
BC Lumber Worker, *20 March 1940*

The Company is good to me,
I'm afraid to join the Union.
They cut my pay and I agree;
I'm afraid to join the Union.
My wages, they are so high,
My family's starving, so am I –
I'm afraid to join the Union.

I get the lowest pay on earth;
I'm afraid to join the Union.
I'm paid exactly what I'm worth;
I'm afraid to join the Union.
I think the Company is fair;
They lay me off but I don't care;
My kids object, but I don't dare –
I'm afraid to join the Union.

Did you hear what we have to say? –
Join up with the IWA.
We're wise to what it's all about,
So let's all sing out –
To boost our pay a dollar a day,
We'll all join up with the IWA.

So now you see it's up to you.
You know what we all can do –
Organize where ever we may be
And march ahead with our brother employee
Don't debate, it's not too late;
The IWA has opened the gate
For better wages, conditions, and security
All join hands and show your solidarity.

Florida, and started to split district councils. Fearing that Germer was on the
verge of orchestrating a complete takeover of the IWA, President Mickey
Orton, a friend and ally of Harold Pritchett, and the union's executive expelled
Germer and appealed to the CIO to reprimand him for his unethical behaviour. "[He] has failed miserably [in his role as director of organization]," Orton
wrote to Phillip Murray, the new head of the CIO and a Germer supporter.
"His actions not only reduced the dignity of his office and his personal pres-
tige in the eyes of the great majority of the responsible officers and the sincere
membership of our Union, but he has aligned himself with a number of noisy
and vociferous individuals who, since our inception as an International Union,
have concerned themselves with disruption and division." CIO president
Murray agreed to hold an investigation into Orton's allegations that Germer
was carrying on a campaign against the duly elected officials of the IWA, disrupting the affairs of local unions, and discriminating against union organizers
on the basis of their political beliefs. After six weeks of hearings before CIO
officials – hearings which were less about the accused's activities and more

about who was and was not a communist – Germer was exonerated. He remained tied to the IWA until 1944, when he was promoted to the upper echelons of the labour movement, first as the CIO's point man in the west and later as its representative to the World Federation of Trade Unions.

At the same time, anti-communists in British Columbia also became active – their activities only intensifying as the BC Coast District Council chalked up some impressive organizational gains in the 1940s. Indeed, in the wake of the successful drive to organize the Queen Charlotte Islands and the signing of a Coast-wide agreement, the council emerged as a powerful presence within the IWA in particular and in the provincial and national labour movement more generally. To those opposed to the presence of a red leadership, it appeared that the province's woodworkers were being delivered snoose, spar, and skidder to the "communistic elements."

The conflict between these two opposing factions took many forms.

**LOCAL 1-85**

# Pioneer Local

WITH ITS ORIGINS in the 1934 loggers' strike against Bloedel, Stewart, and Welch at Great Central Lake, Local 1-85, centred in Port Alberni on Vancouver Island, is one of the original IWA locals. After brief stints in the United Brotherhood of Carpenters and Joiners and Lumber and Saw, Local 1-85 received its charter from the IWA in 1937. Like other IWA locals, it was a hot spot during the Cold War as the red and white blocs struggled for control of the industrial union movement at the local, district, and inter-

**PEOPLE GET READY**
**Members of Local 1-85 prepare for action during the 25-40 Union Security strike in 1946.**
IWA ARCHIVES

national level; more than 50 years after the famous split between the IWA and the Woodworkers Industrial Union of Canada, Maurice Rush, a former leader of the Communist Party, returned 1-85's original charter to the IWA.

But the Cold War is only one chapter of this local's long history. During the past 60 years it has fought many strikes – 1946, 1959, 1972, 1981, and 1986 – for higher wages, improved benefits, and better working conditions. As the forest industry expanded, so, too, did 1-85's membership – the vast majority of which was drawn from MacMillan Bloedel's operations in and around the Alberni Valley. Workers from the north end of Vancouver Island – mostly loggers who plied their trade in isolated camps – signed up as well. By the late 1970s, Local 1-85 represented about 6,400

Organizing drives, such as the one launched in 1942-43 at Fraser Mills, were characterized by divisiveness as anti-communists in the union, in conjunction with the CCF, worked to curb the influence of red organizers by attending meetings, encouraging the company to steer clear of the union, and distributing leaflets that accused President Pritchett of "using the IWA as a racket for his own personal profit." (No evidence of any kind has emerged to substantiate such claims). In other locales, anti-communists attempted to divide large IWA locals into smaller sub-locals so that they might elect more acceptable leaders. In New Westminster, a group called the "Old Timers" kept up an unyielding campaign against the district leadership, "the gang of wreckers that had pulled the 1931 strike [at Fraser Mills]"; on Vancouver Island, veteran faller – and one-time member of the Lumber Workers Industrial Union – John Ulinder spearheaded an effort to "clean house" and to raise the profile of the social democratic alternative.

people, a distinctive combination of town-based members ("home guards") and bushworkers that is captured by the local's crest, which features a logger and mill worker shaking hands. Current national president Dave Haggard served as 1-85's president from 1990 to 1996.

By the late 1970s and early 1980s, however, as the country plunged into an economic recession and MacMillan Bloedel sought to stem its losses, Port Alberni's – and the local's – fortunes took a turn for the worse. Hundreds of woodworkers were laid off, a move that prompted the local union to set up the Organization of Unemployed Workers, which advocated for the six-hour day, as opposed to layoffs, as a way to deal with hard times. The recession was but the opening act in a longer drama of economic restructuring that saw MacBlo reduce its workforce in the area by 51 percent, from 5,386 in 1980 to 2,764 in 1996. "It was kind of like losing your country. That was your livelihood, your way of life, your routine," an employee from Alberni Plywoods recalled after the plant closed down in 1991. "I was 53, I think. Too young to retire but too bloody old

to work anywhere else." Today, Local 1-85 is rebuilding and diversifying its membership base.

At the same time as technological change and globalization of the economy were taking their toll on 1-85, environmental concerns – specifically the fate of old-growth forests in Clayoquot Sound and the Carmanah Valley on the southwestern portion of Vancouver Island – were heating up. The lower Carmanah Valley was set aside as a park by the Social Credit government in 1990. That same year at the NDP convention, Local 1-85, and the IWA as a whole, called on the opposition party to adopt a "compromise solution" to land-use conflicts, the bitter struggles that pitted companies, workers, environmentalists, and First Nations people against each other. The policy adopted by the NDP – which included a commitment to protect a percentage of "representative ecosystems" and the "land base of the working forest in order to maintain employment" – proved to be a key plank in its successful election campaign in 1991. But as the clashes over Clayoquot Sound in 1993 showed, peace in the woods remained an elusive objective in the 1990s.

## LOCAL 1-3567 (INCLUDES 1-357 AND 1-367)

# Heritage of Struggle

AGAINST A BACKDROP of economic recession, industry-wide restructuring, technological change, and reduced timber supply, two of the IWA's oldest organizations – 1-357 (New Westminster) and 1-367 (Maple Ridge) – came together to form Local 1-3567 in 1992.

Originally a sub-local of Vancouver's 1-217 based at Fraser Mills, Local 1-357 was chartered in 1942 and covered a large swath of BC's Lower Mainland – from the industrial city of New Westminster in the south to Port Moody, at the head of Burrard Inlet, in the north. With a heritage of struggle that stretches back to the turn of the twentieth century, when a clutch of industrial organizations (IWW), craft unions (AFL-TLC), and political parties (SPC) were active amongst New Westminster's working class, Local 1-357 was always a hotbed of political activism. Throughout the Cold War it was the standard-bearer of social democracy within the IWA, pro-

viding a staging ground for local whites Stewart Alsbury, George Mitchell, the "Old Timers" group, and their counterparts within the CCF and the CCL-CIO. In 1952, John McRae "Rae" Eddie, a local IWA organizer who helped the union consolidate its hold on the region's sawmills in the 1940s, became the first CCF candidate from New Westminster to be elected to the provincial legislature. Eddie's victory was just the first of many for the party in the "Royal City"; between 1952 and 1983 the CCF – later the New Democratic Party – won 11 consecutive elections in the area. Links between the IWA and the social democrats were forged in other ways, too. Gerry Stoney, who headed the New Westminster local from 1971 to 1982 and the national organization from 1992 to 1997, was also president of the provincial New Democratic Party from 1982 to 1988.

Of course electoral politics was but one part of the local's political game. After securing an organizational breakthrough in the mid-1940s, membership in 1-357 ballooned as the local sawmill and manufacturing sectors expanded throughout the 1950s and 60s. By the early 1970s, certifications with industry heavyweights Canfor, Weldwood, International Forest Products, Fletcher Challenge, and MacMillan Bloedel brought about 7,500 men and women into the IWA fold. By the time merger talks began in the early 1990s, however, 1-357's membership had slipped to about 4,000.

Local 1-367 was carved out of the New Westminster organization in 1956 and given jurisdiction over an area that straddles the Fraser River from Pitt Meadows in the south to Lillooet in the north. From its base at Hammond Cedar – a certification that dated back to World War II and its days as a sub-local – the new organization reached out to loggers and workers in primary breakdown plants throughout the region. It added hundreds of shake and shingle workers to its membership rolls in the late 1960s after Local 28 of the AFL-TLC–affiliated International Union of Shingle Weavers, Sawmill Workers, and Woodsmen decided to merge with the IWA. Throughout the 1970s the local grew significantly, peaking at 3,000 members drawn from the shake and shingle, sawmill and manufacturing, and logging sectors of the forest-dependent economy. Like its counterpart in New Westminster, 1-367 was also politically active, working hand in glove with the NDP at the municipal, provincial, and federal level.

But membership numbers started to slip in the wake of the deep recession in the early 1980s when Interfor, MacBlo, Crown Zellerbach, and other large corporations ditched their shake and shingle operations in order to cut costs and focus on more lucrative and less risky dimensions of the lumber business. Many union jobs were lost, a development made worse by the emergence of smaller, non-union companies attempting to fill the void left by the industry's biggest players, the export of raw materials out of the country, and dwindling timber supply.

In 1986, 1-367, and the IWA as a whole, helped the Canadian government secure a ban on the export of cedar logs, blanks, and boards to the United States, a move that stemmed the flow of unprocessed wood across the border, effectively prevented the shake and shingle industry from going belly-up, and curbed job losses in the region. But membership numbers remained depressed – bottoming out at 700 during the recession of the early 1990s – prompting the local to look outside its traditional strongholds in the lumber industry and consider a merger with Local 1-357. "We recognize that the times are changing and we will be seeing fewer and fewer primary breakdown units, loggers, and the eventual shrinkage of the IWA," the local's president, David Tones, remarked at the time, highlighting the need to pursue both strategies. "[W]e had to wake up and smell the coffee. So we are much more active [organizing] now."

With the approval of nearly 80 percent of rank-and-file members, the two organizations were combined, creating a bigger, more powerful organization that continues to benefit from the collective wisdom both locals have garnered over more than 50 years of struggle and success. Today, Local 1-3567, which represents over 4,000 workers, is one of the largest and most diversified locals in western Canada. ▫

ALL IN FAVOUR, SAY AYE

Delegates from Local 1-367 – including David Tones (left), Barry King (beside him), Joe Fowler (right), and Sonny Ghag (beside him) – attend a regional convention in the 1980s.

IWA ARCHIVES

The appointment of organizers was also a flashpoint for red-white antipathy. After receiving the BC Coast District Council's request for three veteran organizers for the Interior of the province, International executive member George Brown despatched a trio of union activists who were loyal to the whites, not the reds. "I wanted to get that section of British Columbia educated on a program of wages, hours, and working conditions," Brown asserted, "and not on any program in the interests of any political party." The BC Coast

## Ships Spread Union Gospel

*Vancouver Province, 20 February 1943*

DOWN BY THE DENMAN DOCKS in Coal Harbor, sandwiched between pleasure craft, fish boats and barges, the cabin cruiser *Laur Wayne* chafes at her moorings while the crew provisions the 44-foot vessel for a four months' voyage in British Columbia waters. The *Laur Wayne* and her sister ship, the *Annart*, hold a unique place in coastal shipping. They carry no passengers and no freight. The vessels are the property of the International Woodworkers of America. They are used by union organizers to reach loggers in distant camps.

Some of the men call the boats "mission ships" because they carry the gospel of trade unionism to workers in the wilderness. The two boats represent an investment of $6500, and the costs of operation are about $3400 per year. The expenses are defrayed

**MAKING WAVES**

The cabin cruiser *Laur Wayne* was the first ship in the IWA's Loggers' Navy.
IWA ARCHIVES

through union dues…Ernie Dalskog, secretary of IWA Local 1-71, will be in command. Duane Pritchett, a budding unionist of 17 years, will be engineer. He is son of Harold E. Pritchett, president of the IWA in Vancouver…

Members of the IWA feel the *Laur Wayne* has chalked up a pretty fair record as a union organizer. She was purchased in 1936 and has traveled a total of 69,000 miles. On a number of calls at out of the way places the *Laur Wayne* has played the role of hospital ship. Men who have suffered sudden illness and accidents have been carried to cities where they could receive treatment…

Unionists do not see anything particularly romantic about the sea-going union boats. They look upon their ships as a strictly business proposition, and are apt to deny they get any thrills out of their work. "Oh, I guess, in a way you do get a thrill sometimes," admits Dalskog. "It makes you feel good to see as many as 150 men pour out of the bush and pile down to the dock to see the union boat come in. They are pretty lonesome for union talk and newspapers. So there is quite a bit of satisfaction in mission work."

District Council was infuriated by this decision, passing a pointed resolution condemning the action. Pritchett pleaded for labour unity: "We have a job to do that requires the greatest degree of unity and anybody who gets in the way of that unity is going to get their toes stepped on." In this particular skirmish, however, it was the BC Coast District Council that got its toes stepped on as Brown refused to back down. While the campaign would, in time, go ahead – both white and red organizers entered the field – the conflict between the two factions was a sign of things to come as the Cold War intensified in the late 1940s and 50s, eventually engulfing the IWA and other unions accused of being "communist-directed."

## Gender Politics/Class Politics

Union politics at this time were not limited to questions of collective agreements and communist domination. Indeed, the exceptional circumstances associated with the war brought other equally important debates to the fore, including the role of women in the lumber industry and labour movement. For employers across the country, especially those crucial to the war effort, severe "manpower" shortages caused a dramatic, albeit temporary, change in the labour force as working women moved to fill the vacancies left by men serving overseas. As historian Susanne Klausen has demonstrated, the management of Alberni Plywoods, or ALPLY, in Port Alberni, BC, understood

## 'Making Herstory'

WHILE MEN HAVE long dominated the IWA, women have made a substantial contribution to the union as well – helping to build the organization and to broaden its agenda. Early in the IWA's history, when the industry was still a man's world, women's involvement and women's concerns centred around the Ladies' Auxiliary. As the union pushed ahead in the 1940s, organizing workers in all regions of British Columbia, the women's organization expanded too, tackling important issues such as unemployment insurance, family allowances, and government-run health care. "Living standards must be protected," Mona Morgan, the auxiliary's district vice-president, told a women-led protest against the high cost of living in 1946. "The health and physical stamina of our country must be improved."

Equal pay for equal work, a bold position in the 1940s, was also a top priority for the Ladies' Auxiliary and for the union leadership, one that flowed from a principled belief that all workers, regardless of sex (or race), deserved the protection that a union could provide. In 1945, under the auspices of the National War Labor Board, the IWA secured equal pay for equal work provisions in a collective agreement with Hammond Cedar – a deal that lasted for the duration of the war.

Women's contributions to the IWA during the 1940s and early 1950s were not limited to the auxiliary movement. Gladys Shunaman certainly knew that. During World War II, Shunaman, like many women, went to work in the lumber industry, filling the void left by male workers who were fighting overseas. Shortly after beginning at Sitka Spruce, Shunaman, then associated with the Communist Party, set about unionizing her section of the company's operations – the planer mill where many of the women were located. She was assisted in this endeavour by IWA pioneers Nels Arseneau, Harold Pritchett, and, especially, Ernie Dalskog, whom she later referred to as "her coach." In 1942 she was elected secretary of Local 1- 217 – the men at Canadian White Pine, one of the larger operations in the local's jurisdiction, voting for her en masse. "It was a little scary," she recalled years later, thinking back to her unexpected election victory.

For the next six years as secretary, Shunaman worked with local, district, and international organizers in an era when enthusiasm for the IWA-CIO was still high amongst the region's sawmill workers. At the same time, she was a passionate advocate for women's equality. But being a local official who was sympathetic to the reds also meant being caught up in the fractious politics of the Cold

War; Local 1-217 was, after all, Lloyd Whalen's and George Mitchell's political stomping ground. "It was troublesome because I really wanted them [sawmill workers] to get organized. I knew what a union meant and I didn't want splits or anything else. I just wanted them to join the union and stay together," she recalled years later. Initially opposed to the communists' decision to secede from the IWA, Shunaman helped set up the Woodworkers Industrial Union of Canada and, shortly after, left the labour movement. "I grew in that period. In so many ways. It was a new experience. It was a challenge," she told IWA historian Clay Perry in 1997. "I took a different view of politics and of life in general. I just grew, expanded, became a different person, and have never been the same since."

In the wake of World War II, most working women left the lumber industry – some willingly, some not – to make room for the men returning from war, taking with them the critical mass of female workers required to place women's issues at the centre of the IWA's political agenda. It was not that the union no longer supported progressive initiatives. It certainly did – and those stances set the IWA apart from mainstream trade unions. In 1953, former Local 1-71 president and MLA Frank Howard criticized the BC government's Equal Pay for Women Act for its limited scope and cumbersome grievance procedure; in 1958, delegates to the annual convention voted to abolish the separate wage scales for women in the plywood industry; in 1966, the IWA went on strike, in part, to secure equal pay for equal work in the Coast master agreement. What was more, the Ladies' Auxiliary remained active and the IWA continued to be a staunch supporter of the CCF and its successor, the New Democratic Party, organizations with a long tradition of progressive gender politics.

But on the job, the IWA's insistence on equal pay for equal work had contradictory results as the elimination of women's lower wage rates often prompted employers to just stop hiring female workers. While this outcome was certainly not what the IWA had anticipated, the union did not appear to challenge this informal hiring freeze in any concerted way. In Port Alberni, for example, where women were prominent in the plywood mill during World War II, it was not until the late 1960s and early 1970s, when the industry experienced another labour shortage, that women were rehired in significant numbers.

Not surprisingly, as female workers trickled back into the lumber industry (of the IWA's 47,000 members, only 1,000 were women), questions related specifically to women's experience on the job, in the union, and in society came to the fore. At the IWA's 1971 convention, delegates approved a resolution calling for a conference of female members – though it was not until 1973 that the regional executive board in BC actually gave the organizers the green light.

On 21 July 1973, the IWA in BC held its first women's conference; female workers from Locals 1-85, 1-217, and 1-357, including Marge Storm and Alice Persons, were there. "Women in the IWA are beginning to organize, to become active in the union, to ensure that the union fights for the rights of working women," the *Lumber Worker* reported. And they started by criticizing both employers and the IWA for the "systematic discrimination in hiring" taking place in the industry. Delegates called for the creation of an annual conference of women, the elimination of female job classifications in seniority agreements negotiated by the IWA, and a ban on sexist content and cartoons in the *Lumber Worker*.

They also wanted to know more about the experiences of those pioneering women who worked in the industry during World War II. One of the women in attendance was Verna Ledger, a mill worker from Canadian Forest Products, Pacific

Delegates to the quarterly meeting of the Ladies' Auxiliary gather in Lake Cowichan in 1944. The cost of living, accessible health care, equal pay for equal work, and the length of the work week topped the agenda.
IWA LOCAL 1-80 ARCHIVES
W.H. GOLD COLLECTION

Veneer Division, in New Westminster and director of Local 1-357's health and safety department. Buoyed by the emergence of female activism, she organized several women's conferences, joined the BC Federation of Labour's Occupational Health and Safety Committee in 1976, and took on the challenge of National Health and Safety Director for the IWA in 1978, a position she retained until her retirement in 1991. Ledger's rise to prominence in an organization and industry that remained male-dominated was indeed significant; not only did her contribution in the area of occupational health and safety enrich the union's political life, but her success as a woman stood as an important symbol for women throughout the industry.

Progress in the area of gender issues was slow but steady as women remained active on the shop floor, in local unions, and at regional and national conventions. In 1984, the IWA offered to relinquish one of its seats on the executive board of the BC Federation of Labour for a permanent woman's representative. In 1990, IWA locals in Ontario, working under pay equity guidelines laid down by the province, negotiated several collective agreements that included substantial pay hikes for women workers. And it wasn't just women who did the same job as men who received a pay increase; female workers who laboured at jobs of equivalent value also benefitted.

However, as many women in the IWA knew well, many issues remained unresolved, including barriers within the union to women's full participation in political affairs, the existence of sexual harassment in the workplace, and the need for permanent women's committees – problems that have become increasingly important as the IWA continues to expand from its traditional base in the lumber industry into the service sector, where many women are employed. In response, Local 1-424 in Prince George convened a "Women in the Workforce" conference in 1995, a gathering followed by similar strategy sessions sponsored by Local 500 in Ontario in 1998 and 1999 and at the national level in 1997 and 1998. "We want a strong union. We are all very proud of the IWA and we have great ties to it and we feel strongly that we are an integral part of that union," Local 1-207's Esther James stated at the national 1998 gathering. "We all have to go back into our locals and get our sisters involved."

Today, women activists in the IWA are pushing forward with a plan to entrench a women's committee in the union's constitution, a move that would create a permanent forum within which to formulate and adopt policies generated by women's educational conferences, develop and co-ordinate training programs for women, and advise the national union leadership on gender issues. □

the severity of the labour shortage induced by the war. As local men from this Vancouver Island town joined the armed forces, bosses there hired scores of young, usually single women to work in its plywood factory producing ammunition boxes, airplane parts, and other war-related materials. Like working women in industries across the country, the women of Port Alberni responded enthusiastically. As one woman who worked for ALPLY observed years later:

> All the kids in town were down there practically. Most of the women that were down there were older. I lied about my age. I kept going down there for months…Every time I'd go in there they'd look at me and say, "You're too small." I'd say "But I'm strong." You had to BS. I kept going back and back and back, finally they just got tired of me. They said, "We'll let you come in. Try you out."…I was happy. I thought, "I'm on my way now."

By 1943 about 280 women – representing 80 percent of ALPLY's total workforce – were employed at the factory. Like the nearly 250,000 women nationwide who laboured in industries considered vital to the war effort, the presence of the "Plywood Girls" on the factory floor and in the community challenged, at least for a short time, age-old notions of what constituted "men's work" and "women's work." "I think a lot of women, including myself, you always felt the men went away and worked so hard…[He] was the breadwinner, and the women look after everything else. And, 'don't bother him, he's quite tired,'" one Plywood Girl recalled in an interview with Klausen. "After I worked, I thought I'm working hard, because it was hard work. Fast and some of it was heavy. I sort of realized, if this is how hard my father works, where's the big deal? This is good exercise."

As in the wake of World War I, however, the advances made by working women on the job were rolled back in the immediate post-World War II period. As one historian has noted, "the family, not the factory, re-emerged as the centre of women's lives." For the Plywood Girls, as for working women across the country, pressure from governments, employers, returning soldiers, and unions to re-establish "normal" social relationships meant leaving the factory floor for those occupations deemed suitably female: homemaker, domestic servant, nurse, or teacher the most common. Most of the women at ALPLY agreed. "Even in those days, it was logical that once the men came back that they would have to work…We expected to leave," said one former employee.

But others stayed on and, as a result, often found themselves having to justify their presence on the shop floor. "[A male employee] said [to me that] he didn't fight in a war to come to this, to take orders from a damn woman…I said, 'When you learn to do this [task], I'll gladly give it to you.'" Once emblem-

*The presence of the 'Plywood Girls' challenged age-old notions of what constituted 'men's work' and 'women's work.'*

atic of female pride, independence, and camaraderie during the war, by the late 1940s and early 1950s the Plywood Girls had become the "Plywood Bags," a negative term used by working- and middle-class people to show their disapproval of some women's stubborn refusal to relinquish their jobs to those thought to be better qualified, namely men. When the IWA voted at its 1958 annual convention to "eliminate the sub-standard wage rates for females in the plywood section of the industry," it, perhaps unwittingly, excluded women from plywood work altogether. For the union, it was certainly a thorny political calculation. Fearing that ALPLY management might use cheap female labour to undercut men's wages, the IWA went about curtailing the bosses'

## LOCAL 363

# Batco and Beyond

ONCE A PART OF Local 1-80 (Lake Cowichan), Local 363 was created in 1943, just as waves of wartime labour militancy were washing over much of British Columbia. Buoyed by recent changes to the province's labour code, a year later the local signed a union agreement with the Batco Development Company of Campbell River, BC. The deal – which established an eight-hour day, a safety committee, and a joint labour-management "production" committee, and outlawed discrimination against union members – was the first of its kind in the lumber industry in BC and came as part of a wider series of breakthroughs in the 1940s. In 1948, Local 363 was at the centre of the Iron River Strike – a battle remembered by workers and historians alike (see Chapter 4) because of the important role it played in the bitter split between communists and anti-communists who were battling for control of the IWA. From the 1950s to the late 1970s, Local 363 expanded, and successive agreements, which covered everything from increases in base rates and cost-of-living adjustments to better medical coverage, seniority provisions, and holidays, steadily improved the lot of

A BATCO BOY, 1940s

Working in the tall trees near Oyster Bay, a lone faller, standing on a springboard, prepares to swing his axe.

IWA LOCAL 363 ARCHIVES

workers. Of particular importance during this period was the 1972 fallers' strike – spearheaded by Local 363 and Local 1-85 – which replaced the piece rate with a day rate ($83.50 for a $6^{1}/_{2}$-hour day).

Over much of the last 20 years, however, Local 363, like other IWA locals, has been caught between the rock of technological change, corporate downsizing, and wasteful logging practices and the hard place of First Nations' land claims and environmental concerns. In the case of the former, the advent of grapple yarders and hoechuckers has left hundreds of loggers in 363's

ability to do so. But according to Klausen, "with the achievement of wage parity, management ceased hiring women, and so began a fourteen-year drought during which only men could obtain work at the mill." The Plywood Girls' time at ALPLY was short-lived, but their example serves to explode the remarkably durable myth that the lumber industry was (and should therefore remain) a man's world.

While the working men and women of Port Alberni negotiated the politics associated with waged work, the IWA Ladies' Auxiliary was taking up different, though certainly related, issues: the rising cost of living, proper health care and education for workers and their families, and other community-related

jurisdiction out of work. At the same time, most value-added production takes place in other locales. "In the 60s we had two jobs for every 1,000 cubic metres of timber harvested," a local IWAer remarked in 1991. "Now there's not even one job per 1,000." As tough as these losses have been, however, they are not as drastic as those experienced by other locals, where top-to-bottom technological change at larger mills has revolutionized the world of work. Membership of 363 today stands at 1,200.

As many IWAers know well, the Tsitika Valley is synonymous with environmental concerns. This ecologically sensitive, timber-rich region is located on the northeastern shore of Vancouver Island between Campbell River and Port McNeill. It is situated within a MacMillian Bloedel (now Weyerhaeuser) tree farm licence. Set aside by the NDP in 1973, the valley has been under the jurisdiction of several government-sponsored bodies charged with investigating and managing its environmental and economic assets. Local 363 has been an important player in this process. In 1990, approximately 43 percent of the valley was set aside not to be logged. At the same time the Tlowitsis-Mumtaglia First Nation

**HISTORIC AGREEMENT**

**Local 363's groundbreaking deal with Batco Development at Iron River in 1943 was the first in a series of IWA victories during World War II.**

COMMUNIST PARTY OF CANADA ARCHIVES
ERNIE DALSKOG COLLECTION

claimed title to the lower portion of the controversial watershed. Both initiatives prompted Local 363, and the IWA as a whole, to pressure the provincial and federal governments to settle land claims and to bring political and economic stability to the province. □

## 'Irrespective of Race or Colour...'

INDUSTRIAL UNIONISM was not the only tradition that the IWA inherited from its left-wing forebearers. Anti-racism was passed down too. Then, as now, workers in the lumber industry were a racially and culturally diverse group – drawn together in the mills of coastal British Columbia, the camps of northern Ontario, or the plants in New Brunswick from across the country and around the world by the powerful prospect of work and wages. From the get-go, the IWA understood that organizational success and the attainment of wider objectives of social and economic justice required that it reach out to all workers. Employers, after all, had long exploited racial (and gender) divisions within the working class to weaken the labour movement.

Throughout the 1930s and 40s, a time in which intolerance and racism were prevalent in Canadian society, IWAers like Joe Eng, Roy Mah, and Darshan Singh Sangha worked hard to bridge the cultural and linguistic divide between white and non-white workers. "[T]his union is a demo-

cratic organization," the strike committee waging the battle at Blubber Bay, of which Eng was a part, wrote defiantly in 1938. "[T]here can be no differentiation between a worker, whether he be white, yellow, or black." In the mills that dotted Vancouver Island and the Lower Mainland, for example, the IWA pushed employers to abolish differential pay scales, improve conditions in company-owned bunkhouses and facilities for Asian workers' and eliminate the role of the "tyee," or ethnic labour boss, who routinely skimmed money from Chinese, Japanese, and East Indian workers' paycheques in exchange for access to jobs. "The Chinese brothers are now taking a more active interest in the trade union movement," Mah reported. "This will pave the way for closer co-operation with the white brothers in our common endeavour to better our economic and social conditions."

In addition to workplace issues, the union also fought for the broader civil rights of its non-white members. In 1943, a delegation consisting of the IWA, the CCF, and the Khalsa Diwan Society lobbied the BC government to allow East Asians to vote in provincial elections, a right they, along with Chinese and Japanese citizens, had lost decades before. Four years later, the government restored this basic democratic freedom. "One of the greatest achievements of the IWA was the uniting of all woodworkers – white, Indian, Chinese, Japanese – irrespective of race and colour," Darshan Singh Sangha wrote in 1947. "Thanks to the farsighted and militant leaders of the IWA, 37,000 woodworkers are now enjoying relatively good wages and working conditions. In many ways, the minority groups, which were always discriminated against and victimized first, have gained the most."

Like Mah and Sangha, Joe Miyazawa played an important role in forging racial unity, working as an organizer in the BC Interior and later as an IWA staff member between 1945 and 1965. During World War II, Miyazawa's family, like all Japanese residents in coastal areas, was thought to be a security risk and was forced into prison camps and towns in the Interior. During this period of internment, Miyazawa went to work at a mill in Kamloops and like his father, who was a member of the Japanese Camp and Mill Workers' Union in the 1920s, became active in the union movement. Miyazawa helped Mike Sekora, then an organizer

**WITH OUR 'WHITE BROTHERS'**
Edmonton-born Roy Mah assisted Chinese-speaking workers and wrote a Cantonese edition of the *Lumber Worker*.
IWA ARCHIVES

with the IWA's International office, to sign up the ethnically diverse mill workers. After the war ended, he stayed on as a paid organizer in the west Kootenay region, as many Japanese workers took up jobs in the Slocan Valley after they were released from the camps. "Wherever I was I knew somebody. I'd make sure we'd make the contacts and then we'd call a meeting at the farmers' institute or the ladies' institute hall or some damn thing," he recalled.

During the Cold War, Miyazawa, then the only paid organizer in southern British Columbia, canvassed local unions to boost support for the social democratic opposition that was emerging in New Westminster. The issue, for him, was not necessarily anti-communism, but the union leadership's priorities: "I don't think the workers were so worldly wise about these things. We didn't know a communist from a Trotskyite."

After the split of 1948, Miyazawa left the Interior for the Coast, signing on as the IWA's associate director of research. (Ironically, he had to get permission from the RCMP to make the move; although the war was over, they were still skeptical of Japanese residents' loyalties.) From this vantage point, Miyazawa continued to advocate not just for workers' rights, but for human rights, and he did so at the local, national, and international level. In the mid to late 1950s he worked on behalf of the International Confederation of Free Trade Unions, a global labour organization, to secure better ties with non-affiliated unions in Japan. Miyazawa left the IWA in 1965. "I had to work for someone else and make a buck or two," he recollected.

The IWA's tradition of integrating issues of class and race, as epitomized by Miyazawa's contribution, was not limited to questions of wages, working conditions, and organizing. Throughout its history the IWA has also taken up the struggle of First Nations people, some of whom were, and are, union members. In 1941, the IWA supported the Native Brotherhood of British Columbia, a First Nations organization founded in 1931, in its push for what IWA International board member Nigel Morgan called "full citizenship rights and parliamentary representation without interference with treaty rights of land titles." In the 1960s, the IWA fought employers in both Alberta and British Columbia who routinely discriminated against Métis and First Nations woodworkers – paying them less than their white counterparts and denying them equal access to job-training programs and other employment opportunities. In 1978, delegates to Region 2's annual convention endorsed two resolutions: one calling on Ottawa to grant a full pardon to Louis Riel, the leader of the Métis rebellions of 1869 and 1885, who was executed by the federal government for his "treasonous" actions; and the other to "rec-

COMBATING RACISM

**Joe Miyazawa addresses a TLC-CCL anti-racism workshop in the 1950s; Local 1-217's Al Pollard is seated on his immediate left.**
IWA ARCHIVES

ognize Native Peoples' ambitions for complete self-sufficiency through political and economic control of their own resources." Drawing on this heritage, the IWA backed the Nisga'a nation's historic – and controversial – land claim settlement with the British Columbia and federal governments in 1998, which granted the First Nation self-government and control of over 2,000 square kilometres in northern BC. "For a hundred and some odd years, Native people in this province have been trying to get a fair and just settlement of land claims," Dave Haggard, president of the IWA, told delegates at the union's convention that year. "What [the Nisga'a] have accomplished…will finally allow a people that have been treated like a pile of crap by our government…to finally sit down and start to develop a process and programs so that they can live with some pride [and] some dignity." □

concerns – all of this in addition to its ongoing role providing strike support for the IWA. "No one wants to be a moocher. Everyone benefits when the Union wins gains, so everyone should help win those gains," an Auxiliary pamphlet read. "We wives, sisters, and daughters know what a pay increase means in the home. The women usually have the difficult job of making the pay cheque fit the budget. WE must be willing to help our men win these increases. When they win we all win. Can we do it? YOU BET WE CAN!"

The Ladies' Auxiliary at Lake Cowichan, Vancouver Island, was one of the most active groups in a women's movement that consisted of local, district, and international bodies; it was affiliated directly with IWA Local 1-80. Founded in 1935, when the Lumber Workers Industrial Union was active in the area, the "Lake Auxiliary" provided a badly needed support network for both local women and local organizers active in the area. Women such as Myrtle Bergren, Edna Brown, and others – including Indo-Canadian women – sponsored dances and benefits to raise funds and, in some instances, provide a front for covert union meetings. "My first dance at Lake Cowichan, you should have seen the looks I got there. There was loggers' boots, there was everything there, but me, in a long slinky black evening gown, no backing, spike heels, walking along this track and up through the bushes to get to the picket camp," auxiliary member Eva Wilson recounted. "They kept looking at me as if I was something from another world, with a backless evening gown at the picket camp. This was in '36." During the late 1930s, the Lake Auxiliary also lent its voice to the chorus of protest against the many deaths taking place in the mechanized world of logging, and provided aid and comfort to those workers in hospital or recuperating at home. One of its first lobbying campaigns was for an improved road linking the local community to the nearest doctor so that injured workers could be rushed to the hospital with greater speed.

During World War II and the immediate post-war years, the Ladies' Auxiliary, like the IWA as a whole, expanded in size, sophistication, and importance as new branches of the women's organization sprang up on Vancouver Island (Campbell River, Courtenay, and Port Alberni) and in the Lower Mainland (Vancouver and New Westminster) – new union strongholds. In addition to its ongoing role in bolstering solidarity on the picket line, it took strong positions on a wide range of issues affecting men, women, and families. At the 1943 annual convention of the BC Coast District Council, for example, the Lake Auxiliary introduced motions calling for minimum wages for domestic workers, equal pay for equal work, and union support for women in war-related industries; all of the resolutions were passed. At the top of the auxiliary's agenda, though, was the rising cost of living and the length of the work day, issues that women linked directly to the quality of life in the home.

*'They kept looking at me as if I was something from another world, with a backless evening gown at the picket camp.'*

"I didn't marry a meal ticket, and that's what it amounts to if my husband works more than forty hours a week! We just never see our husbands when they work such long hours," one woman remarked at a provincewide auxiliary convention. "Wives also need a shorter work week and the only way that most of us can get it is if our husbands pitch in at home to give us a break, spend a little time with the children and, incidentally, learn a bit of housekeeping."

*The women's auxiliary had emerged as an important player within the trade union movement, fighting for causes crucial to the wider struggle of the working class.*

As this quote indicates, by the mid-1940s the women's auxiliary had emerged as an important player within the trade union movement, fighting for causes crucial to the wider struggle of the working class and, increasingly, to their own lives as women. In the early years of the auxiliary, some male IWAers thought the organization should focus on educating women in the finer points of politics because, as one worker put it, "you cannot fight the boss all day and come home and fight the wife and win." No doubt working women learned a lot about the union movement in the Ladies' Auxiliary, but, in addition to undergirding the IWA's many struggles, the organization had a profound effect on the women who attended its meetings, drafted its resolutions, and politicked on its behalf. "The auxiliary provided women with entry into union meetings and activities, so the power gap between male and female family members began to diminish," historian Sara Diamond concluded, underscoring the auxiliary's wider significance for women. "[It] validated the invisible work in the home and the skills associated with that work." Taken together, the experiences of women in Lake Cowichan and Port Alberni shed some light on the unequal relationship between men and women on the job and in the home. It was a condition that the women in both towns challenged in their own ways – and that the IWA continued to grapple with over the next five decades.

## Consolidation

As working-class women raised the question of gender politics, the BC wing of the IWA set about consolidating its recent gains. While its progress was no doubt slowed by the ongoing feud between white and red factions, success on the Queen Charlottes, coupled with victories by Local 1-363 (Campbell River) against the Batco Development Company and Local 1-80 (Lake Cowichan) against the Lake Logging Company, produced an organizational momentum that even the most bitter internal disputes could not derail. Delegates to the 1944 district convention voted overwhelmingly to extend the union into "unorganized operations and territories" and over the next two years the IWA was successful in this endeavour. On Vancouver Island, Local 1-85 was certified at several mills and camps at Port Alberni, Franklin River,

DOMINION DAY, 1944
From its earliest days, the IWA set its sights on organizing woodworkers across the country.
COMMUNIST PARTY OF CANADA ARCHIVES

and Great Central Lake. Success came in urban areas too. Led by Roy Mah, the District Council's newly appointed director of Chinese organization, Vancouver-based Local 1-217 signed up approximately 2,500 Chinese workers who laboured in the mills that clustered around Victoria and the Lower Mainland. (A monthly Chinese edition of the *BC Lumber Worker* soon followed.) In the Interior – where conditions and wages had long lagged behind the coastal region – the union successfully organized workers in and around Kamloops (Local 1-417), Cranbrook (Local 1-405), Kelowna (Local 1-423), and Prince George (Local 1-424). "[T]he question wasn't 'should we have a union?' one IWAer from the Interior wrote. "It was 'which union do we want?'"

On the sawmill side of the organizational ledger, things were also looking up. Communist Jack Greenall was a carpenter in the 1940s and was active in the union drive. "[O]ne of the first breaks in [the early part of 1942] in the Lower Mainland was in the plywood plant in Vancouver, MacMillan Plywood. It created a bit of a lift," he recalled. "[W]hen I saw that something was going, was breaking, I made the decision...So I quit and I went to a meeting that was called...Don't remember too many who were there, although I do remember Rae Eddie was one and [we] discussed the possibilities of getting an organization going in Fraser Mills and other places." In total about 60 men showed up at that meeting to discuss the possibilities of union work, a large turnout that, according to Greenall, reflected the enthusiasm that workers still felt for the CIO nearly five years after it was founded. "They spread the word around and everybody came. We managed to get hold of a hall, held a big meeting, and organized [the] Mohawk [Lumber sawmill]...All these moves had been propa-

'THE SPIRIT OF HISTORY
IN THE MAKING'

Thousands of
IWA strikers and
supporters march
on the provincial
legislature during
the provincewide
1946 strike; a member
of Victoria's finest
(right) is not amused.

gandized over a series of months with various leaflets and [the] *Lumber Worker* and things like that. So that sort of set the tone and from then on it was straightforward." After this initial burst of activity, Greenall was appointed to the ranks of IWA organizers in BC, an appointment made, ironically, by Adolph Germer.

This process of consolidation climaxed in 1946 when the BC Coast District Council, which had jurisdiction over the Interior as well, mounted a general strike for a 25-cent hourly wage hike, 40-hour week, union security, and the dues check-off – an arrangement already won by auto workers in Ontario. It was a direct challenge to the federal government and employers who wished to maintain the wage controls established during the war into the post-war period. Not surprisingly, neither the boss loggers nor the ruling Liberals in Ottawa were interested in granting the union's demands. Thus, after several weeks of fruitless negotiations, the union set a strike date for mid-May; the federal government countered by appointing an arbitration board under the direction of BC Supreme Court Justice Gordon Sloan. "As far as the camps are concerned the IWA is probably better organized than any other union in BC," an RCMP spy wrote wearily after surveying the situation. "The benefits which these workers have already obtained as a result of belonging to the union are considerable…A strike, as far as the camps are concerned, would be 100 percent effective." He was right.

On 15 May 1946, under the slogan "25-40 Union Security," 37,000 wood-workers – 18,000 of them members of the IWA – walked off the job. "All along the Fraser River, from Hope to Mudpole, in the False Creek industrial area of Vancouver and across on the north shore of Burrard Inlet, great sawmills which had never been closed by strike action grew silent," the *BC Lumber Worker* reported. "[N]ot one major lumber operation in these areas was working, while a few days later the lumberjacks of Prince George joined the mass walkout. Even in the Blue River country east of Kamloops, till then completely isolated from the union, small tie camps and the few larger opera-tions were tied up in a spontaneous worker action uninfluenced by any direct connection with the IWA." In many of these locations, picket lines went up and strike committees, working hand in glove with the IWA Ladies' Auxiliary, organized food drives, tag days, and entertainment for the strikers and their families. In the Fraser Valley and other regions of the province, groups of IWA men – known as "flying squads" – patrolled many of the smaller sawmills to bring the men out, widening the circles of action even further. Within a week the lumber industry, and the better part of the provincial economy, had been shut down. "The operators reaffirm their stand that they do not intend to bar-gain away the basic freedom of their employees by making an agreement with the IWA," an industry spokesperson said. "Well then," replied Harold Pritchett, "the die is cast."

While many idle loggers stayed in the camps and mills to walk the picket line, hundreds of others flooded into Vancouver to raise money for the cam-paign, assist strikers at some of the large mills in the Lower Mainland, and take an impromptu "strike holiday." Indeed, just days after the walkout began, most of the city's waterfront hotels, the loggers' traditional stomping ground, were full. "If any more come to Vancouver it looks like they'll be out of luck," a hotel manager remarked. "Those park benches are pretty hard."

One of those idle loggers was Johnny Olsen, a veteran high rigger from a camp at Spring Creek. Under normal circumstances, Olsen would have spent his time in the city "out dancing in Chinatown or at a night club…generally having a good time" before heading back up the coast. But this time around he was more concerned with just "holding on to [him]self," cutting back on food and other expenses to stretch his savings out for the duration of the strike. Toast and coffee for breakfast instead of hot cakes, bacon, and eggs; two squares a day instead of three. When he was not having a beer with a mate or reading a detective magazine in his hotel room, Olsen was putting in a four-hour shift

THE BADGES
OF COURAGE

During the strike, flying picket squads drummed up support in smaller operations and isolated regions while others raised money for the strike fund in towns and cities.

IWA ARCHIVES

on a local picket line – doing his part to support what he called "the union security angle" at the core of the provincewide walkout. "If I look after myself, I'll be okay for two months," he told the *Vancouver Province*.

Nearly three weeks into the strike, Chief Justice Sloan handed down his final report. He recommended a 15-cent hourly wage increase "across the board," partial reduction of working hours – the exact number depending on whether a man worked in a mill or logging camp and the time of year he was employed – and limited acceptance of the union's security demands. "I am unable to reach the conclusion that the union…will stand in any need of any form of additional 'security' or 'union shop' organization in order to permit it effectively to 'police the contract,'" he wrote. Instead, a "voluntary" – as opposed to a compulsory – dues check-off was the most appropriate and, in his opinion, democratic way to go.

The boss loggers and the provincial premier were quick to accept the Chief Justice's recommendations. The IWA, understandably, was not. "We are always talking about the democratic rights of the people and the virtue of majority rule," a union backer wrote to the *Vancouver Sun*. "As I understand it, there are now 37,000 loggers protesting the stand taken by 147 owners of the industry…Does the voice

HITTING THE
BRICKS IN '46

Support for the
walkout came from
across the province.
IWA ARCHIVES

FACING PAGE

The Ladies' Auxiliary
played a crucial role in
the 1946 strike by
bolstering picket lines,
raising funds, and
bridging the gap – both
personally and politically
– between workplace and
family issues.
COMMUNIST PARTY OF
CANADA ARCHIVES

## 'Death Stalks the Woods'

Along the top of the coffin, a row of 18 white crosses, each numbered, and giving the date and place of fatalities, told of the 17 men killed in logging camp accidents this year. The 18th cross was marked "Tomorrow."

—Lumber Worker *account of a 1,500-strong IWA procession in the 1938 May Day parade*

PERHAPS THE MOST horrifying aspect of the working conditions faced by woodworkers was the extent to which they were injured, maimed, and killed on the job. In *More Deadly Than War*, Andrew Prouty points out that virtually every history of the lumber industry pays little attention to the staggering number of casualties in the industry. Driven by the pursuit of profit, the forest companies accepted bloodshed and death as part of the cost of doing business. Of course, workers and their families paid this price, not employers.

Between 1917 and the IWA's founding in 1937, 1,228 woodworkers were killed in British Columbia. In its organizing campaigns, the IWA emphasized that belonging to the union meant woodworkers were backed up by an organization prepared to fight for safer working conditions. The IWA also hammered home the point that employers who blacklisted IWA members were contributing to the carnage experienced by woodworkers.

The *Lumber Worker* printed detailed accident reports on its front pages in an effort to make members aware of just how dangerous their jobs were. The 15 September 1937 *Lumber Worker* described how "a chokerman named Rowe was beheaded Friday, Sept. 10, when hit around the neck by a choker. The choker had become wrapped around a stump, and a pull taken to unwind it, when it swung back and hit Rowe. He was 23 years of age." The union strategy in these early years was to both educate and warn members of the dangers they faced on the job and to promote safer work practices.

The IWA focused its criticisms of the forest industry's appalling casualty figures on the Workmen's Compensation Board (WCB) and the Department of Labour, which it saw as "contenting itself with dealing superficially with the matter." In 1938 the union demanded that the Department of Labour investigate not only fatalities, but "all contributing factors: the ramifications of the employment sharks and the employment of inexperienced men in place of bona-fide loggers."

Throughout the 1940s the IWA made dozens of submissions to WCB Code of Safety Regulations hearings. Many IWA locals formed safety committees, which developed first-aid courses and emphasized the importance of safe working practices. Despite the IWA's efforts, the carnage continued as more and more workers came into the industry. While 568 woodworkers were killed in British Columbia during the 1930s, in the 1940s this figure jumped to 769 dead. Clearly woodworkers belonged to a profession that remained dangerous and, all too often, deadly.

of all these people carry less weight than that of 147? If so, then what majority rules – people or dollars?"

In the wake of the Sloan report, and with rumours swirling that the government might legislate the strikers back to work, the union orchestrated a march of about 3,000 supporters to Victoria, the provincial capital. With so many workers off the job, the union brass thought, total victory was indeed possible. Writing in *Tough Timber*, Myrtle Bergren described the "spirit of history in the making" that animated the marchers that day as they assembled from across Vancouver Island and parts of the mainland and headed to the legislature:

> The men and women who had labored from the earliest days to build this organization now felt a wave of pride at the respect in which they were held…In the huge parade that marched from the armories in Victoria to the Parliament buildings, through the centre of the provincial capital, the women of the Lake Cowichan auxiliary took the lead, proudly carrying the union banners.
>
> Some of the citizens of Victoria hung from windows shouting their solidarity. Those standing on the sidewalks stopped and shouted, waving and clapping as the great demonstration marched by. The spirit of the lumber workers had never been higher, or more proud of their union.

Shortly after the demonstration, however, the federal minister of labour, at the behest of farmers from the Fraser and Okanagan valleys who badly needed crates to ship their products, ordered sawmill workers and loggers who worked in box production back to work at pre-strike wages. As a consequence, the union executive voted unanimously to end the strike and moved to sign a new contract, a decision that was opposed by many rank and filers.

In the end, the IWA agreed to the terms and conditions laid down by Chief Justice Sloan: a 15-cent raise, a 40-hour week – with some restrictions – and voluntary dues check-off. Although the union's gains fell short of its objective of "25-40 union security," significantly, the terms and conditions of the deal were extended to woodworkers across the province; it was, in effect, a new master agreement for the entire industry. As well, the struggle attracted an additional 10,000 members to the union's ranks, making it the biggest organization in BC and the fourth largest in the country. "It was the best union then that the country has ever seen!" exclaimed one participant.

But perhaps the most far-reaching accomplishment of the 1946 strike was what IWAer Al Parkin called its "sociological" impact. Not only did the 37-day affair draw more and more people into the union fold and cement the legitimacy of the IWA, but the agreement that it produced changed the way in

*The struggle attracted an additional 10,000 members to the union's ranks, making it the biggest organization in BC and the fourth largest in the country.*

which people lived. "For the first time, loggers were able to see their wives once in a while. In many of the camps, if you were working a six-day week and sometimes a seven-day week, there was no possible way you could see your wife," Parkin observed. "And hell, some of them saw their kids for the first time in six months…The boss loggers balked because they were in effect carrying the ball for the rest of the employers all across the country…But we forced it and very soon it spread right across Canada. It was a real revolution." It was a sentiment echoed by an anonymous striker: "It was a wonderful victory. It went right deep into everything. Boom!"

## Looking Forward

Clearly a lot had changed for the IWA. After a decade of struggle, the woodworkers had finally secured a widespread organizational breakthrough, a master agreement on the Coast, and a stake in mainstream political and economic life. But the emergence of a big organization brought with it big challenges as well. New collective bargaining laws at both the federal and provincial level were responsible, at least in part, for the IWA's success and changed the relationship between unions and employers immensely. The bare-knuckle battles of the early years had slowly given way to more legalistic solutions to class conflict – the images of struggle at Blubber Bay contrasting sharply with those from the 1940s. No doubt this shift was welcomed by those who risked their lives daily on the job and fought so hard and so long for social change. But it did present the IWA leadership with the challenge of ensuring rank-and-file participation in union affairs, especially at a time when labour lawyers, judges, and politicians were fast becoming important players in labour relations.

## News Flash

*Jim Nesbitt, CBC Radio, reporting from the provincial legislature in Victoria in 1946*

I have just come from the legislative buildings where I saw thousands of striking BC woodworkers lined three-deep. They had come to petition the government to do something to end the strike which has kept 37,000 persons idle for more than three weeks. The loggers, many of them with their wives, some with their children, waited patiently on the rainsoaked streets while their leaders conferred with the cabinet inside the massive granite seat of government…In the crowd were high riggers, the aristocrats of the trade, the men who climb hundreds of feet to top the forest giants, to make of them the all-important spar trees. There were bullcooks, whistle punks, fallers and buckers, donkeymen, sawyers, and boys who pile lumber. They were all there, the work-a-day representatives of BC's richest industry…The marchers were orderly but they cheered loudly and chanted in unison…[The loggers] came today on deadly serious business – the business of their living.

The IWA faced other important issues as well, perhaps most importantly the Cold War. At the same time that it was chalking up impressive gains amongst woodworkers on the Coast and in the Interior region of the province, it was besieged by an impressive and increasingly powerful array of foes – drawn from both inside and outside the house of labour. In addition to hostile employers and governments, the BC wing of the union faced strident opposition from the CCF, the CIO-CCL, and the international leadership of the IWA; what was more, by the mid-1940s, some rank and filers in its own bailiwick were working hard to "clean house" as well. "[H]istory repeats itself…and in this case there is a repetition [of] the old days of the One Big Union when…the bosses and the government [and others] moved on the OBU and…[it] was forced out of existence," Harold Pritchett recalled, drawing a link between the fate of industrial unionism in the 1920s and its status in the post-World War II period. "We were faced with…something similar to what history already established."

Although the communists' ties to the ever-changing direction of the Communist International provided much grist for the red-baiting mill and fuelled suspicions about their true motives, on the ground the reds' steadfast dedication to the cause of industrial unionism certainly earned them the respect and trust of many woodworkers – something even their harshest critics were willing to concede. But whether that legacy was enough to keep the union from tearing itself apart was yet to be seen.

*The woodworkers had finally secured a widespread organizational breakthrough, a master agreement on the Coast, and a stake in mainstream political and economic life.*

# *Success and Struggl*

# Success and Struggle

IN THE WAKE OF THE 1946 STRIKE, the IWA emerged as the most powerful industrial union on the West Coast. These were heady days, but they were also days of fierce internal confrontation as tensions between the IWA's red and white factions increased. This rivalry – which was played out at the International, district, and local levels of the union and involved actors drawn from inside and outside the house of labour – effectively tore the union apart, a development that cemented the whites' position as leaders in the post-war era.

At the same time as the union was trimming its radical sails, it set about consolidating its gains in BC and expanding its organizational horizons. After a decade of struggle, membership rolls swelled to nearly 30,000 workers and rapid advances were occurring in sawmills and plywood mills. Although the 44-hour week was still technically in place, loggers – spurred by the confidence that came with IWA membership – simply refused to work the extra four hours, so that formal acceptance of the 40-hour week in much of the industry in 1947 was a foregone conclusion. Advances in wages, working conditions, and membership, both on the Coast and in the Interior, followed, marking the 1950s and 1960s as a period of remarkable growth. The union's success was not limited to British Columbia; in the post-war period it extended its reach across the country, from Alberta to New Brunswick, organizing workers in all areas of the lumber industry and, in the process, achieving a long-desired goal: to be national in scope and represent workers from the "stump to the finished product." None of this came easily, of course, as employers never gave an inch without a fight, but as many IWAers no doubt understood, a buoyant economy, coupled with legal protection for unions and the emergence of a welfare state, opened up possibilities for working people that only a decade before were unheard of.

Shaped by both the politics of the Cold War and post-war prosperity, the decades following peace in Europe – from 1946 to the early 1970s – were viewed by many unionists as something of a golden age. For the first time in history, woodworkers achieved security and stability for themselves and their families.

CAUGHT RED HANDED
A crafty IWA member, hiding behind a gravestone, snapped this photo of Thomas Noble of Bloedel, Stewart, and Welch holding money for union member Don McAllister in 1947. McAllister refused the bribe.

COMMUNIST PARTY OF CANADA ARCHIVES
ERNIE DALSKOG COLLECTION

# Internal Conflict

By 1947, governments, business leaders, and the media in the US and Canada had begun an active campaign to attack communists both within and outside the North American trade union movement. Newspapers ran numerous articles about communists and "communist infiltration" throughout society and were quick to take note of reds in the labour movement. In British Columbia, newly arrived journalist Jack Webster wrote some of the most passionately anti-communist stories. Webster later commented in his autobiography that he considered himself "a reasonably fair reporter, except for the way I treated the communists in the early days."

The RCMP infiltrated organizations suspected of being communist fronts, and many labour unions – left wing or not – were placed under surveillance. Major forest companies attempted to recruit informants and anti-red activists. Clyde Perry, the cousin of former IWA staffer Clay Perry, was approached and offered a job as an anti-communist informant, as was John Squire, who later became an active white bloc participant. Thomas Noble, the chief personnel officer for Bloedel, Stewart, and Welch, tried to recruit and bribe IWA member Don McAllister. All three men refused these requests.

In conjunction with the growing mood of anti-communism, politicians on both sides of the border designed legislation to restrict and control union activities. In what John L. Lewis – one-time CIO leader and head of the United Mine Workers – famously referred to as "the first ugly thrust of Fascism in

America," the Taft-Hartley Act became law in the United States in June 1947. The act restricted many rights previously won by labour; one of its most noteworthy features was the requirement that all union officers take oaths declaring they were not communists. Failure to do so meant their union would not be recognized by the National Labor Relations Board, a prospect tantamount to organizational suicide in the increasingly legalistic relationship between labour, capital, and the state. In BC that same year, amendments to the Industrial Conciliation and Arbitration Act, though not specifically anti-communist, restricted the activity of unions and sparked considerable opposition from the province's labour movement.

At the same time as governments on both sides of the line sought to marginalize the influence of communist and communist-inspired unionists, "rumblings of rebellion" from anti-communists in the IWA's ranks were getting louder according to CCFer and IWA member Grant MacNeil. In his 1971 history of the IWA, MacNeil wrote, "This rebellious mood became more pronounced when, in the years following World War II, the Communists in office insisted upon adherence to the Communist 'line' to the point where open cleavage with the trade union movement at large was evident." On one side of this political divide were social democrats who felt it was unacceptable that the policy of the union should be influenced by the Communist Party of Canada. Backed by the IWA's International office, the CCF, and the CIO-CCL, the whites red-baited and disrupted the organizational and political activities of the red leaders at the helm of BC District 1. But much to the whites' collective chagrin, rank-and-file members of the union continued to support the "subversives." In the International officer elections of 1946, for example, the red bloc captured three positions; two years later, in the district's annual ballot, Harold Pritchett and his slate of supporters were returned to power by a margin of more than two to one. It was an overwhelming mandate from the membership, one that flowed from a respect for the concrete contractual gains made by the union leadership, not any deep-seated reverence for communism. Despite the red bloc's electoral success, its members faced serious challenges from the whites as the IWA's cold war turned hot.

In August of 1947, IWA president James "Red" Fadling demanded that all International board members comply with the provisions of Taft-Hartley. The two American communists who served on the executive board resigned, but Jack Greenall of BC District 1, who had been elected as an International trustee, refused to resign. Fadling fired him, heightening the tension that already existed between the International and BC District 1. Explaining his refusal to comply with Fadling's edict, Greenall commented, "The principle involved is very simple and boils down to the fact that a government to which

I owe no allegiance, in a country where I haven't a vote, has no right to tell me or any other Canadian what political principles must be endorsed or rejected." In short order the red bloc had been removed from the International's executive board.

In BC, the CCF and the CCL were working to defeat organized labour's red leadership throughout the province. Former Steelworkers Union organizer Bill Mahoney directed a three-pronged campaign launched in 1947. The CCF/CCL's goal was to take control of the Vancouver Trades and Labour Council, the BC Federation of Labour, and the IWA – the biggest union in the province. Their first success came when they gained complete control of the VTLC. By January 1948, all 21 seats were held by CCL-supported anti-communist delegates.

Given the strength of the IWA in British Columbia, Mahoney realized that the campaign for control of the BC Fed required a simultaneous attack on the BC District 1 leadership. After the March 1948 District 1 elections, only New Westminster Local 1-357 was in the hands of the white bloc. It was from New Westminster that Mahoney ran his campaign to rid the IWA of its red leadership.

At a BC District 1 meeting in April 1948, the white bloc delegates from New Westminster charged that $9,000 of revenue had not been accounted for in the union's annual audit. The district officers denied this accusation and immediately appointed outside auditors to check the union's records for the previous two years. The auditors reported that not $9,000, but $150,000 could

**CALM BEFORE THE STORM**

Delegates to the IWA District 1 annual convention gather in Vancouver in January 1948; within the year, the red-white rivalry would split the union in two.

IWA ARCHIVES

113

not be accounted for. A second audit did not find any misuse of IWA funds, but it also failed to clearly absolve the district leadership of the charges against it.

Ultimately, there was no evidence of personal gain on the part of any IWA officers. Indeed, an analysis of the accounting practices then in use, in which payroll vouchers for 1946-1947 were destroyed following an auditor's report in December 1947, provides a reasonable explanation for the independent auditors' findings. Reflecting on this controversy, IWA historian Clay Perry commented that "the old Red Bloc officers died with less wealth than would have been expected of them if they had simply gone on as good loggers, mill, and shingle workers." Even Bill Mahoney saw little reason to press charges.

In the midst of an intense struggle for control of the union, however, the white bloc wasted little time in exploiting the opportunity to challenge the integrity of the IWA's red leaders in British Columbia. In *The IWA in British Columbia*, Grant MacNeil suggested, "It was useful for the Communist Party, then fighting for its existence, to control an organization which provided salaries for its officials. From time to time, it was found convenient to siphon funds from the IWA to Party purposes, or purposes which were coincident with those of the Party."

To destabilize BC District 1's leadership even further, the International established its own newspaper, as well as "The Voice of the IWA," a radio program through which it could communicate directly with the rank and file. During broadcasts in British Columbia in 1948, commentators continually referred to "missing funds" and "the gross mishandling of funds" and made

other suggestions that all was not well with the district's leadership. One broadcast suggested that if Harold Pritchett, Ernie Dalskog, and Karly Larsen "are not on the bosses' payroll, then the lumber operators are getting a lot of free help." In August 1948, another broadcast demanded that "communists should be criticized and exposed."

By that summer, the CCF/CCL and the IWA International were continuing their efforts to defeat the left in BC District 1. At the BC Fed convention in September 1948, the white bloc captured five of nine seats, including the key post of secretary-treasurer when Harold Pritchett was defeated by one vote. In fact, the decisive blow against the red bloc had been struck prior to the convention, when the CCL suspended the communist-led International Union of Mine, Mill, and Smelter Workers. Mine-Mill was the IWA red bloc's major ally in British Columbia, and its suspension cost the reds 22 delegates at the BC Fed convention. The white bloc now controlled the central labour bodies in British Columbia, and BC District 1's red leaders were facing a crisis.

Rumours were rife that the IWA International planned to put BC District 1 under trusteeship and take control of the IWA's affairs in British Columbia. This raised the possibility that the district would disaffiliate –

PEACE, PROGRESS, SECURITY

With the BC Fed's float at the 1947 May Day parade were Fed executives, left to right, Malcolm McLeod, Cory Campbell, Dan O'Brien (BC Fed president), the IWA's Harold Pritchett, and Alex McKenzie.

IWA ARCHIVES

COLD WAR CASUALTY
The WIUC – the
"Wooies" for
short – held its
first convention
in October 1948,
just weeks after
seceding from the
International.
IWA ARCHIVES

break away from the International. The pressures on the red leadership were intense, made worse by the fact that American border authorities had denied permission to the entire red bloc of the Canadian delegation to enter the United States for the IWA International convention, to be held in Portland that fall.

Looking back years later, Ernie Dalskog described the events leading to BC District 1's secession from the IWA:

> Nigel Morgan came to see me one night in my hotel room. It was in September of 1948, and we knew the International convention was coming, and we couldn't get down there, couldn't get visas. We thought they were going to take us under trusteeship. So he outlined his plan, which was complete, complete breakaway, what to do with the money and records and everything.
>
> He asked me what I thought, and I said I'd have to think about it. He said I would have a day to think about it; the next evening there was to be a meeting of the provincial executive of the Labour committee [of the Communist Party], and I would have to make up my mind before the meeting and go to it.
>
> I said I wasn't a member of the committee, so I couldn't go. He said he would make me a member just so I could go, which was funny, because I'd never had any aspiration for office in the Party. He told me that he and Harold had talked about it with [Tim] Buck [Communist Party of Canada leader] in Toronto the previous week, and Buck "hadn't disagreed."
>
> I went home, [but] I couldn't sleep. It was such a big decision, and I didn't like it, but then I couldn't think of anything else to do, any alternative. So I went to the committee meeting the next night. There was Tom McEwen, Charles Stuart, Harvey Murphy, Harold, Bill Stewart, Nigel, and [Bill] Rigby.
>
> Nigel wanted me to make the motion, but I refused, so he did. Harold spoke against it, but not strongly. He didn't have any alternative either. I couldn't make up my mind, but could not think of reasons not to do it, although it was such a big thing.
>
> Anyway, the motion passed, and that was it. Harvey Murphy was very much behind it, and I think he spoke for it. Anyway, it passed, and we all fell in line. Me and Harold and everyone.
>
> Buck opposed it, later, but by then it was too late. Nigel had drummed up the idea among a lot of the local people, and they supported it, and the ball was rolling so fast that even Buck couldn't stop it.

So that was it, a terrible mistake. And we all knew within a few months that it was a terrible, terrible mistake. We could have handled it in other ways. I'll never forget the next morning I went to the office and told Jack Clarke and Al Parkin what had been decided. "What a bloody fool thing," they said, both of them.

On 3 October 1948, the members of IWA BC District 1 voted to secede from the IWA. They took the district's assets and formed the Woodworkers Industrial Union of Canada (WIUC).

The next day, IWA International President Fadling and Stewart Alsbury, president of Local 1-357, applied for a court order to freeze the funds and assets of the IWA. It took several months for the courts to sort out the case, and eventually the IWA did manage to recover some of the funds. Alsbury was named provisional president of BC District 1, and the International declared it would use all its resources to "protect and preserve all the rights and privileges of B.C. woodworkers as members of the IWA, under their Local Union charters and industry contracts which remain in effect."

Immediately after the split, newspaper reporter Jack Webster, CCLer Jack Williams, and IWA eastern Canada director Harvey Ladd worked all night to produce an IWA edition of the *Lumber Worker* in order to lay claim to the newspaper's title. "We got the paper out and down to the post office and we registered the paper," recalled Ladd. "The opposition went down [to the post

OCTOBER REVOLUTION
Delegates to the WIUC inaugural convention hoped to organize 40,000 new members. Wooie leaders (inset) were, left to right, Hjalmar Bergren, Harold Pritchett, Ernie Dalskog, and Jack Forbes.
IWA ARCHIVES

office] with its bundles of paper named the *Lumber Worker* and were refused because you can't have two different outfits with the same name [according to post office regulations]."

The WIUC renamed its newspaper the *Canadian Woodworker* and continued attempting to establish itself. The first WIUC convention was held on 23 October 1948, and Harold Pritchett compared the WIUC's split from the IWA to the IWA's break from the United Brotherhood of Carpenters and Joiners in 1937. Pritchett declared, "In spite of what Fadling said in 1948, and in spite of the bosses, the Woodworkers' Industrial Union is here to stay and to grow and to represent the best interests of woodworkers across the length and breadth of this great country."

Despite the conventioneers' enthusiasm, the WIUC faced many serious hurdles. The CCL refused to accept its application for affiliation, and most

**CLASH AT IRON RIVER**

**The marshalling yard near Iron River where the RCMP escorted 150 men past WIUC pickets.**

CAMPBELL RIVER MUSEUM
PHOTO 15471

## The Iron River Strike

IRON RIVER WAS A MacMillan logging camp south of Campbell River on Vancouver Island. The 100 men on the crew were staunch supporters of the WIUC, and when two loggers were fired in November 1948, they called a wildcat strike, shutting down the Iron River operations. In the midst of the IWA/WIUC's "divorce and custody" battle, Iron River became a focal point for the power struggle between the two unions. This struggle also involved the Labour Relations Board, as well as employers, who quickly took advantage of the dissension in their workforce. The events at Iron River exposed

the ugly side of the split that tore the IWA apart in British Columbia and also foreshadowed the ultimate demise of the WIUC.

In the wake of the IWA/WIUC split, the IWA had maintained control of mills, while the WIUC's strength was with loggers in the woods. The Iron River situation gave the IWA leadership a chance to establish its credibility by demonstrating it could control the lumber industry workforce beyond mill workers. On the other side, the WIUC believed the Iron River strike was an opportunity to demonstrate its strength, build a solid base of membership amongst loggers, and show it was a legitimate, strong union. The battle for status and credibility proved to be nasty.

companies would only honour contracts with the IWA. In the wake of the split, the IWA moved to retain its collective bargaining rights and agreements. The two unions were competing to organize camps, and WIUC organizers were confronted with the rank and file's confusion and allegiance to the IWA. Employers had little tolerance for the new organization, and WIUC members experienced serious harassment and intimidation. Moreover, the IWA and WIUC were battling in court over union certifications, and employers were only too happy to exploit the division in their workforce.

By the time of the second WIUC convention in April 1949, the IWA represented the majority of British Columbia's woodworkers. The WIUC had only certified nine operations. A strike at Iron River in the spring of 1949 saw the struggle turn violent, with the employer hiring IWA members to do what striking WIUC workers felt was scab labour. Employers, the provincial Labour

WOOIE BADGE

By the early 1950s, all WIUC locals had returned to the IWA fold.

IWA ARCHIVES

Although Iron River was a WIUC stronghold, the IWA attempted to settle the dispute by negotiating directly with the MacMillan company and encouraging the crew to go back to work. In response, WIUC loggers shut the camp down on 15 November 1948. At the IWA's request, the LRB declared the wildcat strike illegal and the IWA began efforts to break the strike.

On 8 December 1948, Tom Bradley, Stewart Alsbury, and Lloyd Whalen of the IWA attempted to lead 25 loggers through the WIUC picket line. Incensed WIUC loggers attacked the IWA men. Alsbury suffered broken ribs, and tensions escalated considerably. That night the IWA shipped in 150 men, most of whom were allegedly not loggers, to challenge the WIUC strikers. The WIUC's *Canadian Woodworker* stated, "this mob was escorted to the picket line…by 26 provincial police…Unable to provoke a fight with the token picket line of 14 men and three women facing them, they burned down the lean-to shelter used by strikers."

Five WIUC strikers were charged with assaulting Alsbury and Bradley, and the resulting trial

provided evidence of the measures the IWA's white bloc leaders used in their power struggle with the WIUC. Under oath, Alsbury admitted that the company had invited him to bring IWA men to Iron River. It was revealed that the IWA had been looking for white bloc volunteers to infiltrate Vancouver Island operations where WIUC support was strong. Moreover, the leaders of District 1 had used strike funds to finance the attempt to strike-break the Iron River dispute.

The WIUC maintained a steadily shrinking picket line at Iron River until April 1949. Meanwhile, the dispute was being settled through the courts and the LRB and by a membership that was gravitating in increasing numbers towards IWA affiliation. By May 1949, the WIUC had certifications in only nine jurisdictions. It had become evident that while it had been easy to declare a breakaway from the International, it was considerably more difficult to build the new union. A year later, the WIUC gave up. While the circumstances were somewhat uneasy, the IWA once again was the driving force behind the ultimate goal of "One Union in Wood."

Relations Board, and the IWA were all against the WIUC, and the bell began to toll for the upstart organization.

By 1950 it was apparent that most woodworkers had decided to stay with the IWA. In August 1950, WIUC officers endorsed unity with the IWA, and the WIUC was abandoned. The WIUC locals made their way back to the IWA, and the communist leadership was blacklisted. The "terrible mistake" Ernie Dalskog referred to had been fully realized.

The red bloc was gone, but it had left its mark on woodworkers and their union. As Clay Perry observed:

> The old leadership had many admirers who were far from the Communist Party. In the District Officer elections held in March of 1948, thousands of such members voted for them as dedicated, determined, and able trade unionists. There was a sense that the hard-nosed employers had to be confronted by equally hard-nosed union reps. A sense that since companies, in their heart of hearts, did not believe that there should be unions, it was not a bad thing that they be matched with union reps that did not believe there should be companies. The white bloc's triumph…was in changing the question from "Do you want hard-nosed union leaders and negotiators?" to "Do you want a communist-dominated union?"

To men like John McCuish, being a red was not about using trade union involvement to do Moscow's dirty work; rather it was a way of looking at politics, economics, and class relations – a way of being a trade unionist at a time when few were willing to gamble, sacrifice, and struggle on behalf of those thought to be too unskilled, too rough, too uncouth to belong to a union. "Do you think we walked over the Malahat and up the Queen Charlottes, on all rough water, without a Marxist theory?" he asked years later. "We might have made eighteen thousand mistakes, but there is one thing: we done it. We built the organization…I didn't give a god damn [what job a worker did], what we had to do was organize workers." And in many ways they did.

In spite of the schism between the white bloc and red bloc, divisive and upsetting as it was for IWAers on both sides of the split, there was still some measure of respect for what the communists had accomplished. Thomas Barnes, an IWA member and white bloc supporter from Port Alberni, said:

> Having made [it] clear that I find myself violently opposed [to the red bloc], I think it's only fair to say that in my observation, there were many dedicated and sincere individuals within the Communist Party who did undergo great hardship in some earlier efforts to get the trade unions organized. Over a period of time I've known quite a large number of

*'We might have made eighteen thousand mistakes, but there is one thing: we done it. We built the organization.'*

those people who did a lot of initial spade work in trying to get unions organized in the woods, in the sawmills, and in the mining industry in this province.

The defeat of the communist leadership led to the establishment of a social democratic leadership that continued the fight for improved wages and benefits on behalf of IWA members. Stewart Alsbury was elected to office in 1949, and the reds referred to by Grant MacNeil as "traitors" were barred from membership in the IWA. In the booming post-war economy, the IWA achieved steady gains in wages and benefits, and championed social programs designed to aid working people. As always, prosperity would not be attained without struggle.

## Opening Round

With the IWA/WIUC battle raging in 1949, employers had been in a position to exploit the dissent in the workforce, and IWA loggers and mill workers did not win any wage improvements that year.

By mid-1950, however, the union's finances and membership numbers were healthy, and members made it clear they were not going to let another year go by without a wage increase. The union rejected a conciliation board recommendation of a nine cent per hour increase. Instead, the IWA demanded, and got the Labour Relations Board (LRB) to conduct, a supervised strike vote – the first government-supervised strike vote in the British Columbia woodworking industry. With 70 to 75 percent of woodworkers voting to hit the bricks, the owners caved in and gave union members $12^1/_2$ cents per hour, as well as a modified union security clause.

In 1951, the union consented to extend the agreement for another year, with a cost-of-living bonus adjustment. Union members received wage increases of about 12 percent in both 1950 and 1951. Given that inflation was low at the time and there was the possibility of a wage freeze as a result of the Korean War, the union brass were quite pleased with their successes at the bargaining table. However, more than one third of the members voted against the 1951 agreement.

By 1952, the IWA strike fund was in good shape and a confrontation with employers appeared inevitable. Member-generated wage and contract recommendations were carried forward to the bargaining table. The union wanted a 14-cent cost-of-living bonus, a 35-cent raise, and a union shop security clause. Conversely, the employers were demanding a wage cut because of falling sales.

The LRB felt that neither side had bargained in good faith, and it refused to hear the IWA's demand for a supervised strike vote. The union decided to

While serving time in jail in 1952 for defying a court injunction against picketing, Tony Poje (standing) was elected president of Local 1-80.

IWA ARCHIVES

FACING PAGE

A member of Local 1-85 operates a mechanical debarker at MacMillan Bloedel's Alberni Plywoods in the 1950s.

PHOTO COURTESY
GEORGE MCKNIGHT

conduct its own vote, even though the IWA leadership was reluctant to strike. On 12 June the IWA announced that more than 85 percent of those voting were set to walk off the job. On 15 June 1952, 32,000 members downed tools.

Members of Duncan Local 1-80 picketed at the docks in Nanaimo to prevent ships from being loaded with timber. When longshoremen honoured the IWA picket lines, employers obtained an injunction that prohibited picketing. Local 1-80 Business Agent Tony Poje defied the injunction and was fined $3,000 and jailed in Oakalla prison for three months. Poje was jailed despite a condition in the strike settlement that all court actions emanating from the dispute would be dropped. While he was in jail, the members of Local 1-80 elected Tony Poje as their president.

The 1952 strike lasted until 28 July and ended in failure for the union. Chief Justice Gordon Sloan mediated a settlement that did not come close to the IWA's terms. A cost-of-living bonus was maintained, there was a 5$^1$/$_2$-cent wage increase, and three more statutory holidays were added in lieu of larger wage gains. Full union recognition was denied because the government had not mandated the strike vote, thus making it "illegal."

In the aftermath of the strike, IWA president Stewart Alsbury came under fire for the union's failure to make concrete gains. Joe Morris had risen to prominence in BC District 1 during the red-white split, and his actions during the strike effectively superseded those of Alsbury.

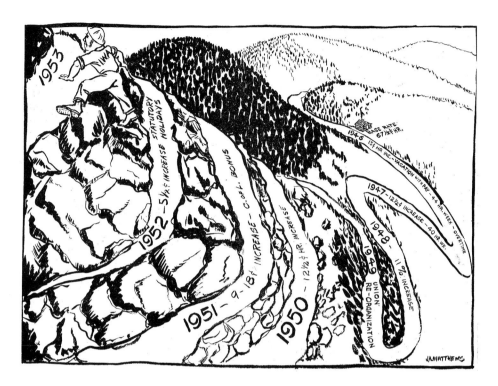

ONWARDS AND
UPWARDS

During the 1950s,
the IWA made slow,
steady gains at the
bargaining table.

IWA ARCHIVES

Charges and counter-charges flew between the two men, and the 1953 campaign for the district leadership turned into a fierce battle between Morris and Alsbury. Ultimately, Morris eked out a victory when the votes were counted, winning by less than 300 votes from more than 13,000 cast ballots. Morris led District 1 until 1962, when he was elected an executive vice-president of the CLC (he became president of the labour central in 1974).

In 1953, a conciliation board decision produced a master agreement for the IWA on the Coast. Although the union was still unable to get full union shop recognition, the agreement consolidated 1951's cost-of-living bonus into the wage structure. International Vice-President Carl Winn encouraged the membership to accept this agreement and emphasized the need to co-operate with the industry. Winn argued that owners of forest industry companies and their workers had common interests, and that these interests would form the basis of their relationship.

"Unions were becoming more and more respectable in the public's view, more acceptable to management and more responsible. Both sides had realized they had to keep the industry going," said employer's representative Bob Gallagher. Gone was the red leadership that challenged the very legitimacy of corporations and the capitalist system. But regardless of the union leadership's political views, it was inevitable there would be clashes between woodworkers and bosses.

## Into the Interior

The IWA's strength had always been centred around the coastal forest industry, but in the mid-1940s, British Columbia's District 1 officers decided to further their organizing efforts in the Interior. Like the Interior forest industry itself, union organization in the Interior had been scattered. Now IWA organizers found that wages and working conditions in major mills near larger communities were comparable to those on the Coast. However, in more isolated mills and logging camps, conditions ranged from worse to terrible – loggers organized at a Canal Flats operation had to make demands for such basic needs as fumigation to destroy bedbugs, proper ventilation in the bunkhouse, and more than one shower per 40 men.

Inspired by the success of the 1946 Coast strike and spurred on by increased production, IWA Interior locals began to grow in Cranbrook, Kelowna, Kamloops, Nelson, and Prince George. In the late 1940s and early 1950s, production at Interior camps and mills was expanding much more quickly than it was on the Coast, and Interior locals were unhappy with their wages, low in comparison to those on the Coast. There seemed little reason that wage parity was denied to the Interior union members.

The lumber market was weak in 1953, and coastal IWA members had won relatively small gains in their contract that year. This played into operators' hands when Interior locals decided to pursue big improvements in their contracts. In the northern Interior, operators represented by the Northern Interior Lumberman's Association were only offering an extension of the previous year's agreement. Although a conciliation board suggested a 6 percent increase, three more paid holidays, and a modified union shop contract, the operators refused to consider the proposal.

As a result, the Interior locals decided to take a strike vote in September 1953. LRB regulations called for strike votes to be taken in each bargaining unit, and the results of the strike vote were uneven. In the north, 20 out of 34 units voted to walk off the job on 28 September. In the southern Interior,

**LOCAL 1-424**

# Northern Stronghold

STRETCHING FROM THE YUKON border in the north to Alberta in the east to Smithers, BC, in the west, Local 1-424 covers more territory than any other BC local in the IWA, and with over 5,400 men and women in its ranks, it is also one of the largest locals in terms of membership.

ON STRIKE

Members of Local 1-424 at Weldwood of Canada's Quesnel Division hit the bricks in 1951.

IWA LOCAL 1-424 ARCHIVES

Local 1-424 received its charter in 1945, at a time when demand for lumber was huge, labour shortages were acute, and working people were on

19 units out of 39 voted to strike, and on 23 October they began to walk the picket lines.

Local 1-424 was based in Prince George and represented 1,500 workers. "I came up here then," one woman commented about Prince George, "took one look, and got out fast. There was nothing but loggers and prostitutes." Local 1-424 members worked at mills controlling 90 percent of the lumber shipments in the Interior, and with the promised co-operation of the railroad

the offensive in BC and across the country. Initially, the bulk of the union's support came from the men who lived in Giscome and worked for Eagle Lake Mills, but after the provincewide strike in 1946, the local's ranks swelled, reaching 1,700 by the end of the decade. Wages and conditions improved steadily too. Like the IWA as a whole, Local 1-424 was swept up in the rivalry between communism and anti-communism in the late 1940s and 1950s. At a pivotal meeting of the BC Federation of Labour in 1948, a gathering in which the red and white blocs were running for leadership positions, it was Howard Webb, a shop steward from Giscome, who cast the deciding ballot to elect a "white" secretary-treasurer, a move that tipped the balance of power on the provincial body's executive in favour of the social democrats tied to the CCF and the Canadian Congress of Labour. Webb went on to become secretary of the Prince George Labour Council and, with the local's backing, a city councillor.

During the early 1950s the local's membership improved modestly with victories in Quesnel and Dawson Creek. But in 1953 its future appeared to be in jeopardy as it battled local mill operators for stronger closed-shop guarantees, including compulsory dues check-off, and higher wages. Dubbed

by one writer as the "most serious episode" in 1-424's history, the strike lasted for over 100 days. In the end, the local secured some modest concessions on both fronts, but it had done so at a considerable cost: membership constricted, many woodworkers and their families went broke, and several small operators went out of business. In the wake of the strike, the local steered a less confrontational approach and was, in time, able to secure compulsory dues check-off and a menu of other improvements, including wage hikes and better vacations, safety provisions, and grievance procedures.

By the late 1950s the local was back on solid ground – membership was increasing, albeit slowly, and labour relations were, on the whole, peaceful. Throughout the next three decades, 1-424, like other IWA locals, added thousands of new members, reaching an all-time high of 7,000, and negotiated successive collective agreements that included better base wage rates and pensions for retired workers. Today, as the economy of the northern Interior changes and environmental concerns persist, Local 1-424 has successfully reached out to workers in other industries, including value-added and secondary manufacturing and the service sector.

unions they vowed to shut down the northern Interior industry to support their demands. The bosses did not blink. It was a tough strike as the cold fall and winter weather began.

In his history of Local 1-424, Ken Bernsohn vividly recalled the gut-level reaction to the onset of the strike:

> If you were a union member you were angry. But you were also confused. You know what it's like when a strike starts. You worry about money. You wonder what's really happening…What's going on? How long will the strike last? What's the strike pay? What's this I hear about the Northern Planers? Better go down to the office and find out about picket duty.
>
> Everyone's there you know, plus a lot of others. Lame jokes. People moving fast through the crowd…are they really that hassled or just try-ing to look important? Guys with instant speeches. The men who leave the room when someone catches their eye and nods toward the door. It's the opening scene of the strike, but you feel like you walked into a play halfway through the third act and spent the afternoon trying to sort it all out…
>
> Too much time to sit and worry. What about your car payments? Your house payments? On the 28th, a lot of husbands and wives stayed up late talking. Worrying. Some people responded by buying lots of canned goods. Some stocked up on cigarettes. A few stocked up on booze (their supply didn't last as long as they thought it would). The union executive responded by meeting with strike captains, setting up committees, plan-ning, and got home only long enough to change their clothes.
>
> By the time three days had passed, a soup kitchen had been set up in the CCF Hall. The menu was moose stew and coffee, three times daily, for as long as the strike lasted. That took a lot of moose, and during [hunting] season, the members brought them in. After the season was over they were supplied by other sources. A phone would ring late at night, "There's a moose out back of the CCF Hall. Do you think you can get it off the street?" Allegedly, the local conservation officer made midnight deliver-ies of moose that had been hit by trains or cars. Farmers offered free vegetables if the strikers would pick them. Merchants donated food. The first day over 200 men registered for picket duty and strike benefits. By the end of the week over 400 men, including non-union types who had been thrown out of work when the strike started, were eating at the soup kitchen. Everyone in the union who was married ate there as a matter of course. It would help the food last at home a little longer.

The IWA quietly encouraged single men to leave the area and look for work elsewhere in order to extend the strike fund. Union locals from the Coast

*'It was goon squads against goon squads. It wasn't safe to have two or three men out picketing. There had to be at least a dozen or they'd end up battered.'*

128

donated almost two tons of clothing, most of it for children. Local car dealers
agreed to suspend strikers' car payments for the duration of the strike. The
local economy was seriously affected by the strike and there appeared to be no
end to hostilities in sight.

The northern operators essentially wanted to bust the union in their
region. They hired goon squads, and violent clashes ensued. While many IWA
people knew it was crucial to maintain public sympathy, others were angry
and frustrated with the companies' actions and did not shy from confrontations. "It was goon squads against goon squads," commented Ken Bernsohn. "It
wasn't safe to have two or three men out picketing. There had to be at least a
dozen or they'd end up battered."

Aggravating these frustrations was the blatant anti-union bias in the
media. A *Prince George Citizen* story about a confrontation between strikers
and a mill owner illustrates this bias:

> A group of pickets overturned a mill owner's car and tore his clothing
> following a brief altercation. A shot was fired in an effort to disperse a
> group of about 80 pickets near a planing mill. The manager was alone in
> his car when pickets overturned it and dragged him to the ground.

The same incident, according to a striker on the scene, unfolded this way:

> We heard this guy was going to start up, so we drove out to the mill. As we
> went toward the office, this guy opens up with a .303. As you can imag-
> ine, we didn't like this. So we waited until he ran out of shells, then
> dumped his car in a ditch and went home. We'd called the RCMP when

he started shooting, but they didn't show up all the time we were there. It turns out they showed up two hours later.

The employers' use of the courts and the law against the strikers was also a problem for the union. The operators filed a series of injunctions in the courts in an attempt to wear the IWA down. Alex Macdonald, later attorney-general of British Columbia, was the sole lawyer for Local 1-424 and was run ragged trying to keep up the fight against the flurry of injunctions. "The real issue wasn't union shop or union wages. It was union recognition," Macdonald recalled. By the late autumn of 1953 there was serious concern about the impact of the strike on members. The IWA's Tage Morgenson observed:

> People were frantic. They couldn't feed their families, they couldn't get jobs, they had no hope…We began to have trouble with people stealing from the soup kitchen. If your children are really starving, you do things you'd normally be shocked by. I was lucky. I had money in the bank and

**LOCAL 1-423**

# Strength in Diversity

LOCAL 1-423 IS LOCATED in BC's southern Interior and represents about 2,400 workers in many different occupations, including logging, sawmilling, plywood and secondary manufacturing, and silviculture. Chartered in 1945, this organization, like its IWA counterparts in other regions, was caught up in the politics of the Cold War; in 1948, the year the International union split, Grand Forks Sawmills saw battles between those tied to the IWA and those sympathetic to Harold Pritchett and

'A ONE AND A TWO...'
**Local 1-423 members belt one out on the picket line during a strike against Grand Forks Sawmills in 1953.**
IWA LOCAL 1-423 ARCHIVES

the breakaway Woodworkers Industrial Union of Canada. In the wake of this struggle, District 1 placed all three southern Interior locals under the authority of the newly created Interior Regional Office in hopes of bringing about financial and organizational stability.

Of particular interest during this early period is the local's relationship with the region's large Doukhobor community. Originally from Russia, the Doukhobors came to the Kootenay region in the early 1900s in search of a more hospitable environment for their unique brand of Christianity. The Doukhobors do not recognize any secular power, they oppose integration with the dominant society, and they embrace pacifism and non-violence. Many Doukhobor men worked in the region's lumber industry, a sector of the economy

planned to buy a new truck for Christmas. Then the strike started. When it was over, I had less than $100 in the bank and no truck.

In December 1953, Justice Arthur Lord was appointed to look into the dispute and make recommendations, and on 6 January 1954 the strike came to an end. The IWA's goal in the Interior had been to fight for wages and benefits closer to those being paid on the Coast. Lord's terms of settlement fell far short of that goal. Members received a 5¹/₂-cent per hour increase and a "maintenance-of-membership" clause, but did not obtain full union shop recognition. The Interior members had been out for three to four months in difficult, cold weather, but received less than their coastal counterparts had obtained months earlier. It was a bitter and violent strike and ended with only 800 IWA members remaining in Local 1-424. "It would take years to rebuild the union [in the north]," commented Ken Bernsohn. In the ensuing years, the gap between Interior and coastal wage rates actually *widened*, setting the stage for another pivotal strike by Interior woodworkers in 1967.

*'The real issue wasn't union shop or union wages. It was union recognition.'*

that by the late 1940s and early 1950s was the scene of many union drives sponsored by Local 1-423. In 1951, during an organizing campaign at Boundary Sawmills in Midway, BC, the local sought to draw the mill's Doukhobor employees into the union fold. The Doukhobors were wary as their religious beliefs expressly forbade involvement in any "political" movement or "taking an oath of allegiance to anybody other than God Almighty." In response, the IWA agreed to exempt them from political matters, picket line duty (where violence was a possibility), and swearing an oath to the union. As a result, the Doukhobors agreed to sign IWA cards. "May peaceful life prevail in the midst of the labour ranks," William Chiveldave, one of the Doukhobors' representatives, remarked.

Local 1-423 regained its autonomy by 1964, when the IRO was finally disbanded, and three years later it played a key role in the IWA's seven-month battle for parity with the Coast. "Seventeen years from now, two thirds of the lumber cut in the province will be from the Interior," local president

Bill Schumaker told striking woodworkers, underscoring the historical significance of the strike. "[I]t is for this reason that the fight taking place in the Interior on parity is similar to the fight on the 40-hour week, the eight-hour day, and seniority." In the wake of the Interior conflict, 1-423's membership expanded – from a modest 500, located largely in the Okanagan Valley, to a peak of about 2,600 in 1975, drawn from a region that included the area between Hope and Princeton. Although the region's forest industry has contracted significantly over the past 20 years, Local 1-423 has maintained certifications with Weyerhaeuser and other forest companies and a visible presence in many local communities. In 1995 it became the first IWA local to fly an IWA Canada union flag on company property – a Weyerhaeuser sawmill in Okanagan Falls – and three years later IWA members at Chaparral Industries built their local a new headquarters in Kelowna. "We are looking to build our local union bigger and stronger in the years ahead," Troi Caldwell said after the new office opened.

**LOCAL 1-417**

# Ups and Downs

IN 1945, WOODWORKERS in the Kamloops/Salmon Arm area were designated Local 1-417. Although the young local was able to secure a handful of certifications, the instability of the industry, coupled with recalcitrant employers and internal financial difficulties, left it in dire straits. So, too, did the divisive politics of the Cold War. As a result, the IWA created the Interior Regional Office in 1953, and Local 1-417, along with Kelowna's Local 1-423 and Cranbrook's 1-405, were brought together under this new co-ordinating body to better navigate the rough political and organizational seas ahead. After a hard-fought victory over Birch Island Lumber (now Vavenby Division, Slocan Group) in the mid-1950s – a strike that secured union representation, a shorter 44-hour work week, and a modest wage increase – Local 1-417 was on a more secure footing. It chartered a women's auxiliary in 1957; held its first convention in 1959; started publishing a monthly news bulletin; and sponsored education classes in Merritt, Revelstoke, Clearwater, and other communities. Membership stood at 775.

"Organizing is the growth mechanism of any union," Rob Jankiewicz wrote in the IWA's 1996 *Annual*, recounting the local's early history, "and two of the most prominent practitioners in Local 1-417 were Bob Schlosser and Gil Johnson." Both

men were active throughout the 1960s and 70s – "when forest jobs were so plentiful they could be found at the beer parlor" – and were the driving force behind many successful campaigns, including the bitter Interior strike of 1967-68. Schlosser was the local's president at the time, joining Jack Munro from Local 1-405 and Bill Schumaker from Local 1-423 on the negotiating committee. Many veterans of this battle recall that opposition from employers was fierce – KP Wood Products in Avola, for example, fired workers who supported the union and turned off the heat in the bunkhouse to make sure no one misunderstood its position. But after seven months, the IWA emerged victorious, securing partial parity with the Coast and other important gains. By the mid-1970s, 1-417's membership peaked at 3,000.

As Kevin Kelly, local president in the 1980s, recalled, however, although membership was high at that time, some unsettling trends in the industry were already evident: "Weyerhaeuser's closure of Avola, Blue River, and Kamloops Lumber was the start of our membership decline." Throughout the 1970s and 1980s, the local was squeezed by employers' aggressive push to both modernize the mills and contract out bush work, a dynamic that put thousands of woodworkers out of work and cost the local about 1,000 members. Despite this economic reversal, Local 1-417 has retained certifications with major forest companies, including Weyerhaeuser, Tolko, Slocan, Ainsworth, and Federated Co-op, and some of the membership losses have been offset by significant victories amongst logging truck drivers in 1994 and, four years later, employees of Naya Natural Spring Water in Revelstoke, BC. □

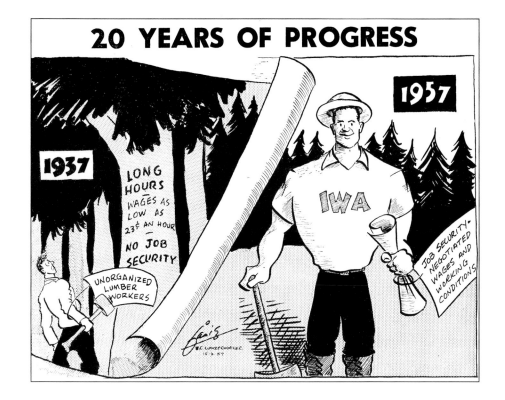

**20 YEARS OF PROGRESS**

1937

LONG HOURS
WAGES AS LOW AS 23¢ AN HOUR
NO JOB SECURITY

UNORGANIZED LUMBER WORKERS

1957

IWA

JOB SECURITY·NEGOTIATED WAGES AND WORKING CONDITIONS

POST-WAR PROSPERITY

As this cartoon suggests, the IWA was bullish on the prospects of better wages, working conditions, and job security.

IWA ARCHIVES

## 'Twenty Years of Progress'

Through the mid-1950s, negotiations and contract settlements across the province went relatively smoothly. In 1954, lumber prices were at a low ebb, and the union chose to forego wage increases in favour of establishing statutory holidays with pay. "You know," one coastal logger told the IWA's Joe Miyazawa, "as far as I'm concerned, the best things you guys ever did for us was when you got paid statutory holidays. You don't know how good it feels laying in bed, looking at the bloody ceiling, and thinking 'I'm getting paid today.'"

The union was militant about enforcing the hard-won rights in its contracts. In the Interior, bitterness over the employers' 1953 attempt to bust the union only furthered the determination of the remaining members to assert their rights under the contract. "For the first time, the contract was enforced down to the last comma and semi-colon. Grievances were rare before 1953, suddenly they were common," said Ken Bernsohn.

The IWA also remained active in the political arena, providing staunch support to the CCF. By 1954, four IWA members had been elected to the BC legislature and one was a member of Parliament. Rae Eddie of New Westminster, John Squire of Alberni, Tony Gargrave of Vancouver, and Frank Howard representing the mid-north Coast were CCF members of the legislature. Tom Barnett of Local 1-85 was a CCF member of Parliament, and Frank Howard also became an MP in the late 1950s. (A District 2 staff member, Arnold Peters, was elected to the Ontario legislature in 1957.) The IWA's support for the CCF resulted in the union having a presence on the mainstream political scene it had never previously enjoyed.

In 1957 the IWA finally won the long-sought right to a full union shop. There were major contract improvements that year, and union membership continued to grow substantially in BC and across the country. District 1 had 35,000 members, and over half of British Columbia's workforce belonged to a union.

After long and often bitter negotiations resulted in no wage gains for 1958, the left showed a minor resurgence in the union. Syd Thompson had been a communist throughout the 1930s, although he resigned from the Communist

**RAISING AWARENESS**

**Standing proudly with a crew from Kootenay Forest Products in the early 1960s is job steward – and future local president – Wayne Nowlin (second from left).**

IWA ARCHIVES

**LOCAL 1-405**

# Strength in Community

WITH ITS HEADQUARTERS in Cranbrook, Local 1-405, represents about 2,100 blue- and white-collar workers in the mountainous southeastern region of BC. It was chartered in 1944, and shortly after being admitted into the IWA it secured agreements with many logging and sawmilling companies throughout the region. In the following decade the local was active in both the 1946 provincewide 25-40 Union Security strike and the

1953 Interior strike, sending members from Canal Flats, Waldo, Fernie, and other towns to Creston to bolster solidarity and prevent scabs from working in local mills. At the same time, Local 1-405, like other BC organizations, was caught up in the fractious politics of the Cold War. When the communist-led Woodworkers Industrial Union of Canada split from the IWA in 1948, it took all of the certifications from this region with it. It was not until 1957, after IWAers George H. Mitchell, Clayton Walls, Ernie Boulet, Bob Ross, and J.W. Reibin conducted an intensive organizational campaign in the region, that the last WIUC local, located at Kootenay Forest Products in Nelson, returned to the IWA fold. "The IWA is the undisputed leader

Party in 1949. He became a job steward and eventually the plant chairman at Western Plywoods (later Weldwood Kent) in Vancouver. Frustrated by the 1958 contract, he ran for president of Vancouver Local 1-217, the largest IWA local with over 6,000 members. Thompson narrowly won the election over incumbent president Lloyd Whalen in 1958. Thompson's election helped push the moderate IWA leadership, and especially District President Joe Morris, to become more militant. The immediate result of this militancy was a 70-day Coast strike in 1959 that ended with solid gains for union members, including a 20-cent per hour wage increase, with an additional 10 cents per hour for tradespeople. Thompson did not hesitate to challenge Morris or his successor, Jack Moore, when he felt it was necessary, and he played an important role in making the IWA a vigorous, aggressive union in the 21 years he led the Vancouver local.

among the workers in the BC lumber industry," district president Joe Morris stated triumphantly after the votes were tallied.

During the 1960s and 70s, the lumber industry in the east and west Kootenays expanded; so, too, did Local 1-405, securing certifications at operations in, among other locations, Cranbrook, Jaffray, Castlegar, and Golden. In 1967 it spearheaded a strike for wage parity with woodworkers in the coastal regions, a 228-day battle that was led, to a large degree, by 1-405's new business agent, a millwright from Kootenay Forest Products named Jack Munro. But victories in the lumber industry were not the only signs of the local's newfound strength. In the mid-1970s it opened the East Kootenay Labour Centre, participated in an important experiment in workplace democracy – placing two members on the board of directors of Kootenay Forest Products and running a shift at the Crown corporation without line supervision – and helped to elect Lyle Kristiansen, the local's financial secretary and member of the NDP, to the federal parliament. It also extended its reach into the white-collar workforce by successfully unionizing the Castlegar and District Savings Credit Union, an

organizational trend that has continued to this day, with other credit union employees joining the IWA fold. By 1980, about 3,300 people in the region had signed IWA cards.

The local's membership declined substantially over the 1980s and early 1990s as economic slumps, coupled with sweeping technological change, resulted in job losses across the industry. Kootenay Forest Products, for example, closed down in 1985. Although pockets of high unemployment and the proliferation of small, portable mills has made it difficult to organize in the region, Local 1-405 still retains strong support amongst woodworkers in the Kootenays. One recent victory took place in Golden in 1996 where, after the Evans Forest Products plywood mill went bankrupt, it looked as though 600 people, many of them IWA members, were going to be out of work. But Local 1-405 and the IWA, in co-operation with the provincial NDP government, Forest Renewal BC, and private sector investors, struck a deal to keep the mill alive by making it more efficient and diversifying its product line. As one IWA official remarked in 1999, "[W]e believed in the workforce and in the community."

ALBERTA'S RISING STAR

Korean War veteran Keith Johnson helped to build the Alberta local before moving to the highest ranks of the IWA as International president in 1973.

IWA ARCHIVES

## Across the Rockies

The IWA had a brief success organizing woodworkers in Alberta following World War II, but the red-white split of 1948 forced the International to relocate all organizers and staff in Alberta to British Columbia in order to shore up the union. The result was the temporary collapse of the union in Alberta. With the situation in BC District 1 stabilized by the mid-1950s, the IWA decided once again to expand into Alberta. By the spring of 1955, Alberta had two new IWA locals. Local 1-206 had jurisdiction in the province south of Red Deer, and 1-207 covered the province north of Red Deer. In recognition of its expansion into Alberta, BC District 1 changed its name. It was now simply District 1 and included both BC and Alberta.

With an office established in Edmonton, International representative Mike Sekora and District 1 vice-president Bill Gray spearheaded the IWA's efforts in Alberta with the active assistance of Joe Morris, Research Director Joe Miyazawa, and Clayton Walls, all of District 1. Officers from the two Alberta locals were installed by July 1955 and the union turned to the task of securing contracts for its new members. Ongoing resistance from several employers resulted in the Alberta's LRB becoming involved in Local 1-206 and 1-207's efforts to represent the hundreds of workers from mills, plants, and logging operations who had joined the union. The IWA enjoyed considerable success during these LRB proceedings, with twelve operations from five companies certified by January 1956.

Keith Johnson was an Alberta-born IWAer who in 1973 became the IWA International president. After returning home from the Korean War, Johnson worked briefly in a Victoria plywood plant, where he first joined the IWA. In 1955, he made his way back to Edmonton, found work at a new plywood plant, and helped the IWA organize workers.

"I found out they were building a plywood mill in Edmonton," Johnson recalled years later. "That was the old Western Plywood, which is now Weldwood of Canada. They were building a plywood mill and I went in and made an application and they hired me on a construction crew there and I ended up being a lathe operator. Mike Sekora, who used to be an old organizer, came walking by one day…and he said, 'You guys organized – you want to get organized?' I said, 'Gimme some cards' and we signed that thing up in about 10 days."

One of the major reasons to organize Alberta's woodworkers was to eliminate the low-wage area adjacent to British Columbia. By 1956, Local 1-207 had established a base rate of $1.10 per hour in most operations it represented – a considerable improvement over the 70 to 75 cents per hour typical of non-union workplaces, as well as the 85 cents per hour earned by Local 1-207 members employed by the Imperial Lumber company.

## LOCAL 1-207 (INCLUDES 1-206)

# On Tough Terrain

IN THE EARLY DECADES of the twentieth century, organizers from the Industrial Workers of the World, Lumber Workers Industrial Union, and the Communist Party of Canada, including Doc Savage and IWA stalwart Syd Thompson, were active amongst Alberta's woodworkers and for good reason. According to a report completed by the IWA in 1947, conditions in Alberta were "revolting." "Most of the Alberta woodworkers live in remote and scattered camps. The workers are provided with wooden bunks with no springs," it observed, detailing a living and working environment reminiscent of turn-of-the-century coastal operations in BC. "Straw and hay replace the mattress. Sheets and pillow-cases are denied them. Blankets are not regularly cleaned and are infested with vermin and bed-bugs."

Before the IWA could establish itself on a permanent basis, however, the district leadership withdrew all its organizers from the province in the late 1940s and redirected its human and financial resources to battle the communists in British Columbia. "It all fell apart when we had the great stupid war with [IWA leader and communist Harold] Pritchett," Keith Johnson, former Alberta leader and International head of the IWA from 1973 to 1987, recalled. "Organization fell flat on its face." In the early 1950s, with the white bloc fully in control, IWA organizers Mike Sekora and Bill Grey rebuilt

FIGHTING THE TOUGH FIGHTS
Over its history, members of Local 1-207 have battled hostile employers and successive right-wing provincial governments.
IWA ARCHIVES

the Alberta local and received two charters from the International in 1955: one for the region south of Red Deer, Local 1-206, and the other for the area to the north, Local 1-207. The two locals later merged, retaining 1-207 as the official designation.

By the end of the 1950s, Local 1-207 had achieved its first large-scale breakthrough in the province organizing 450 pulp cutters (many of them former members of Lumber and Saw from Ontario) in and around Hinton. In the decades that followed, workers from many towns, including Slave Lake, Hines Creek, Grande Prairie, Fort Macleod, and High Level, signed IWA cards. "It was hard work," Johnson observed, perhaps thinking of the superlative efforts of organizers like John Smithies and Gil Johnson, who are credited with bringing hundreds of new members into the organization in the 1970s. "Let's face it. Alberta has never been a hotbed of labour activity. You know it's a conservative, bible-punching province. You know the old Social Credit governments of [William "Bible Bill"] Aberhart and then [Ernest] Manning and all that. There was no friendliness in the department of labour at all. They would screw you over ten different ways to keep the peace. Probably it's not any different today."

Indeed, it's not. From April 1986 to January 1994, Local 1-207 fought the longest strike in IWA history against the combined opposition of Zeidler Forest Industries of Edmonton and Slave Lake and the province's Tory government (see Chapter 6 sidebar "Hard Times in the Land of Plenty"). Today the Alberta local represents about 1,600 workers, men and women labouring in and out of the forest industry.

**IN THE BUSH**

A camp grievance committee set up by Local 1-207 gathers in a plywood bunkhouse at North Western Pulp and Power's Camp 10 in 1958.

IWA LOCAL 1-207 ARCHIVES

In August 1956, 120 workers at Imperial Lumber walked off the job in pursuit of a first contract and a significant wage increase. When IWA members at Western Plywood in Edmonton won a base rate of $1.26 per hour in September 1956, the writing was on the wall for Imperial Lumber. In October, the company agreed to sign a collective agreement that raised the base rate to $1.15 per hour by the end of the two-year contract. This contract was a breakthrough for the IWA, as Imperial Lumber had a long history of successfully turning back attempts by its workers to join a union.

However, the IWA's efforts to establish a new wage pattern in Alberta were tempered by the intense anti-union mindset of that province's employers and politicians. In southern Alberta, Local 1-206 had particular difficulty with employer hostility as the years wore on. In 1955, it burst on the scene, representing workers at a number of operations, but by 1963 it had been reduced to representing members at only one sawmill in Blairmore. In the spring of 1964, Local 1-207 was in the midst of a long strike at Grande Prairie and demanded that the Alberta government launch an official inquiry into the conditions of Alberta's lumber industry. The IWA's demand was met with stony silence as Ernest Manning's Social Credit government condoned the Alberta Lumberman's Association's efforts to block the IWA organizers.

BROTHERS IN ARMS –
SOMETIMES

Although the IWA's
Joe Morris (right) and
Saskatchewan's premier
Tommy Douglas agreed
on most issues, the
union nearly struck a
Prince Albert operation
run by the CCF-created
Saskatchewan Timber
Board in 1955.

IWA ARCHIVES

"Wages are low and conditions are disgraceful, but in Alberta today, the employers are determined to make it a low-wage paradise for runaway business from British Columbia," commented the *Lumber Worker*. "Until the advent of the IWA in Northern Alberta, the Métis Indians who relied on the lumber industry for their livelihood were cruelly exploited." One contractor's payroll records indicated that while the median wage for local white workers was $191 per month, Métis workers were paid only $83 per month. IWA strikes were undermined by scab labour at Grande Prairie and Blairmore in 1964, a problem that was ongoing in the regressive climate of Alberta labour relations.

Nonetheless, the IWA had established itself in Alberta and carried on with its organizing efforts. District 1's Bob Schlosser went to Alberta in 1963 to shore up Local 1-206's sagging fortunes and helped organize members in several new operations. In Edmonton, Hinton, Slave Lake, Fort Macleod, Lloydminster, and numerous other communities, the IWA established itself as a positive force for workers, steadily expanding its membership throughout the 1960s and bringing the benefits of union representation to hundreds of workers across the province.

## Big Sky Country

Despite the perception of Saskatchewan as a vast treeless land, almost two thirds of the province is blanketed by forest. Commercial forestry was established in the Prince Albert area in 1876, and the provincial forest industry developed in a piecemeal fashion over the following decades. During World War II, operators had been allowed to "cut out and get out," overcutting for "emergency" use and leaving vast tracts of land on which regeneration was difficult. In Saskatchewan's climate it takes 130 years to grow marketable white spruce, and it became apparent that the industry needed to take serious steps to balance this tremendous loss of timber.

In September 1944, Tommy Douglas's newly elected CCF government consulted the operators of Saskatchewan's lumber industry about creating a

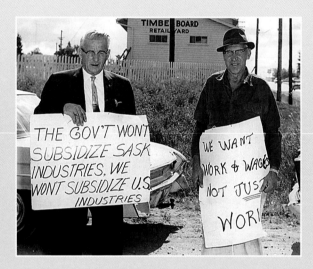

### STALWART OF THE STRUGGLE

**Glenn Thompson, pictured here (left) on a picket line in front of a Saskatchewan Timber Board retail operation in 1967, was a veteran of the On-to-Ottawa Trek and the CCL-affiliated National Union of Woodworkers.**

IWA ARCHIVES

**LOCAL 1-184**

# Prairie Local

LIKE THEIR WORKING-CLASS counterparts across the country, woodworkers in Saskatchewan were swept up in the labour militancy during World War II and the immediate post-war period. Glenn Thompson, a representative from the Canadian Congress of Labour, organized about 80 workers into the Prince Albert Woodworkers Union in 1944. A year later, the new union – which was chartered directly by the CCL – affiliated with the Prince Albert Labour Council and has remained an active member ever since. In 1953, the Prince Albert Woodworkers Union – along with several National Union of Woodworkers outfits located at Meadow Lake, Carrot River, and Hudson

Bay – banded together to form Local 184 of the IWA. Originally a part of District 2, eastern Canada, it moved to District 1, western Canada, in 1959. Today, with jurisdiction over the entire province, Local 1-184 has a membership of almost 1,300 men and women who work in many different sectors of the economy, including sawmilling in Meadow Lake, Big River, Carrot River, and Prince Albert, a plywood mill in Hudson Bay, secondary manufacturing in Saskatoon, Moose Jaw, and Estevan, and public services in Hudson Bay.

One of the new local's first certifications in the 1950s was with The Pas Lumber Company in Reserve, a company town located northeast of Prince Albert near the Manitoba boarder. "The company was reluctant to the idea of the IWA because it was a big union," Abe Pahlke, one-time woodworker and member of the local's negotiating team, recalled. "However, after a few months they accepted the IWA." Shortly after signing a contract with the new International union, the company pulled out of Reserve around 1955, selling its inter-

lumber and forest products marketing board. The new Canadian Wheat Board had been of great benefit to provincial farmers, and the government suggested that a similar development would help the forest industry. A year later, in September 1945, the CCF established the Saskatchewan Timber Board.

The Timber Board handled the processing and sale of all the main forest products taken from provincially owned land in Saskatchewan. It signed contracts with operators and guaranteed them a set price, thus minimizing the risks of the volatile timber market. It also calculated sustained yield volumes

ests to the Saskatchewan Timber Board, the body set up by the province's CCF government to manage the lumber industry. "It was a struggle to keep working conditions maintained," Pahlke stated. The Crown corporation operated in Reserve until 1971, when it closed its operations, a development that pushed Pahlke and many other woodworkers in the area to move to Hudson Bay to continue working in the industry.

Hudson Bay has long been the local's centre of gravity, providing a large portion of its membership. Located southeast of Prince Albert, about 50 kilometres from the Manitoba border, the town was home to several large forestry companies, including Seattle-based Simpson Timber Company and Saskatchewan Forest Products (Saskfor), a division of the Timber Board. Simpson Timber built its Hudson Bay mill in 1965; Saskfor's plywood plant, which depended on peeler logs from Simpson's bushworkers, started operation in 1973. Workers at both outfits were members of Local 1-184. Throughout the 1970s and 80s, Simpson Timber and Saskfor, with the help of a sweetheart deal on stumpage rates from the provincial government, expanded considerably to meet the demands of the North American housing market. "In most cases being a union member had positive results," Pahlke recollected, "but there were times when the company was hard-nosed at negotiations and the workers paid the price." Indeed they did. In the late

1980s and early 1990s, a deep economic recession forced Simpson Timber to close down its mill and Saskfor to curtail production. About 900 jobs, both directly and indirectly linked to the forest industry, were lost; of that 900, about 165 were IWA members. But as bleak as things looked in 1990 – "We're in desperate straits here. The whole economic base of the community has fallen out from beneath us," a Saskfor plant chairman remarked at the time – woodworkers, their families, and the IWA never gave up on Hudson Bay, fighting hard over the decade to keep the community alive. Weyerhaeuser recently announced that it plans to expand production with a new superplant at Hudson Bay and an expansion of the old MacMillan Bloedel oriented strandboard plant, first built in the 1960s.

Local 1-184 is also involved in Wapaweeka Lumber, a unique joint venture with Weyerhaeuser and the Woodland Cree First Nations of Northern Saskatchewan. Located a stone's throw from Prince Albert, Wapaweeka's new mill, which produces dimensional lumber from small-diameter logs, employs about 35 workers, of which 24 are First Nations people. Before the mill started up, Local 1-184 secured a voluntary certification and later helped to negotiate a unique collective agreement that promotes a consensus-based approach to decision making and long-term employment for First Nations workers.

PRAIRIE COLD

**Members of Local 2-184, employees of The Pas Lumber Company in Reserve, Saskatchewan, monitor hydraulic arms as they carry logs over a sleigh in January 1954.**

IWA LOCAL 1-184 ARCHIVES

and reformed logging practices so every part of harvested trees would be processed to its maximium potential use.

The Timber Board's forest management policies were credited with bringing stability to the province's forest industry. A 1956 federal government report compared forestry practices in Saskatchewan and eastern Canada and found there was far less logging waste in the Saskatchewan forest industry than in the east. Because maximizing profit was not the only consideration in Saskatchewan's provincially controlled industry, the IWA saw the Timber Board's well-integrated forest policy as a progressive development to be encouraged in other regions of the country.

The Timber Board was also seen as a positive step towards increasing harmonious relations between employers and woodworkers. The Board took over the Saskatchewan Box Factory at Prince Albert in 1945, and employees there immediately gained wage increases, sick pay, WCB benefits, and holidays with pay. As well, amenities were provided within the plant that contributed to other improvements in working conditions.

The CCF government's introduction of progressive labour legislation was another step towards providing balance in the industry for working people.

Saskatchewan's woodworkers participated in the rush of union organizing that occurred during World War II, forming a union in 1944 with the aid of CCL organizer Glenn Thompson. Thompson had been a participant in the

TOO CLOSE FOR
COMFORT
A sawyer at The Pas
Lumber Company
operates a 54-inch
bottom saw in 1954.
IWA LOCAL 1-184 ARCHIVES

famous On-to-Ottawa Trek of 1935, and he later organized workers at a
Co-Op oil refinery in Regina. In 1953, the Prince Albert Woodworkers Union
received a charter as Local 2-184 of the IWA. Thompson was elected president
and Local 2-184 remained under the jurisdiction of eastern Canada District 2
until 1959, when the union redrew its boundaries and included Saskatchewan
and Manitoba in District 1. (When the IWA revamped the structure and geographical boundaries of its districts, it also renamed them. The former District
1 became known as Region 1, with jurisdiction extending from the Manitoba-
Ontario border to the coast of British Columbia; District 2 became Region 2,
with jurisdiction over Canada east of the Manitoba-Ontario border.)

Despite the IWA's staunch support of the CCF and the improvements it
brought about, the Timber Board was still an employer in the eyes of the
union. In 1955, Local 2-184 prepared to strike a Timber Board-owned operation in Prince Albert. District 2 Director Harvey Ladd recalled, "We took a
strike vote and we had more phone calls from unions all over Canada…that it
was a terrible thing. 'For God's sakes, you're not going to strike against the
Saskatchewan CCF government,' and I said I'd strike against the Queen, it
doesn't matter. My job is to see that the welfare of these workers is cared for
and that's it…This is the greatest example we can give the working class of
Canada that we stand for the working class, regardless of anything else."

Ultimately the strike was averted with the aid of Premier Douglas.
"Tommy Douglas and I sat down in his office in the legislative building to the
wee hours of the morning, trying to solve, settle up some problems in this little
plant…We formed a formula that settled it," said Ladd.

Glenn Thompson and Ladd organized loggers at Smooth Stone Lake and

"Teamwork and Solidarity" conferences, like this in Kitchener, Ontario, in 1955, helped forge an active grassroots organization. Long-time IWA member and Region 2 executive Bill Pointon is in the front row (second from left).

IWA ARCHIVES

workers at the Timber Board's Big River sawmill. The IWA had begun to forge a presence in the province's lumber towns, including Reserve, which was located amidst forest lands south of Hudson Bay. Prior to World War II, lumber cut for commercial use in the area was shipped via rail to The Pas, Manitoba, and local farmers often had their own small mills for producing fence posts and a supplementary income. In the 1940s, Reserve became a company town when a mill was established by The Pas Lumber Company. Abe Pahlke recalled starting work at the local mill at age 15 in 1946, being paid 45 cents per hour for 10-hour days, and working 12-hour days when the employer demanded. The CCL originally organized woodworkers in Reserve in the late 1940s, and in 1952 the IWA's Jack Moore convinced them to join the union. Conditions quickly improved as the union negotiated higher wages and chipped away at the 60-hour-plus work weeks, reducing them to 40 hours.

By 1960, Local 1-184 represented approximately 450 IWA members, the majority of them located at Hudson Bay near the Manitoba border. The Saskatchewan local also represented workers at a plant in The Pas, Manitoba, in this period. With the 1964 election of Ross Thatcher's Liberal government in Saskatchewan, labour relations between woodworkers and the industry took a sour turn. The CCF government had promoted the use of voluntary conciliation to settle labour disputes – with considerable success – but Thatcher's Liberal government was more concerned with meeting the needs of industry. As a result, the IWA was forced to strike several times in the 1960s to win

contracts with Simpson Timber company holdings, Domtar operations in Saskatoon, and the Timber Board. An August 1967 strike against the Timber Board erupted when the Thatcher government refused to grant Local 1-184 members parity with agreements reached with MacMillan Bloedel and Domtar operations. By the end of August 1967, the government had capitulated and Local 1-184 won its demands.

Local 1-184 also had to contend with raids from the Laborer's International Union in the late 1960s. The LIU had woodworker members in a number of companies, but chose to raid IWA operations rather than organize the unorganized woodworkers of Saskatchewan. By 1972, the superiority of Local 1-184 contracts and ongoing efforts of IWA organizers succeeded in winning over the last woodworkers represented by the LIU to the IWA.

## From West to East

The IWA's origins in eastern Canada were linked to the red-white schism of the 1940s. With the red-led Lumber and Sawmill Workers union already in control of northern Ontario's unionized woodworkers, the IWA International officers wanted to ensure that communist influence did not spread. Harvey Ladd recalled that "the International wanted to keep the officers and organizers of British Columbia out of eastern Canada. There's no doubt about that."

Ladd had been active in the CCF as the party's trade union secretary in the

**IWA BOUND**

Delegates to the National Union of Furniture Workers convention gather in Hanover, Ontario, in 1946; a year later they joined the IWA en masse.

IWA LOCAL 500 ARCHIVES

early 1940s and had joined the Workers Educational Association (WEA) as assistant national director in 1943. The WEA was engaged in educating workers about the trade union movement and assisting unions in their organizing and educational efforts. (Bora Laskin, later to become chief justice of the Supreme Court of Canada, was among the teachers who ran classes for the WEA.)

Ladd's work in the realm of education so impressed the Mine, Mill, and Smelter Workers union that it hired him as a staff member, but Ladd left Mine-Mill in early 1947 when the International president insisted the union support the Liberal party rather than the CCF. Ladd was immediately hired by the CCL as a general organizer and enjoyed considerable success in northern Ontario, organizing workers in all occupations. Within weeks, Claude Ballard and George Brown of the CIO approached Ladd about becoming director of the IWA in eastern Canada. Ladd was hired and began to organize

**LOCAL 500**

# The Finished Product

WITH A HERITAGE OF STRUGGLE that stretches back to 1919, when the workers at Knechtel Furniture Manufacturing Company in Hanover, Ontario, joined the United Brotherhood of Carpenters and Joiners (UBCJ), this local's roots run deep. Following its tenure in the UBCJ, the men at Knechtel broke with the mainstream trade union movement during the Depression, when communist organizers were busy organizing industrial

**LISTEN UP!**

**In 1952, the IWA began a 13-month battle against Durham Furniture for a better collective agreement.**

IWA ARCHIVES

unions. (In southwestern Ontario, where agricultural co-ops were well developed, members of the United Farmers of Ontario and the CCF were also active.) After furniture workers in nearby Stratford opted for the red-led Furniture Workers Industrial Union, workers at Knechtel in Hanover – and at other furniture companies in Listowel, Kincardine, and Kitchener – followed suit. When the communist unions were disbanded in 1935, the Furniture Workers Industrial Union rejoined the UBCJ as Local 1002. After fighting several unsuccessful strikes in 1937 to secure a "New Deal" for furniture workers in Ontario, it bolted to the newly formed centre for industrial union-

Ontario workers into the IWA. His initial organizing efforts were aimed at furniture workers.

Southern Ontario furniture workers had originally been organized several years earlier by the Workers Unity League, an offshoot of the Communist Party. The WUL eventually abandoned them and they re-formed under the banner of the National Union of Furniture Workers (NUFW), chartered directly to the CCL. By 1947, the NUFW units were no longer being properly serviced by union representatives and several were interested in joining the IWA. Knechtel furniture workers in Hanover received the charter for Local 2-486 in April 1947, becoming the first IWA local in eastern Canada.

The 1947 IWA International convention passed a resolution that assessed members from District 1 a one-dollar fee. About $20,000 was raised from this assessment, earmarked specifically to help build the IWA in eastern Canada,

*The IWA's origins in eastern Canada were linked to the red-white schism of the 1940s.*

ism, the Canadian Congress of Labour, in 1945. It was then known as the National Union of Furniture Workers. This long and winding journey in and out of the craft and industrial union movements ended in 1948, when it joined the IWA – one of the powerful new affiliates of the Canadian Congress of Labor – and was designated Local 2-486. It received its Local 500 moniker in the late 1960s.

From its beachhead at Knechtel, the local organized Heintzman Piano, Saugeen Veneer, Maple Leaf Veneer (now Interforest), and other operations in and around Hanover over the next 20 years. "We were the only organized union in town," pioneer IWAer Wilf "Chally" Chalmers recalled years later. Like other locals, 500 fought many strikes, including battles against Knechtel in 1948, Hanover Kitchens in 1963, Simmons in 1989, Koolatron in 1990, and more recently, Interforest Veneer in 1999. It was also active on the cultural front, opening the "Woodworkers' Club" in 1960; part meeting hall, part beer hall, the club was (and still is) a popular spot for dances, card games, and

other important union affairs and is a sign of the local's presence in the community.

By the late 1970s and early 1980s, membership in the southwestern Ontario local was still drawn primarily from the furniture industry. With the advent of free trade with the United States, however, and the reduction of the high-tariff barriers that had protected the industry since the time of John A. Macdonald, this sector of the economy went into a tailspin, closing down operations and laying off thousands of workers, including many IWA members, in order to compete with low-wage, low-cost operations in the United States. "Since the emergence of the free trade agreement there has been a helluva lot of nervousness in the industry," fourth vice-president Bill Pointon observed in 1990. By the time the economic shakedown was completed, the local lost most of its certifications in the furniture industry save for Hanover Kitchens, a company that specialized in "high-end" products. Since that time, however, Local 500 has clawed its way back with a handful of successful organizing drives. Today, its membership stands at 2,300.

NO FOOLING!

**Durham Furniture strikers take time out from the picket line to pose for the camera in 1952.**

IWA ARCHIVES

and organizing offices were opened in Toronto and Montreal. The motivation behind this fundraising push is illustrated by George Brown's comments at the 1946 International convention, where he had criticized District 1's red leadership for its strategy towards eastern Canada. "They [District 1 leaders] said we had promised not to go into Ontario, and there was no such promise. They wanted us to skip it entirely and move into Quebec. Why? Because the Labor Progressive Party was in control of what organization there was in Ontario…Bruce Magnuson [communist leader of Lumber and Saw] was in full control. They wanted us to jump over to Quebec to form a link there whereby they would leave the control to whatever organization there was under the domination of the Labor Progressive Party."

By September 1948, IWA District 2 had organized 11 operations in Ontario and 1 in Montreal, accounting for approximately 350 members. Although the IWA inherited several NUFW locals, much basic organizing work remained to be done as these locals were in disarray and had not been certified with the provincial Labour Relations Board. Complicating matters further was the "October Revolution" in District 1. Harvey Ladd recalled, "The night the split took place, I was on an airplane to Vancouver…I figured I would be out there for about a week, but I was out there for three months and then for most of the whole year." With Ladd gone to British Columbia to shore up District 1, District 2's organizational activities were put on hold.

CRAFTSMEN'S
SPECTACLE

An IWA float in a
parade in Stratford,
Ontario, in the 1950s
displays union-made
fine furniture from
Preston Noelting.

IWA ARCHIVES

By the time he returned, Ladd said, "the organization wasn't on a particularly good footing."

Ladd's goal was to stabilize the IWA's presence in the furniture industry
and then work on organizing in northern Ontario. He had already had initial
successes in November 1947 in northern Ontario when he and local unionists
were able to organize the Roddis Lumber Company in Sault Ste. Marie and the
Blind River Lumber Company in Blind River – the first sawmill local in
District 2. The IWA negotiated a 1952 contract at Roddis Lumber that saw
members earning $1.10 per hour at a time when standard wages in the
Ontario industry ranged from 65 to 95 cents per hour.

By the mid-1950s, the IWA was well established in furniture factories;
lumber mills; planing, veneer, container, and plywood plants; as well as other
wood-related industries in Ontario and Montreal. The diverse number of
workplaces made it next to impossible to create a master contract, and most
workplaces created their own locals and sub-locals. Like their counterparts in
British Columbia during the 1950s, IWA locals in eastern Canada won modest
wage gains, but made great strides in achieving union shop recognition and
securing fringe benefits such as improved vacation, holiday, and medical
benefits. The average minimum wage in Ontario IWA operations was $1.04 in
1957, considerably lower than that of British Columbia, and the five contracts
held in Quebec that year saw average minimum wages that were another
12 cents lower than those in Ontario.

The diverse nature of IWA locals in eastern Canada necessitated a strong
education program in order to foster solidarity among members. Harvey
Ladd's background as a trade union educator was crucial to the union's growth

## LOCAL 1000

# 'Educate to Agitate.'

IN THE SPRING of 1959, representatives from 16 different wood-related operations in north-central Ontario attended the founding convention of Local 1000 in North Bay. Drawn from the ranks of several IWA sub-locals – like Local 57, based at Roddis Lumber and Veneer in Sault Ste. Marie, and a former National Union of Woodworkers outfit located at Pembrooke Shooke Mills in Pembrooke – they came together to form an amalgamated local, an arrangement that allowed for co-operation on industry-wide issues but gave each outfit the autonomy to negotiate its own collective agreements. It was a novel set-up at the time, a geographically based structure created long before the amalgamation of Regions 1 and 2 prompted the merger of other independent locals and sub-locals throughout the province.

For the better part of its life, the bulk of Local 1000's members – about 70 percent – were employed by G.W. Martin, one of the largest processors of hardwood and pine in North America, with operations in Harcourt, Mattawa, Huntsville, Rutherglen, and Sault Ste. Marie, among other north-central Ontario locales. At its peak, Martin employed about 1,800 people, 1,100 of which were IWA members. In 1989, however, the company went bankrupt, a development that brought about a drastic restructuring of its operations and, in the end, hundreds of job losses. These losses were compounded in the early 1990s by the closure of other manufacturing operations in the province – victims of a strong Canadian dollar, high interest rates, and the free trade agreement with the United States.

Despite this industry-wide shake-up, Local 1000 has maintained a presence in wood-related primary and secondary manufacturing. Five of its original sixteen sub-locals – Staniforth Lumber (Columbia Forest Products), Wilberforce Veneer (Ontario Veneer), Roddis Lumber and Veneer (Domtar), Hay and Company (Tembec Inc.), and MacMillan Bathurst – are still going strong. It has also successfully diversified its membership base, a trend underway since the merger of Regions 1 and 2, which was boosted considerably by a new dues formula unveiled by the IWA national office in 1998. Stretching from Sault Ste. Marie in the west to Hawkesbury in the east to Belleville in the south, Local 1000 now represents men and women who labour in a wide range of workplaces, including credit unions, nursing homes, car dealerships, and synthetic fibre plants. It is also responsible for servicing the IWA's sole Quebec organization, Local 400.

Significantly, the local has taken a leading role in educating its members about their rights, responsibilities, and history. In 1990, it negotiated an employer-paid education fund as part of a collective agreement with Amoco Fabrics, the first of its kind in the IWA. After securing this arrangement at the local level, the north-central Ontario organization brought forth a successful resolution to make it policy on a national basis. Today Local 1000 spends more than $100,000 a year on education. ◻

in eastern Canada during the post-war era. Ladd recalled that "the educational part was pre-eminent…the single greatest effort we put forward…and we took our people through from beginning to end, not just the job of steward and arbitration and the rest of it…We had lecturers from all over the place. We had tremendous support from the labour movement because we probably had one of the very few real education programs. Without it, the organization would never have survived. Without it, we never would have had this militancy." Despite scarce resources, District 2 initiated a "Teamwork and Solidarity" education program that served IWA members from Quebec to Saskatchewan.

By December 1958, over 400 new members from three Bathurst Containers plants in Quebec had joined the IWA, and the *IWA News*, Region 2's newspaper, proclaimed that further "progress and growth were planned for the sixties." While this progress and growth did take place, the IWA was first involved in one of the most monumental strikes in Canadian history.

## On the Rock

For years, Newfoundland's loggers had coped with conditions that hearkened back to the worst traditions in the industry. Over 14,000 loggers and several thousand more mill workers were represented by unions that were little more than company-dominated organizations. A Royal Commission established in 1959 found camp and sanitary conditions in Newfoundland barely improved over those described in a report 30 years earlier:

PARLEZ-VOUS FRANÇAIS?

In order to serve its francophone members better, the IWA held a "Teamwork and Solidarity" conference for French-speaking activists in Montreal in the early 1950s.

IWA ARCHIVES

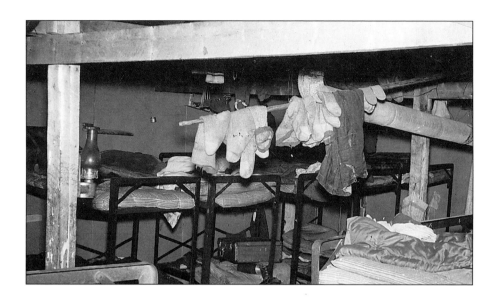

Dark and squalid hovels which would not be used for hen-houses except by the most primitive farmer. Dirt is everywhere. Rats are common. Dilapidation is the rule. There is nothing to do in the evenings but sit around on the bunks talking. The light is from a limited number of flat wicked kerosene lamps. Men have been passed down to a dead level of a flat rate and have grown resigned. If a man kicks there are just now only too many to take his job.

Newfoundland's loggers were being paid ten dollars a day (30 percent less than wages in northern Ontario) and working a 60-hour week.

In October 1956, Harvey Ladd was invited to address a convention of the Newfoundland Lumberman's Association (NLA). The NLA was run by Joe Thompson and was the most prominent of the ineffectual company unions that represented Newfoundland woodworkers. As events developed, the NLAers at the 1956 convention voted to join the IWA, but were outmanoeuvred on procedural grounds invoked by Thompson. Ladd recalled what happened next:

Well, I just moved up and said, "I want to thank you for your interpretation of trade union democracy, and incidentally, if there is anyone here who wants to move away with us, we will have a meeting outside, and we will start the rolling of the International Woodworkers of America; we are not buying any unions, and we have won this convention fair and square, and we are here to stay and we are going to build a union in Newfoundland for the loggers." And that's precisely what we did.

But the company refused us the right…of our representatives to meet with the loggers. [So] we walked through to the camps and our people

LOGGERS' NAVY –
EASTERN STYLE

With a generous
donation from Local
1-217 (Vancouver), the
IWA in eastern Canada
bought a vintage World
War II snowmobile to
organize loggers.
IWA ARCHIVES

went thirty, forty, fifty, and one of them went seventy-two miles on foot
…we hired airplanes and landed our people in. We had our own snow-
mobiles and we hired a schooner to go around the island.

From late 1956 through January 1958, the union put in an extraordinary
effort to organize Newfoundland woodworkers. The IWA created a special
"Newfoundland Section" in its constitution and in April 1958 was granted
certification by Newfoundland's Labour Relations Board. When not organizing, IWA staff helped loggers file unemployment insurance and workers' compensation claims. Over $3,000,000 in unemployment insurance back pay was
collected for Newfoundland loggers, and workers who could not obtain proper
medical treatment in Newfoundland were sent as far as Toronto for rehabilitation and treatment.

Despite the loggers' overwhelming support for the IWA, there remained
big hurdles facing the union in its fight to improve conditions. The Anglo-
Newfoundland Development Company (AND), with headquarters in Grand
Falls, and Newfoundland Pulp and Paper Mills (Bowater's) based in Corner
Brook were not at all pleased that the IWA now represented their workforce.
The companies actively tried to crush the union, denying access to company
camps and using their influence to have IWA ads removed from newspapers.
Moreover, public support for the union was minimal. Even mill workers, who
could have provided invaluable assistance, were cool to the IWA and at times
openly opposed the new union. The IWA did not waver.

Demands for wages and working conditions were drawn up and presented
to AND in the summer of 1958. The loggers' modest demands included a 25-
cent raise and a 44-hour work week, bacon and eggs for breakfast, and a regular
change of straw in the bunks. By October 1958, negotiations had bogged down
and a conciliation board was brought in to make recommendations.

## The Post-War Compromise

FROM THE CLOSING STAGES of World War II until the mid-1970s, IWA members, along with other unionized Canadian workers, enjoyed unprecedented economic prosperity as governments granted unions legal rights and recognition that fostered tremendous gains at the negotiating table. In exchange for these gains, organized labour in Canada agreed to be governed by industrial relations legislation that essentially narrowed its interests to achieving wage and benefit improvements, while restricting the possibility of a working-class revolt that would threaten the capitalist system.

The immediate roots of this post-war compromise lay in the militant union activity of the 1930s and 40s. During the Great Depression, workers had suffered as governments insisted they were unable to help their citizens, but with the onset of World War II and the mobilization of state resources for the war effort, it became all too apparent that the government was capable of playing a progressive

A JUST SOCIETY

During the 1950s, 60s, and 70s the CCF/NDP, working with the labour movement, was a driving force behind the creation of social programs and the expansion of collective bargaining rights.

UBC SPECIAL COLLECTIONS
BC 1902-5

role in the economy. With full employment during wartime production, workers did not hesitate to fight their employers for the right to a dignified existence. The resulting strike waves of the 1940s were accompanied by a huge leap in the popularity of the CCF.

The CCF's demand for social security programs for all citizens caught the attention of workers across the country. By 1943, the CCF was a powerful force on the political scene, with opinion polls indicating it was more popular than both the ruling federal Liberal government and the opposition Conservative party. In 1943, the CCF came close to winning provincial elections in British Columbia and Ontario, and in 1944, the Tommy Douglas-led CCF was elected in Saskatchewan. Prime Minister Mackenzie King and the Liberals were forced to pick up a number of CCF policy planks in order to maintain their credibility with voters – the federal government introduced family allowance, old age pensions, health insurance, and housing programs.

In early 1944, Privy-Council Order 1003 was passed, enshrining in federal law the principle of compulsory collective bargaining. This meant employers under federal jurisdiction could no longer duck negotiations with a union after it had been certified as the legal representative of workers. In 1945, Justice Ivan Rand furthered the legal recognition of unions when he ruled that union dues must be deducted from all workers in a union-certified workplace, regardless of whether they chose to join the union or not. The "Rand Formula" at once provided unions with unprecedented financial stability and eliminated the onerous duty of collecting dues from individual members, thus freeing union officials to focus on other pursuits.

Canadian workers remained militant in the immediate post-war period, with the IWA and Lumber and Saw strikes of 1946 among many prominent labour disputes that confirmed workers were determined to fight in order to maintain their hard-won gains of the war years. However, the context of these battles was no longer simply a union-employer dispute. With government recognition of union rights came labour laws that created a legal framework outlining the parameters of union activity. Labour relations boards became powerful regulators of union activity. Strikes were illegal during the life of a contract, and grievances were handled through a formal system designed to eliminate work disruptions. These developments entrenched the tendency towards a bureaucratic, legalistic relationship between workers and employers. In essence, unions were now required to limit their demands to issues of wage and benefit improvements. As Craig Heron observed, "The new labour legislation, like its predecessors, was primarily concerned with keeping workers on the job and away from the picket line."

After the dreadful experiences of the 1930s, most workers were delighted with the gains they made under the new regime of "industrial legality." For IWA members, the establishment of a union shop, seniority recognition, statutory holidays, shorter work weeks, pension plans, and increased pay meant the period from 1945 to 1975 was a time of affluence. But in this era the industrial relations system also served to rein in the power of working-class opposition to capitalism. Working-class solidarity was quietly undermined as traditional tactics like direct action on the job were replaced by negotiated settlements and legal constraints. The conflict between social democrats and communists also disrupted the possibility of broad support for a massive workers' movement.

The post-war compromise, then, was a trade-off: workers gained a higher standard of living through improved wages and benefits, while employers maintained greater control over their workplace technology and the work processes, thereby ensuring increased productivity and profits. In the early 1970s, the onset of advanced communications technology and an increasingly global economy sparked economic disruption that caused employers to clamp down on the gains workers had made. Free trade deals, profit-driven economic and social policies, and a tax system that dramatically shifted the burden of taxes away from corporations and onto the backs of workers marked the end of what had been the most prosperous era workers in Canada had ever known.

UNION DEMOCRACY
IN GRAND FALLS

Newfoundland
members attended a
wage and contract
policy conference in
1958. "For the first
time, their union was
treating them like they
mattered," observed
historian and activist
Bill Gillespie.

IWA ARCHIVES

Harvey Ladd wanted to avoid a strike, hoping to have a longer period of time in which to build and consolidate the union in Newfoundland. Although the conciliation board's recommendations were disappointing, the union agreed to accept them. AND, however, which had stockpiled pulpwood and was prepared for a strike, rejected the recommendations, largely because it wanted to bust the union before it had a chance to become further established in Newfoundland. With AND's rejection of the recommended improvements, Newfoundland IWA members voted to strike on 1 January 1959.

Ladd and the IWA were under no illusions about the negative press coverage they would receive. The Newfoundland media had been looking for a chance to smear the IWA. As historians Jerry Lembcke and William Tattam observed in *One Union in Wood*, the *Grand Falls Advertiser* was so fanatically opposed to the IWA that AND made copies of its editorials for redistribution.

"Do you honestly think these leaders in their swanky hotels are interested in the Newfoundland logger and what he gets and how he lives?" one *Advertiser* editorial began. "No, unfortunately there are too many James Hoffas, too many Dave Becks in labour circles nowadays." (Hoffa and Beck were American labour leaders under investigation by the United States government.) As deluded as such pronouncements were, they nonetheless

NO HOFFAS HERE
IWA Local 254 president George Stoodley (front, left) shakes hands with organizer Jeff Hall as loggers show their support. Hall later played an important role in organizing mill workers in New Brunswick.
IWA ARCHIVES

helped shape public opinion and neutralize support for the loggers. The union fought back to the best of its ability and had considerable success in the early weeks of the strike. It distributed a massive number of pamphlets and news releases, and Ladd was on the radio giving the union's side of the story. AND had hoped its workforce would give up the strike and abandon the IWA, but the loggers stood solidly behind the union.

In his history of the Newfoundland labour movement, *A Class Act*, Bill Gillespie described how the loggers responded to the IWA and the strike:

> For the first time, their union was treating them like they mattered. The IWA held a convention at which democratically elected delegates told the union negotiators what they wanted in their contract. It was a far cry from the days of Joe Thompson. So when the loggers headed into the strike they possessed a growing sense of confidence in themselves and a faith in their leadership.
>
> Every day the loggers watched as the police escorted strike-breakers across the picket line. There was plenty of verbal abuse but little violence …five weeks into the strike the RCMP officer in charge of policing the picket lines reported that the lack of violence was "one of the better aspects of the strike"…
>
> Gradually, though, signs began to appear that the loggers were winning. The strike-breakers began to leave the camps. The woodpile at the mill was diminishing…Very early in the strike the Newfoundland Federation of Labour abandoned its neutrality and began defending the IWA in the press and organizing financial support. Unions from all over Newfoundland sent money and messages of encouragement.

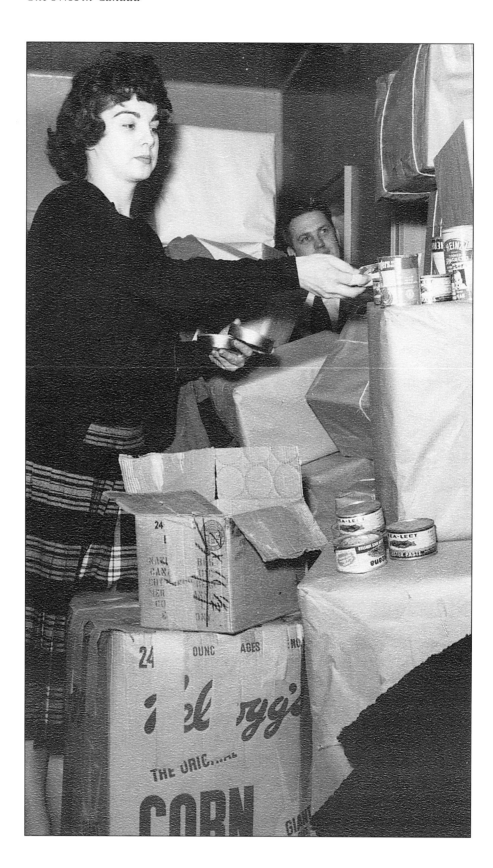

COME FROM AWAY

Chris Everson of the Ontario Federation of Labour and Harvey Ladd prepare boxes of donations for shipment to the Newfoundland strikers and their families.

IWA ARCHIVES

**Women and children joined the union's picket lines along the Trans-Canada Highway.**

IWA ARCHIVES

Pickets stretched for 200 miles along the Trans-Canada Highway in Newfoundland. Sixty-six year old Annie Noel gave up her house for as many as 100 loggers per day. Welfare committees were created in each logging town, with women making up the majority on the committees. Material support in the form of cash, food, blankets, and clothing flowed in from across the country. By February 1959, there were indications that the companies were considering a settlement and that the IWA was going to win the strike.

It was at this point that the Newfoundland premier, Joey Smallwood, a former labour organizer who had been conspicuously silent since the strike began, broke his silence. Smallwood was a popular premier whose opinion carried considerable weight among Newfoundlanders. He first declared himself to be Newfoundland's minister of labour. Then, in a well-advertised radio broadcast delivered on 12 February 1959, Smallwood ferociously attacked the IWA. The premier vilified the union, constantly referred to its leaders as "gangsters" and "outsiders," and announced he would drive the IWA out of Newfoundland. Smallwood cloaked his rhetoric with pro-labour language, but made it clear the IWA was the enemy in this particular strike. He announced he would create a new union for Newfoundland's loggers, the Newfoundland Brotherhood of Woodworkers (NBWW).

Smallwood's attempts to set up a union flopped. When it became apparent that Newfoundland loggers would remain loyal to the IWA, Smallwood resorted to drafting some of the most outrageous legislation ever passed in Canada. On 6 March 1959, the provincial government passed two laws that were obviously designed to whip up anti-IWA hysteria.

The first law decertified and outlawed the two IWA locals in Newfound-

land. The second law permitted the government to dissolve any trade union in the province whose leaders had been "convicted of such heinous crimes as white slavery, dope-peddling, man-slaughter, embezzlement, such notorious crimes as these." Of course no IWA leader had ever been charged, let alone convicted of such crimes. Smallwood's ridiculous innuendos underscored just how determined he was to taint the IWA in any way he could.

Three days after Smallwood rammed through his bizarre legislation, the IWA suffered a serious and arguably lethal blow with the onset of the first real violence of the strike.

Located in the interior of the island, west of Grand Falls, Badger was a loggers' town and IWA stronghold. Reporter Ray Timson of the *Toronto Star* was present as a large battalion of police escorted strikebreakers to work and then suddenly turned on the crowd of strikers lining the street. Timson described the events in Badger:

> Marching three abreast and carrying nightsticks, a column of sixty-six policemen waded into a throng of striking loggers last night, clubbed two of them unconscious, [and] flattened dozens more while wives and children screamed for them to stop. I watched the attack on mainly defenseless men for nearly an hour.
>
> One Newfoundland policeman was hit with a two foot long piece of birch wood and is in hospital in Grand Forks in critical condition. One Mountie was punched in the face. Both blows were struck after the police started wielding billy clubs. The police sticks were eighteen inches long. I heard three sickening skull cracks.

None of the loggers were arrested; most had been beaten to the ground, handcuffed, and dragged to their feet. At the height of the club-swinging, which occurred beside the Full Gospel Church, children stood watching and began crying. Their mothers cried with them. One shouted, "The men can't do anything, there are too many police."

At another point, a logger standing in a backyard bordering the road watched the police escorting handcuffed, dazed loggers away. He shouted, "You sure have guts, haven't you?" An officer pointed to him and yelled "get that man, get him now." The logger turned and fled and about 25 mounts and policemen cleared the fence like jackrabbits and chased him down toward a row of houses. He was beaten to the ground and arrested.

In this melee, Constable William Moss died from a blow to the head. Logger Earl Laing was charged with murder, but the case was dismissed. No evidence was produced at trial that Laing or the other loggers had a weapon capable of killing a man. Indeed, in the confusion of the police riot it is

UNION BASHING
Strikebreaking RCMP officers, spurred on by the Smallwood government, gang up on an IWA member in the Newfoundland strike.
IWA ARCHIVES

UNITED WE STAND

**With many men in jail, women bolstered the picket line.**

IWA ARCHIVES

possible that Moss was struck by a fellow officer. Regardless, the events at Badger led most Newfoundlanders to rally around their premier's anti-labour stance. The government exploited the death and funeral of Constable Moss in order to push anti-IWA sentiment to a fever pitch. Prime Minister John Diefenbaker was among those from across the country condemning Smallwood for provoking confrontations and violence. In Newfoundland, this criticism was largely unheard or ignored, and mobs repeatedly destroyed the IWA office in Grand Falls.

On 12 March 1959, Smallwood's NBWW union negotiated a settlement with AND. The settlement conformed to the December 1958 conciliation board recommendations the same terms that AND had rejected. The outlawing of the IWA meant loggers who wanted to work had to join Smallwood's union. Although the strike dragged on for several more months, its effectiveness was undermined by the double whammy of draconian legislation and intensified public hostility after the death of the police officer. The strike petered out and in March 1962 the NBWW was absorbed into the United Brotherhood of Carpenters and Joiners at Joey Smallwood's invitation. Contact between Smallwood and the UBCJ dated back to 1959, and collusion between the two occurred throughout 1961 as they negotiated a takeover of the NBWW. In March 1962, the union announced it had signed up a majority of Newfoundland loggers as members. Smallwood biographer Richard Gwyn

BRAND NEW DIGS
Local 700 president John Doskotch
shows off the local's new office in
Toronto in 1967.
IWA ARCHIVES

## LOCAL 700

# Industrial Heartland

STRETCHING FROM BELLEVILLE in the east to
Niagara Falls in the west, Local 700 spans the most
populated region in the country: southern Ontario.
The Toronto-based local was established in 1956
when 18 workers at a MacMillan Bloedel outfit in
Etobicoke, then a suburb in the west end of Toronto,
signed IWA cards. Between 1956 and 1976, 700's
membership increased to approximately 1,500
workers – with its support drawn from a wide range
of industries, including wood manufacturing and
road building/paving machinery manufacturing.
By the late 1970s and early 1980s, as the long post-
war boom ended and the nation's economy went
into a deep recession, a rash of plant closures cut
deeply into the local's membership base; there were
fewer than 300 people in the local in 1982. Between
1986 and 1989, 700's fortunes took a turn for the
better as a wave of local and sub-local mergers,
brought about by the reorganization of Districts 1
and 2 when the IWA's Canadian wing withdrew
from the International union, added members to
the local. "It was a rebirth," President Tony
Iannucci remarked at the time, looking back on

nearly a decade of organizational stagnation and
corporate downsizing.

During this period, Local 700 fought for better
wages and working conditions – and took up important race and gender issues as well. In 1987, for
example, it won a case before the Ontario Labour
Relations Board against Hanford Lumber, a
Rexdale-based company that had fired an East
Indian worker, just days before his work visa
expired, to keep him from joining the IWA. Because
of the IWA's challenge, the OLRB ordered the company to rehire the worker and pay back wages. Three
years later, 700 successfully negotiated a contract
with MacMillan Bloedel in Weston that established
pay equity for women workers in the plant. The IWA
*Pay Equity Training Manual*, an important resource
for front-line negotiators, was developed shortly
thereafter. In addition to securing this pioneering
contract, the first of its kind in southern Ontario,
700 made advances on the membership front as
well. In the early 1990s, it extended its reach into
the burgeoning retail sector with certifications at
three Loeb supermarkets, and it waged a successful
five-week strike against ALCARB Resources of
Hamilton in 1996, fighting contracting out.
Although two successive terms of Conservative government have dampened union activity in Ontario
– the ruling Tories under Mike Harris have gutted
the province's labour code – Local 700 has more
than held its own: in April 2000 it doubled its membership from about 650 to nearly 1,300 with the
addition of Canac Kitchens in Thornhill and the
Durham Victorian Order of Nurses in Oshawa.

noted the UBCJ ballot was unsupervised and its results were never released. That same year, Joey Smallwood met with the infamous dictators Francisco Franco of Spain and Antonio Salazar of Portugal. "Did the premier go to learn or to teach?" mused the *IWA News*.

The Newfoundland strike cost the IWA over a million dollars. Thousands of Newfoundland loggers and their families wintered in hardship and suffered grievously for their efforts to improve the horrible conditions under which they worked. However, in their struggles they did not forget the IWA's tremendous effort on their behalf, and thousands of Newfoundland loggers maintained a strong loyalty to the IWA for years. The scale and drama of the Newfoundland strike illustrated the depth of the IWA's commitment to improve the lives of those who worked in wood.

ON TARGET

In 1961, Region 2 successfully negotiated pensions for workers at four Hanover, Ontario, furniture plants – the first deal of its kind in the IWA.

IWA ARCHIVES

## Advances in Region 2

While the long, difficult battle was being waged in Newfoundland, Region 2 continued servicing its members, organizing new workplaces, running education programs, and negotiating contracts. The union had been encouraging its many locals to consider amalgamating wherever practical, with the aim of strengthening their bargaining power. In 1960, representatives from 16 operations in northern Ontario met at a convention to found Local 2-1000, and Local 2-486 combined with other Hanover-area locals to represent furniture workers as Local 2-500. Most other locals in Ontario were content to maintain their autonomy and rely on pattern bargaining to win wage and benefit increases.

MARITIME MATTERS
New Brunswick Local 306
was organized in the
wake of the failed
Newfoundland campaign.
IWA LOCAL 306 ARCHIVES

**LOCAL 306**

# Beachhead at Burchills

IN THE WAKE of the IWA's bitter defeat in Newfoundland in 1959, several of the men involved in the campaign, including Harvey Ladd, John McCool, and Jeff Hall, turned up in New Brunswick in the early 1960s. Workers in several sawmill and plywood mills in and around Newcastle (now Miramichi) — Frank Girouard, Bert Blackmore, Laurie Richard, George Bradford, and Eric and Yvon Barrieau among them — wanted a union. After a short, but effective, period of organizing, they had one.

Local 306 was chartered in 1963, and within a year it represented approximately 250 workers at six different operations; the core of its support was drawn from the Burchill and Acadia sawmill and plywood operations. "We had several plants on the go [at the same time], organized into the IWA," Frank Girouard recalled years later. "We were negotiating at all these companies at the same time. We got all the wording in the contracts approved, but when it came to discussing money, all the companies went their separate ways." As a result, the young local fought a lengthy strike against Burchill in 1964, securing a 15-cent raise

and, significantly, a guarantee that if the plant was ever bought by another company, the new owner would have to honour the collective agreement.

Although 306 remained solid during the 1960s, in the late 1970s and early 1980s its membership eroded as mills shut down and, in some cases, workers opted out of the IWA. "They were not serviced like they should have been," Eric Barrieau, a long-time Burchill worker and IWAer, recalled. But thanks to workers' ongoing commitment to the IWA and the protection of its original 1964 agreement, the local maintained its presence at Burchill despite periodic closures and many different owners. After a four-year shutdown from 1990 to 1994, for example, a tough time for workers, many of whom were forced to accept government assistance to weather the economic downturn, Burchill was bought by Nelson Forest Products. Local 306 also represents workers at Repap New Brunswick's stud mill.

Today the local is looking to expand its presence in the province, where less than 25 percent of the workforce belongs to a union and wages for woodworkers still lag behind those paid in other locales. It opened a new office in Miramichi in October 1999, and just two months later it successfully unionized workers at Northumberland Co-operative, a company that, among other endeavours, operates a dairy facility and sells hardware throughout New Brunswick.

In 1961, Local 2-500 made a significant breakthrough when it won a
pension plan for workers at four Hanover furniture factories. IWA members at
Knechtel, Wright-Spiesz, Pepplar Brothers, and Knechtel Kabinet Kreations
were the first workers in the union in Canada to win a pension package. Given
the range and diversity of Region 2's workforce and the existence of so many
small locals, the establishment of the plan was a major achievement.

A year later, workers from Bathurst Containers' four plants in Hamilton,
Whitby, St. Laurent, and Montreal formed a Paper Council within the IWA
and consolidated their efforts at the bargaining table.

The IWA expanded into New Brunswick in 1963 with the founding of
Local 2-306. Poor wages and working conditions at several forest industry
operations in the Miramichi region of the province created a ripe organizing
opportunity, and by 1964 the local represented 250 woodworkers. A strike
eventually won a first contract at the Burchill Brothers' plywood mill that
same year and cemented the IWA's presence in New Brunswick.

There was another fight for a first contract in 1963 when a strike began at
Hanover Kitchens. Region 2 organizer Wilf "Chally" Chalmers recalled that
Hanover Kitchens was determined not to recognize the IWA – the result was a
scrap. IWA members remained solid throughout the strike and eventually
decided to organize a boycott of the entire town of Hanover. The union hired
buses to carry the citizens of Hanover to neighbouring communities like
Walkerton and Durham to do their shopping on the weekends. "You could
have fired a cannon down the main street in Hanover and you wouldn't have
hit a thing," Chalmers told the *Lumber Worker* in 1990. The resulting political
pressure brought to bear on the employer helped end the strike.

With ongoing organization, Region 2 represented over 6,000 members by 1966. As ever, education remained a fundamental aspect of Region 2's efforts. Regressive labour laws in Ontario and Quebec made education about the IWA and the function of the trade union movement a crucial part of the drive to organize new workers. "We Canadians in Eastern Canada live in a jungle of fear," Harvey Ladd said in 1965. "When you look at the face of a woodworker, when you ask him to sign a card, all over that face is written a horrible chapter in Canadian democracy." Union members passed a resolution that year calling for a 25-cent per capita fee to be collected for educational purposes, and Region 2's commitment to education for union members became one of its enduring legacies. It brought the same commitment to its locals in Quebec. In recognition of the French-speaking members in Region 2, the *IWA News* was published in both English and French, and the union constitution was also translated into French.

Harvey Ladd stepped down as president of Region 2 in 1969, when he was elected an International vice-president. In 1973, he was appointed the director of the IWA International's education department, bringing his years of experience with labour education to the fore for all IWA members.

## Lumber and Saw in Northern Ontario

In Ontario's northern woods, Lumber and Saw remained the union of choice for woodworkers. As in the IWA's District 1, Lumber and Saw had purged its communist leaders in 1951, and the task of re-establishing the union's leadership fell to Bill Sawyer. By 1953 he had recruited and hired Lothar Bode,

Andre Wellsby, and Tulio Mior, all of whom quickly established themselves as skilled, capable organizers and union leaders who enjoyed the strong support of members. Even the companies expressed their approval of what historian Ian Radforth described as an "efficient, democratic organization." Like the contemporary IWA leadership in British Columbia, Lumber and Saw leaders were staunch supporters of the CCF/NDP and urged their membership to support the party.

In the 1950s, expansion in the industry and a scarcity of labour in the northern Ontario woods saw Lumber and Saw's membership go from 2,000 in 1951 to an all-time high of 16,000 in 1957. New members were attracted to the union by its demonstrated ability to establish good wages and working conditions. In the mid-1950s, the union established the right to a union shop,

## A 'Red' Purge in Lumber and Saw

BRUCE MAGNUSON was a young emigrant from Sweden when he arrived in Canada in 1928. While working as a teamster in Saskatchewan, he became interested in left-wing politics. Shortly after arriving in Port Arthur (now Thunder Bay) in 1933, he joined the Communist Party of Canada and became an organizer for the Lumber Workers Industrial Union. Upon the LWIU's demise, Magnuson moved on to the Lumber and Sawmill Workers Union and had much success organizing northern Ontario bushworkers. When the CPC was declared illegal in 1940, Magnuson, with his well-established reputation as one of the prominent red union leaders, was subjected to harassment from Canadian authorities, who ultimately detained him. From August 1940 until September 1942, Magnuson was held at a prisoner-of-war camp in Petawawa. On his release, he was welcomed back into his position as president of Port Arthur Local 2786. Like IWA members in British Columbia, northern Ontario's loggers respected the toughness and negotiating abilities of

RED PIONEER
**Lumber and Saw's Bruce Magnuson.**
PROGRESS BOOKS

their leaders and were not overly concerned about their political stripes.

By the time Lumber and Saw members won a decisive victory over timber operators in 1946, opposition to communist trade unionists was becoming formidable. The media denounced communist union leaders like Magnuson and Dan MacIsaac, by then president of Local 2786, northern Ontario's largest local. Red delegates were being removed from their seats on local trades and labour councils. Pressure mounted against the leaders of Lumber and Saw. The union's parent organization, the United Brotherhood of Carpenters and Joiners, was increasingly intolerant of Lumber and Saw's leadership and by 1950, was openly committed to purging its communist leaders.

The 1950 contract had a condition stipulating that any union officer who wanted to visit a camp had to have the approval of the UBCJ general representative. The UBCJ used this condition to deny Lumber and Saw's union representatives permission to attend to their membership. The protests of Lumber and Saw's red leaders were ignored by the Carpenters' union.

seniority clauses, and ever-improving living conditions in the camps. In 1960, it won a 44-hour week at the same rate of pay for the old 48-hour week, and by 1965 a 40-hour week had been obtained. While industry-wide bargaining and a master contract were lost with the rapid expansion of the industry, pattern bargaining soon evolved, with the Abitibi company typically setting the standard for the union in its negotiations with other companies.

Technological change came slowly in the period immediately following the war, but increased substantially through the 1950s and 1960s, driven in large part by the shortage of labour that was helping Lumber and Saw members achieve big gains at the bargaining table. The use of horse-drawn sleighs and river drives as methods of getting wood to the mill had largely ended by the late 1950s as mechanization of the work process became established.

In May 1951, the UBCJ escalated its campaign. Armed with a court injunction, General Executive Andy Cooper and four international officers from the UBCJ's Indianapolis headquarters put Local 2786 under trusteeship, charging its leaders with the misuse of union funds. This allegation appears to have been unfounded, but it served the purpose of undermining the credibility of Lumber and Saw's red leadership. Newspapers carried headlines proclaiming "Action Taken In Supreme Court to Rid Union of Red Influence," "Probe Sawmill Union Here for Communist Affiliation," and "Mismanagement of Funds Also Under Investigation." In response, Harry Timchishin of Local 2786 referred to the International's actions as nothing less than an illegal takeover of the local. The end result of the UBCJ's efforts was the removal of the red leadership from Lumber and Saw. But the deposed leaders were not about to go without a fight, and like their red colleagues in British Columbia they chose to form a new union.

In June 1951, the Canadian Union of Wood-workers (CUW) was created, with locals in Port Arthur, Timmins, and Sudbury. A fourth local was brought into the CUW from Quebec. Marc Leclerc, Bruce Magnuson, Harry Timchishin, Jack Quinn, Harry Raketti, A.T. Hill, and a number of other ex-Lumber and Saw leaders appealed to bushworkers to join their organization. The CUW hoped to offer an alternative to what it perceived as conservative unionism. Like the Woodworkers Industrial Union of Canada in British Columbia, the CUW ran into a wall of opposition.

In the summer of 1951, Ontario Provincial Police arrested CUW organizers who tried to enter camps and organize workers. While the Ontario government and its Labour Relations Board responded to the CUW with indifference, Maurice Duplessis, the premier of Quebec, suggested that CUW members be thrown out of the camps. Meanwhile, Andy Cooper and the Carpenters union were negotiating contracts and solidifying their hold on Ontario's loggers. By the autumn of 1951, the CUW had collapsed, its leaders purged from their positions of influence in the woods of northern Ontario. The defeat of the reds in both British Columbia and northern Ontario marked the end of communist-led unionism in the woods.

FOREST AS
FACTORY, 1952

A logger in northern
Ontario unhooks
chokers from logs
moved with a diesel
engine.

Chain saws and power skidders replaced bucksaws and horses. Fred Miron, a Lumber and Saw union representative in the mid-1960s, recalled, "One day they would be on a horse, the next day on a tractor skidder. One thing that I'm proud of is that the conversion to the new technology was made with the same people. We insisted that the company train our existing members."

Tulio Mior, president of Local 2693 from 1958 to 1983, commented, "In the 1950s, we knew it [technological change] was going to happen. The extent was a guessing game, but it was an accepted factor." Like the IWA, Lumber and Saw was never opposed to technological change, but maintained that workers had to be trained on the job for new machines and work methods. According to Mior, workers "accepted new methods easily," and the evolution of mechanization in the workplace was not a problem for Lumber and Saw members.

With the exception of minor disputes with individual companies and an occasional wildcat strike to bring a stubborn operator into line, Lumber and Saw members made solid gains throughout this period without having to mount a major strike. Tragically, this period of relative peace between labour and the industry was violently interrupted in 1963.

## The Reesor Siding Massacre

In early 1963, the first major dispute to hit the northern Ontario logging industry in years erupted near Kapuskasing. The 1,500 members of Lumber and Saw Local 2995 launched a wildcat strike against Spruce Falls Power and Paper Company on 14 January. The strike reached a horrible climax nearly a month later when three strikers lay dead from gunshots and eight more were wounded at Reesor Siding, a railway siding and depot 37 miles west of Kapuskasing. The Reesor Siding Massacre remains the deadliest labour action in the history of the Canadian woodworking industry.

The circumstances leading up to this tragedy were not unique. Indeed, they were typical of many labour disputes that have taken place before and since in the forest industry. For months, Spruce Falls Power and Paper loggers had been unsuccessful in their efforts to get a new contract with the company. Their frustration was exacerbated by the fact that loggers employed in nearby Abitibi mills had recently won a 10 percent wage increase and the 40-hour week.

Spruce Falls refused to negotiate a deal with its loggers, largely because one of its parent companies, the *New York Times*, was itself being struck. The *Times* purchased 30 percent of its newsprint supply from Spruce Falls, and because of the *Times* strike, the demand for newsprint had fallen off. Complicating matters further was the fact that the Spruce Falls mill received an ongoing supply of wood from farmers in the area, so it was not entirely dependent on union loggers for its timber supply.

LIVES LOST
From top to bottom are Irenée Fortier, Joseph Fortier, and Fernand Drouin.
PROGRESS BOOKS

173

**MASS ARRESTS**

After the Reesor Siding Massacre, 138 Lumber and Saw members marched to the Kapuskasing Inn and were charged with unlawful assembly.

IWA LOCAL 2995 ARCHIVES

In *Reesor Siding: A Labour Dispute in Northern Ontario*, Martin Champoux described how farmers supplied the Spruce Falls mill with 25 percent of its wood. As an incentive to settle the region, the Ontario government had offered these farmers low-cost permits to cut up to 100 cords of Crown timber. Given the poor conditions for farming in northern Ontario, the local farmers banded into co-ops in order to make wood harvesting a profitable practice.

Local 2995 President Joseph Laforce knew that if the union wanted to get a settlement from the company, it was crucial to gain the farmers' support. He worked hard to convince the farmers that if the union got a good settlement, they would be able to increase their prices and further their own profits. Laforce promised to provide support to the farmers if they would stop supplying wood to Spruce Falls.

Despite Laforce's arguments, the farmers refused to co-operate with the union. Mainly French Canadian Catholics, the farmers' anti-union stance had its roots in the church's conservatism and intolerance of anything

IN THE MEDIA GLARE

Following charges, Lumber and Saw members were escorted to a waiting bus while local and national media watched.

IWA LOCAL 2995 ARCHIVES

that remotely smacked of communism, including trade unionism. The farmers ignored the union and continued to do business as usual with the Spruce Falls mill.

Spruce Falls recognized the leverage it had over its loggers in negotiations and refused to offer a wage increase. Moreover, the company demanded that a seven-day work week be put into effect, if necessary, to ensure delivery of wood before the spring thaw. Consequently, on 14 January 1963, Local 2995 loggers launched a wildcat strike, even though it was against the wishes of the union executive and in defiance of Ontario labour law. Eleven hundred employees of the Spruce Falls mill struck in sympathy with the loggers. In response, the company refused to negotiate with the strikers until they returned to work.

As the strike wore on, relations between the three parties became increasingly tense. The farmers relied on independent contractors to haul their wood to the Spruce Falls mill, and the strikers focused their efforts on stopping the contractors from delivering wood. In one instance, when union patrols found a contractor's trucks loaded with wood, 400 loggers showed up to "unload" the wood, scattering it far and wide.

Local police were too undermanned to deal with the conflict and escalating confrontations. On 4 February, the Ontario government appointed Bora Laskin to mediate the dispute. As Laskin's first hearing began on 10 February, farmers began to gather at Reesor Siding to protect 600 cords of wood awaiting delivery. Strikers had previously scattered 1,100 cords of wood at Reesor Siding. In anticipation of further confrontation with the strikers, the farmers armed themselves with rifles, shotguns, and a revolver.

BROTHERLY LOVE

Wally Dubinsky, Local 2995 lawyer, holds a cheque issued by the UBCJ head office to cover the fines handed out to Lumber and Saw members convicted of unlawful assembly.

IWA LOCAL 2995 ARCHIVES

Shortly after midnight on 11 February, between 400 and 500 strikers arrived at Reesor Siding and immediately crossed the rope police had strung up around the farmers. The farmers opened fire and within seconds three strikers were dead and eight more were wounded. Killed were Irenée Fortier, Joseph Fortier, and Fernand Drouin. Seriously injured were Harry Bernard, Ovila Bernard, Joseph Boily, Alez Hachey, Albert Martel, Joseph Mercier, Léo Ouimette, and Daniel Tremblay.

Twenty farmers were charged with illegal use of firearms with intent to injure, and three charges of non-capital murder were laid shortly thereafter. Ontario's attorney-general sent in 200 police as reinforcements and charged 237 strikers with illegal assembly. Their bail was paid by the union and they were set free.

Organized labour, the Ontario NDP, and a Liberal MPP all demanded inquiries be held to determine why the dispute turned into a bloodbath. There were indications that the police had at minimum handled the situation ineptly and further indications that the police had bungled their investigation of the shootings. Ultimately, a jury found insufficient evidence to convict the farmers of non-capital murder. They were instead convicted of possession of dangerous firearms and fined $150 each. The Ontario ministry of labour assumed control of the dispute and forced the strikers to return to work under an extension of their 1962 agreement.

REESOR SIDING
REMEMBERED

In April 1996, the
Ontario Heritage
Federation erected
a plaque in front of
the Reesor Siding
Memorial statue.
Pictured from left to
right are Norm Rivard
(Local 2995 president),
Ken Signoretti
(Ontario Federation
of Labour executive
vice-president),
Mercedes Steedman
(Ontario Heritage
Federation),
Wilf McIntyre
(Local 2693 president),
and Len Wood
(NDP Member of
Provincial Parliament).
IWA ARCHIVES

ACTION IN THE
INTERIOR
Pictured here at
the IWA's annual
convention in 1956,
Clayton Walls (on
far right) met with BC
Interior delegates.
Walls oversaw the
administration of
the Interior Regional
Office from 1954
to 1962.
IWA ARCHIVES

Thirty-three years later, on 25 April 1996, the Ontario Heritage Foundation unveiled a plaque commemorating those killed and injured. The ceremony was attended by IWA officials and numerous representatives from organized labour in Canada.

## 'Parity With the Coast'

In the 1960s, the IWA continued to assert itself as one of the most aggressive unions in the country. Brief economic recessions in the late 1950s and the early 1960s caused only a stutter in the momentum developed by the union. Its strength resulted in steady improvements in each contract it negotiated. Unprecedented economic prosperity meant union members were enjoying a quality of life barely imaginable when the union was formed in 1937, and they were prepared to fight for more.

Low levels of unemployment helped create conditions in which union members were not reluctant to down their tools, whether in job actions sanctioned by union leaders or in numerous wildcat strikes. The willingness of union members to challenge the bosses and even the law was indicative of a vigorous, healthy union. The IWA's successes in the 1960s did not always come easily, but conditions were generally favourable to the union.

It was in this setting that the IWA's BC Interior locals decided to once

INTERIOR LEADERS
At the helm of the IWA and Interior locals during the 1967 "parity strike" were, from left to right: Bob Schlosser (Local 1-417), Jack Moore (Region 1 president), Bill Schumaker (Local 1-423), Jack MacKenzie (regional vice-president), and Jack Munro (Local 1-405).
IWA ARCHIVES

again fight for wage parity with coastal IWA members in 1967. After the difficult 1953 strike, Interior members were still lagging well behind their coastal counterparts. By 1964 the Interior locals made 19 cents per hour less than Coast members, and the agreement the southern Interior locals negotiated that year gave them only a 36-cent increase over three years. This was less than what the Coast locals had received earlier that year, and many southern Interior members were angry with the regional leadership for urging them to accept an inferior agreement. It was grudgingly accepted by a majority of only 200 votes.

By 1967, Interior workers were earning $2.26 per hour, 50 cents less than the Coast members, and they demanded two key items in negotiations that year: wage parity with the Coast and a contract that expired on the same day as the Coast agreement, which traditionally expired several weeks before the Interior agreement. A common expiry date meant all members could strike at the same time, allowing the union to threaten a provincewide shutdown if employers were recalcitrant.

In the mid-1960s, Jack Munro was an IWA business agent in the southern Interior. Munro had been opposed to the 1964 agreement and was determined that southern Interior members would gain significant improvements in 1967 to bring them in line with their coastal counterparts. In his autobiography, *Union Jack*, Munro recalled that he was in favour of achieving parity with the Coast by the end of the proposed agreement. However, most of the negotiating committee wanted parity immediately. When the judge serving as mediator in the dispute brought down his report, he rejected both the demand

HIGH YIELD
IWA locals across
the country grew
steadily in the 1960s.
Shown here is the
new executive of
the Loggers' Local 1-71,
sworn in during 1969.
Ernie Freer, seventh
from right, led the
local during this
period of expansion.
IWA ARCHIVES

for immediate parity and the change in contract expiry date. A thousand Interior workers from the north and 4,000 from the south voted to strike. Subsequent negotiations failed and by early October 1967 the IWA was on strike in British Columbia's Interior.

In the northern Interior, the IWA had been reluctant to strike. "Sure, we could get half a dozen plants to close," commented Tage Morgenson, "but at all the others we'd lose. Our people had been through some tough years and now they at last had steady jobs. Forty-four cents an hour looked pretty good, and we didn't think they'd want to strike just to change the contract date." Because the law stated that only those operations voting to strike could walk off the job, the northern Interior strike of 1967 hit only two operations: the mill in Mackenzie and Northwood company operations.

In 1967, Mackenzie was still a "new" town and the mill was the sole reason for its existence. "The company put up new homes as soon as possible," observed Ken Bernsohn, "but for the first wives who arrived, living on an island of tract housing in the wilderness was more than they could take…When negotiations opened in 1967, the people in Mackenzie wanted more. More money to make it worth their while to stay. More amenities. More things to do. More stores."

"Frankly, what we had to do was let these guys let off steam," said an IWA executive board member. "They'd be furious if we tried to get them back to work…No contract, no matter how good, could solve the problems in Mackenzie." Five weeks into the strike, the northern region reached an agree-

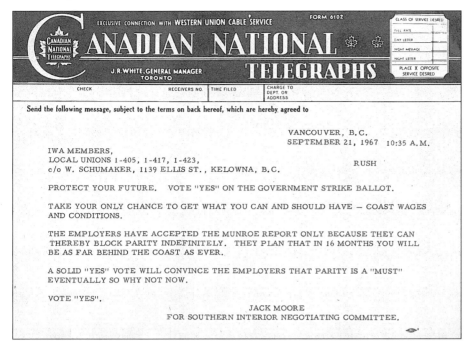

VANCOUVER, B.C.
SEPTEMBER 21, 1967   10:35 A.M.

IWA MEMBERS,
LOCAL UNIONS 1-405, 1-417, 1-423,
c/o W. SCHUMAKER, 1139 ELLIS ST., KELOWNA, B.C.          RUSH

PROTECT YOUR FUTURE.   VOTE "YES" ON THE GOVERNMENT STRIKE BALLOT.

TAKE YOUR ONLY CHANCE TO GET WHAT YOU CAN AND SHOULD HAVE — COAST WAGES
AND CONDITIONS.

THE EMPLOYERS HAVE ACCEPTED THE MUNROE REPORT ONLY BECAUSE THEY CAN
THEREBY BLOCK PARITY INDEFINITELY.   THEY PLAN THAT IN 16 MONTHS YOU WILL
BE AS FAR BEHIND THE COAST AS EVER.

A SOLID "YES" VOTE WILL CONVINCE THE EMPLOYERS THAT PARITY IS A "MUST"
EVENTUALLY SO WHY NOT NOW.

VOTE "YES".

JACK MOORE
FOR SOUTHERN INTERIOR NEGOTIATING COMMITTEE.

**VOTE YES!**

In the fall of 1967, President Jack Moore urged Interior members to "get what you can and should have – Coast wages and conditions."

IWA ARCHIVES

ment. It called for a 44-cent per hour wage increase, with another wage increase in 1969 equal to that received by Coast members. While this did not give IWA members in the north parity with the Coast, they had closed the gap considerably.

In the south, negotiations broke off and picketing continued, with operators continually applying for injunctions against the union's activities. In Nelson, a mill manager advertised for scabs to re-open a Kootenay Forest Products mill. "We had a meeting in Nelson when this goofy bugger put this in the paper," said Jack Munro. "We decided to march through town and give the city of Nelson a message – that we were united." Union members rallied and paraded through the streets and convinced the employer to re-think his efforts to open the mill.

Four months after the strike began, the owners of a mill in Castlegar announced they were withdrawing from the Interior Forests Labour Relations Association, the employers' bargaining association. "The Castlegar mill was the most militant of all the mills, and this was a prime example of how that militancy paid off," said Munro. The employer agreed to grant Castlegar members parity with the Coast, as well as their requested contract expiry date. While the Castlegar members were delighted that their employer had caved in and they were back to work, the rest of the southern Interior continued to endure a long strike through the winter, with negotiations going nowhere and no end in sight.

In mid-April 1968, the employers were beginning to soften. They offered

LONG MARCH

In March 1968, Jack Munro led picketers from Kootenay Forest Products down the streets of Nelson to focus the public's attention on the company's stated intention to open its mill and "obtain workers where it could."

NELSON DAILY NEWS

wage parity, but were adamant they would not adjust the contract expiry date. The IWA negotiating committee rejected this offer, but the government forced the committee to put the employers' offer to a vote by the membership. Jack Munro recalled what happened:

> It was another overwhelming rejection by the membership – by a higher number than the original strike vote. We were in a bargaining session with the employers at the time, and after we read the results of our vote, we sat in that room for over an hour without anyone saying a word, not a word. It wasn't up to us to say anything, we had answered. It was up to them.
>
> It was that incredible no vote, that rejection of the offer, that won the strike for us. The employers knew we were serious. We finally started talking and shortly thereafter we settled. We didn't end up getting parity, but we got within 14 cents of parity. We got the expiry date changed to June 30. That strike lasted 224 days and it was tough on a lot of people. But it was a good strike.

On 10 May 1968, southern Interior members voted to accept the proposed agreement. The IWA spent over $3 million in support of the strikers, and while the goal of parity was not reached, the union had sent a powerful message to employers. Parity with the coast remained a demand for Interior members, and the 1967-68 strike did not lessen their determination to obtain that goal.

## The Long Boom Ends

The quarter century that followed the IWA's crucial breakthrough in 1946 was a dramatic period of upheaval, militancy, and considerably more success than failure at the bargaining table. It was a time of unrivalled prosperity for union members in both Region 1 and 2 as government, employers, and the labour movement – buoyed by vigorous economic growth and the expansion of the social safety net – forged a post-war compromise shaped by big government, big unions, big wages, and big profits.

All of this came at a price, however. Logging remained a dangerous occupation. Between 50 and 100 men died on the job each year in BC alone in this era, prompting the union to urge its members to refuse work they thought unsafe, lobby for helicopter ambulances, and challenge employers to beef up their own safety procedures. One of the ongoing culprits behind all the carnage was technological change – mobile steel spars, skidders, feller-bunchers, and smaller chain saws all made their appearance in this era – and the increased demands employers subsequently made of their workers. As productivity in the industry rose, spurred on by the sweeping technological changes, workers continued to be injured, maimed, or killed on the job in staggering numbers. (The number of days lost to injury outpaced the number of days lost to strikes, a grim statistic when one considers just how militant the IWA was during this period.) Not surprisingly, safety on the job, in addition to wages, benefits, and logging practices, remained a key issue for the union.

THE GOOD OLD DAYS

**Pictured with a Tyee yarder and a Local 1-80 logging crew on Vancouver Island in the 1960s are local union officer Jack Mumm (left), local president Weldon Jubenville (fourth from left), and regional president Jack Moore (right).**

IWA ARCHIVES

## 'Follow the Rules and Don't Get Killed'

*New Westminster I think it was, or some place in the Haney local outside of the Vancouver local, there was a shingle worker and he fell into the cut-off saw. Oh, we were just as much to blame, our cut-off saws were open wide, that poor devil there he is mangled in half. Half his body there had to be operated on and everything. The rib cage was gone, shoulder was gone and everything. Well, that is the stuff that is going on and this safety is a farce. It is a bloody disgrace!*

– IWAer Scotty Rough,
1968 Region 1 convention

IN THE POST-WAR ERA, the IWA remained deeply concerned about the dangerous and deadly toll its members experienced while trying to earn a living. Increasing mechanization and technological change resulted in speedups on the job, and IWA members were well aware of the dangers they faced as employers demanded more production. In 1949, the IWA launched a safety program based on a tri-partite model of co-operation between labour,

industry, and government. Joint labour-management safety committees were set up at every IWA-organized operation, and the union launched an aggressive educational campaign. In 1951, long before health and safety laws acknowledged the workers' right to refuse dangerous work, the IWA told its members in British Columbia to stop work on all jobs that did not meet the union's safety requirements.

In January 1952, John Atkinson of Local 1-80 was appointed as District 1's first full-time safety director. With Atkinson's appointment, the IWA became the first union in North America to have a full-time safety director. Atkinson emphasized education as a key to reducing casualties, and the *Lumber Worker* expanded its coverage of safety issues from a small corner of the paper to a two-page spread. In the early 1950s the *Lumber Worker* published hand-drawn illustrations of fatal incidents; by the mid-1950s it was running graphic photos of mangled corpses trapped in machinery and other gruesome images of death, driving home the point that every worker was at risk of injury and death. Headlines such as "He Forgot The Rule And Died" put the initiative on workers to follow safe working practices.

Despite these efforts, the carnage continued. The IWA safety campaign had some success at

# another man died...

**OCCUPATION:** Mill Hand
**AGE:** 33
**EXPERIENCE:** One Month

January 2, 1958—The workman was attempting to replace the chain on the sprocket of a slow moving wood conveyor. The sprocket was turning at approximately 32 revolutions per minute.

It is assumed that his clothing became caught on the sprocket and he was wrapped around the shaft several times, causing instant death.

**DON'T GAMBLE YOUR LIFE WITH SLOW MOVING MACHINERY.**

reducing accident rates, but the number of fatalities increased throughout the 1950s – 777 forest industry workers lost their lives in BC during the decade – and many union members questioned the industry's commitment to the tripartite safety program. In 1959, injury and death rates jumped significantly. Region 1 president Joe Morris demanded the WCB play a stronger role in promoting safety education and charged employers with falsifying accident reports to maintain good records.

In the early 1960s the IWA was infuriated when many companies began asking job applicants if they had ever received WCB benefits; the obvious implication was that to answer "yes" meant a worker would likely not be hired. While the IWA continued to work with the WCB in the 1960s, the tripartite model had begun to unravel.

By 1968, the union's safety program was no longer focusing on the worker's responsibility for safe work practices to the degree it had a decade earlier. "An accident is very seldom due solely to unsafe behavior," commented an October 1967 *Lumber Worker* article. IWAers cited production speedup as a primary cause of casualties, flayed the WCB for ignoring violations of accident prevention regulations, and attacked the industry's lack of commitment to safety. Another 601 woodworkers died in British Columbia in the 1960s, despite a drop in the overall number of workers employed in the industry.

The IWA's emphasis on safety and the well-being of its members grew tremendously in the 1950s and 1960s. Workers at IWA-organized operations were less likely to be injured or killed than those at non-union worksites, a testimony to the success of the union's safety education campaign. While the tripartite safety model ultimately failed, the union's commitment to safety and health expanded considerably. No longer did safety issues only deal with overt physical injury and death. The IWA was aware of newly emerging concerns about the hazards of sawdust and air pollution, excessive noise levels, and the long-term effects of operating machinery, and fought to have these once-invisible issues addressed.

Scotty Rough's anger and despair was, sadly, all too justified, and the IWA would increase its efforts in the coming decades to confront the dangers its members faced.

April 2nd, 1964.

Fair Harbour

Carl Schenkeveld - Age 32 - Married

Steel spar engineer was hired on March 29th
and killed on April 2nd.
Large chunk shaped like a walking stick was
picked up by mainline while it was slacked
off. When mainline tightened it slid down
and flew through the air striking the
engineer.

\* \* \* \* \* \* \* \* \* \* \* \* \* \* \* \* \* \* \* \* \* \* \* \*

September 10, 1964.

Greenwood contractors at Great Central (non-
Union) Fedje & Gunderson contract falling
under agreement to us.

Henry Kubera - Age 34 - Single

Killed at 10:45 am while bucking a log.
Cat was making grade - pushed a log off the
road it brushed against a tall cedar that was
green at the top but rotten at the roots -
it fell on top of Kubera killing him instantly.

\* \* \* \* \* \* \* \* \* \* \* \* \* \* \* \* \* \* \* \* \* \* \* \*

June 3, 1965.


Northern Hemlock Logging

Terry McCaffery - 19 years - single

U.B.C. Student hired as a chokerman
first time in the woods.
Was struck by a falling sapling
at 10 a.m. Died instantly.

**DEATH STILL STALKS
THE WOODS**

Accident reports filed
by Local 1-85 detail
the human cost of
"getting the wood out."

IWA LOCAL 1-85 ARCHIVES

186

In the years ahead employers and the government launched a renewed assault on the gains working people had made in the years since World War II. IWA members and the rest of the working class were forced to confront problems such as inflation, unemployment, and corporate downsizing in a setting that was increasingly hostile to working people and their organizations. The era of post-war affluence was about to come to a close; hard times and new challenges lay ahead.

# *Consensus* to *Conflict*

# Consensus to Conflict

*The union's annual conventions were testimony to the bottom-up, member-driven democracy that informed the decision-making processes of union leaders.*

AS THE 1970s DAWNED, the IWA in Canada was a healthy, vigorous, and battle-hardened union. In western Canada's Region 1, over 40,000 workers were IWA members, the vast majority in BC. In eastern Canada's Region 2, IWA locals and sub-locals represented over 10,000 workers in diverse operations, including the corrugated cardboard plants of Quebec and Ontario, with another large block of membership in the fine furniture factories of southwestern Ontario. The union's annual conventions were testimony to the bottom-up, member-driven democracy that informed the decision-making processes of union leaders. Union members hashed out issues on the convention floor and did battle with employers when necessary.

By mid-decade, however, as high inflation, interest rates, government deficits, and unemployment emerged across the country, the long economic boom wound down and working people, IWA members among them, faced a tough new reality as the post-war compromise between government, industry, and organized labour unravelled.

As the decade began, however, Region 1 found itself grappling with an old issue – piecework – in a strike that showed both the strength of local autonomy in the union and its potential for divisiveness.

## The Highest-Paid Woodworkers in the World

Since its inception in 1937, the IWA had adopted a policy of eliminating piecework in the forest industry. Thirteen years later, the most prominent group of workers in the IWA still being paid on a piecework scale was the tree fallers – they had traditionally been paid according to how much timber they felled. In the early 1950s, the union demanded a standard day wage for tree fallers, but companies staunchly refused to change the method of payment. Because the principle of piecework pay was well-established and popular among most fallers, the union instead worked to negotiate pricing formulas on a camp-by-camp basis to protect fallers from being cheated by their employers. Over the years, pay-rate disparities became an ever-increasing source of aggravation, and fallers went out on wildcat strikes with increasing regularity.

In 1972, the IWA's Wage and Contract Conference again called for the abolition of piecework and the establishment of a day rate for fallers. Local 1-217's president Syd Thompson observed that fallers were earning anywhere between

$50 and $200 a day, "and the $50 a day man worked just as hard." IWA president Jack Moore was hopeful that bringing in a day rate would cut down on the high number of fatalities among fallers by eliminating the need for speed-ups.

Unhappy with the IWA wage and contract proposals for 1972, and insistent on maintaining the piecework system, a group of fallers from Vancouver Island set up a 17-member special steering committee. The legitimacy of this committee was called into question by some IWA officials, including Jack Moore, who argued that the fallers' meetings were unconstitutional because open voting was held on contractual matters when secret ballots should have been used. Other prominent IWAers like Syd Thompson said that the fallers "weren't given the leadership [from IWA officials] they should have had, which is the reason they went out on their own."

On 18 April 1972, the fallers' steering committee called for a wildcat strike and 800 fallers went off the job on Vancouver Island and the Coast. The fallers wanted to maintain the piecework system and establish a standardized pricing formula for all camps based on the number of board feet felled. In an attempt to appease the fallers, the IWA's Coast Negotiating Committee proposed a piece rate of $1.10 per thousand board feet. If this proposal had

**FALLERS' REVOLT**
Prior to the 1972 strike, fallers on Vancouver Island, like the men pictured here in Campbell River in 1969, founded the Fallers' Society to air their workplace grievances and criticisms of the union.
UBC SPECIAL COLLECTIONS BC 102-44

# THE FALLERS' PRAYER

Our Father, Billings, who art in a concrete heaven,
Overwhelming is thy ignorance.
Thy kingdom is falling,
Thy will isn't being done
In the B.C. woods, as Bonner wishes.
Give us this day our daily injunction,
And forgive us our determination
As we forgive the parasites that make money off us,
And lead us not into poverty
But deliver us from thy greedy clutches.
For ours is the skill, the knowhow and the production
As will be forever and ever. Amen.

—Shorty Undercut,
Forest Drive.

1972

GET SHORTY

During the fallers' strike, one logger poet celebrated workers' determination and "knowhow" while skewering the "parasites that make money off us."
IWA LOCAL 363 ARCHIVES

been accepted and won from employers, it would have brought huge wage increases for every faller on the Coast, but the fallers' steering committee rejected it as inadequate.

This put the Coast Negotiating Committee in a bind. There were 28,000 Coast woodworkers waiting for a new agreement, but a rebellious minority of fallers were upending the recommendations that the wage conference had put forward. Third vice-president Stan Parker was a former faller who described the fallers as "a little group who said, 'negotiate what we want or we won't accept anything.'" Faced with an impossible situation, the negotiating committee decided it had to act in the interests of the majority of the membership. The committee chose to proceed with negotiations, and the elimination of piecework was once again on the agenda. The fallers carried on with their strike, which was starting to curtail coastal logging operations. Layoffs mounted throughout the forest industry.

The employers used the fallers' strike as an excuse to duck contract negotiations. Consequently, the union asked its membership for a strike vote. When a solid result showed that members supported the union, employers agreed to negotiate, and IWA Coast locals reached a new deal in mid-July. Included in the settlement was the elimination of piecework for fallers. They would initially be paid at the rate of $80.52 per day based on a six-and-a-half-hour day; higher-earning fallers would be guaranteed 90 percent of their previous year's earnings. The fallers, however, were not impressed. Their strike continued.

Through a series of flying pickets and by creating a shortage of logs, the fallers effectively shut down much of the industry. Rumblings of discontent over the continuing job action began to emerge. Faller Bill Goodwin offered an explanation for the fallers' reluctance to return to work. In a letter to the *Vancouver Sun*, Goodwin described the true motivation of fallers as lost "in a quagmire of evasive verbiage from all sides including their own." Goodwin went on to explain:

> [The work of fallers is] one of the last bastions of true capitalism to be found today. The faller is motivated by greed, and sustained in the sure knowledge that he is separate and unequal from other men. He is paid for the amount of logs he produces, and the more skillful he becomes and the harder he works, the more money he makes; the reverse also being true. He works alone, and in common with all loners, his eccentricity increases with his age. He is a maker of quick decisions, and the hazards of his trade are such that almost daily his life depends on these decisions being both correct and acted upon promptly. When he is wrong he accepts the fact with a strange fatalistic resignation and pays the penalty, which too often turns out to be his life. Such then is the type of man around whom the issue revolves.

Despite the fallers' objections to the new contract, the newly negotiated day rate remained in place. Most fallers were back at work by the end of August 1972, ending their four-month wildcat strike.

At the Region 1 convention in October, the split between the 800 fallers and other Coast woodworkers was a hot topic. Faller delegates told the union leaders they "hadn't heard the end of this yet" and defended the right of minorities within the union to have the leadership take up their problems. *Vancouver Sun* reporter George Dobie took note of a point made by many IWA members when he wrote, "If the regional officers had capitulated to them [fallers], every minority group in this great, big democratic union would have had the right to break off and fight its own battles without consideration for the total membership."

In the wake of this dispute, a faller from Franklin River suggested fallers should become "contract fallers" and set up their own independent businesses.

*Through a series of flying pickets and by creating a shortage of logs, the fallers effectively shut down much of the industry.*

# Why Are 800 Fallers in Court?

## WHAT ARE THEY GUILTY OF? . . .

1. *They are Guilty of:* Trying to implement the boss's own agreement.

2. *They are Guilty of:* Trying to make their jobs safer (accident rate of 108%).

3. *They are Guilty of:* Refusing to take a pay cut.

4. *They are Guilty of:* Trying to equalize the wages of all fallers throughout the coast, as in all other trades.

5. *They are Guilty of:* Stopping an industry from making a mockery of a Union Contract.

6. *They are Guilty of:* PROTECTING THEIR BASIC UNION PRINCIPLES.

*Canadian working men are being made criminals by the actions of American-controlled corporations.*

# WHO IS <u>REALLY</u> GUILTY?

WHO'S GUILTY?

Fallers lashed out at "American-controlled corporations" during the 1972 strike.

IWA LOCAL 363 ARCHIVES

However, the vast majority of fallers stayed with the IWA. Max Salter, president of Courtenay Local 1-363, called for both sides to bury the hatchet and concentrate on improving the fallers' day rate and working conditions. Stan Parker later observed that the introduction of a day rate smoothed out production fluctuations and that in some camps, fallers had worked ten straight working days for the first time ever. Despite lingering differences of opinion and philosophy, the fallers begrudgingly accepted their newly regimented wage scale.

The dispute with the fallers almost overshadowed the substantial gains won in negotiations during 1972. After years of frustration, the long-sought goal of parity with the Coast was finally achieved in both the north and south Interior. The British Columbia locals won wage settlements that made them the highest-paid woodworkers in the world. As well, they had negotiated a pension plan, fully funded by the employers, for the first time, along with an employer-funded health-and-welfare plan and a number of other fringe benefits. Complementing these gains was the election of British Columbia's first New Democratic Party government.

## The IWA and the NDP

In the 1950s, many tradition-bound CCFers still felt that trade unions and political parties should not mix, perceiving their respective goals as too distinct. But as the legalistic, regulated relationship between labour and capital evolved in the post-war era, it became increasingly apparent that the needs of organized labour needed to be addressed through legislation. Region 1 president Joe Morris, and Stu Hodgson and Syd Thompson of Local 1-217 were among the labour leaders who helped convince Tommy Douglas, the CCF's national leader, that a new coalition between organized labour and the CCF would be a valuable undertaking. This reinvigorated alliance resulted in the creation of the New Democratic Party (NDP) in 1961.

Throughout the 1960s, the IWA advocated a strong program of political action. The union was a driving force behind many of the NDP's policy planks, including calls for a universal minimum wage, increased aid and improved facilities for retraining workers displaced by technological change, and the removal of existing legislation that crippled legitimate trade union activities like organizing and negotiating collective agreements. The IWA's Jack MacKenzie served as president of the British Columbia NDP in the mid-1960s and wrote numerous columns in the *Lumber Worker* that explained the importance of IWA members' support for labour's political party. A number of IWA members had won election to the provincial legislature as CCF candidates in the 1950s and 60s, and IWA member Frank Howard was elected several times from the north coast as a CCF/NDP Member of Parliament.

In Manitoba, the 1969 election of an NDP government and subsequent changes to that province's labour code were crucial to the IWA's success in organizing forestry workers in The Pas. Similarly in Saskatchewan, where Allen Blakeney's NDP government was elected in 1971, amendments to labour legislation made it easier to organize and win certification for new units. In BC, Dave Barrett (who later proclaimed, "I'm an IWA boy, and proud

*IWA member Frank Howard was elected several times as a CCF/NDP Member of Parliament.*

of it!") led the NDP to victory and joined the other provincial NDP governments in setting out progressive labour and occupational safety legislation.

Local 1-357 president Gerry Stoney was one of the NDP's strongest supporters within the IWA. Stoney lobbied the Barrett government incessantly during its tenure, fighting for extended health care benefits and financial assistance for senior citizens and encouraging the development of a vibrant education system. Dave Barrett later recalled that "Gerry Stoney came to Victoria and presented his ideas, his issues, and his demands – none of which held any personal benefit for him." Accompanying the efforts of IWA officials was solid grassroots support from the rank and file.

Lyle Pona was one of those rank-and-file members who joined the NDP in 1963. Pona, who later became the IWA's director of organizing and then its director of education, worked diligently on behalf of the NDP and recalled that in the 1970s the IWA conducted "on-the-job canvasses" of IWA members through job stewards. These canvasses created a dialogue between the NDP and IWA members, and surveys indicated the IWA rank and file provided more support to the NDP than any other trade union in British Columbia.

BUILDING BRIDGES

One-time president of Local 1-357 and future leader of IWA Canada, Gerry Stoney, seen here at the BC NDP's 1978 convention, was a staunch believer in close links between the IWA and NDP.

DEMOCRAT PHOTO
DENNIS McGANN

However, the successes of the NDP in the early 1970s were accompanied by ongoing political battles between unions. Tensions emerged between the BC Federation of Labour and the IWA after the NDP's election in British Columbia. Region 1 president Jack Munro, who succeeded Jack Moore in October 1973, openly disagreed with the BC Fed when it criticized the NDP's new labour code. Munro suggested that "before we started attacking Bill King [NDP labour minister] and the NDP government, we should sit down and read the thing and give it a chance to see if it would work or not." Munro suggested that the BC Fed was mistaken in treating the NDP government as though "it was there to do the bidding of organized labour." Consistent with the IWA's unwavering support for the CCF and NDP, the union recognized that although disagreements with the government were inevitable, the interests of labour and working people were best represented by the NDP. Therefore, for organized labour to engage in a nasty public spat with its political party of choice was just plain bad politics. Although the IWA's support for the provincial government remained solid, the BC Fed and most of its affiliates continued to openly criticize the NDP. Organized labour's frustration with the Barrett NDP government contributed to its defeat in December 1975.

IWA members maintained their solid commitment to the NDP through-out the 1970s and 1980s. In 1979, Lyle Kristiansen of Local 1-405 was elected to the federal Parliament in the riding of Kootenay West, and Gerry Stoney served as president of the British Columbia NDP from 1982 to 1988. While

Dave Barrett, BC's first NDP premier, pledges his support for the IWA at the union's 1973 convention.

PACIFIC TRIBUNE COLLECTION

the IWA-NDP relationship was on solid ground, this era was marked by serious divisions in the house of labour, as Canadian-based unions attempted to raid the IWA's membership.

## Wrapped In the Flag

By the late 1960s, as American economic and cultural dominance increased, English Canadians were expressing a patriotic desire to have an identity distinct from the United States. For many Canadians in the trade union movement, American-based international unions, including the IWA, came to represent one more example of American encroachment on Canada's sovereignty. This emerging Canadian nationalism created a backlash within some sectors of the Canadian labour movement against international unions.

By the late 1960s, several all-Canadian unions were formed after break-aways from American parents. Among the new unions were the Pulp and Paper Workers of Canada (PPWC) and the Canadian Paperworkers Union (CPU), both of which spent considerable time and effort raiding or attempting to raid IWA-organized mills in BC and Alberta respectively. In Saskatchewan, the Laborer's International Union (LIU) attempted to take over IWA operations throughout the province. *Lumber Worker* editor Pat Kerr commented in 1971 that "the tragedy of the whole matter is that there is no need for any union to raid another in the forest industry with the thousands upon thousands of millworkers and loggers still unorganized."

The PPWC and CPU were notorious for wrapping themselves in the

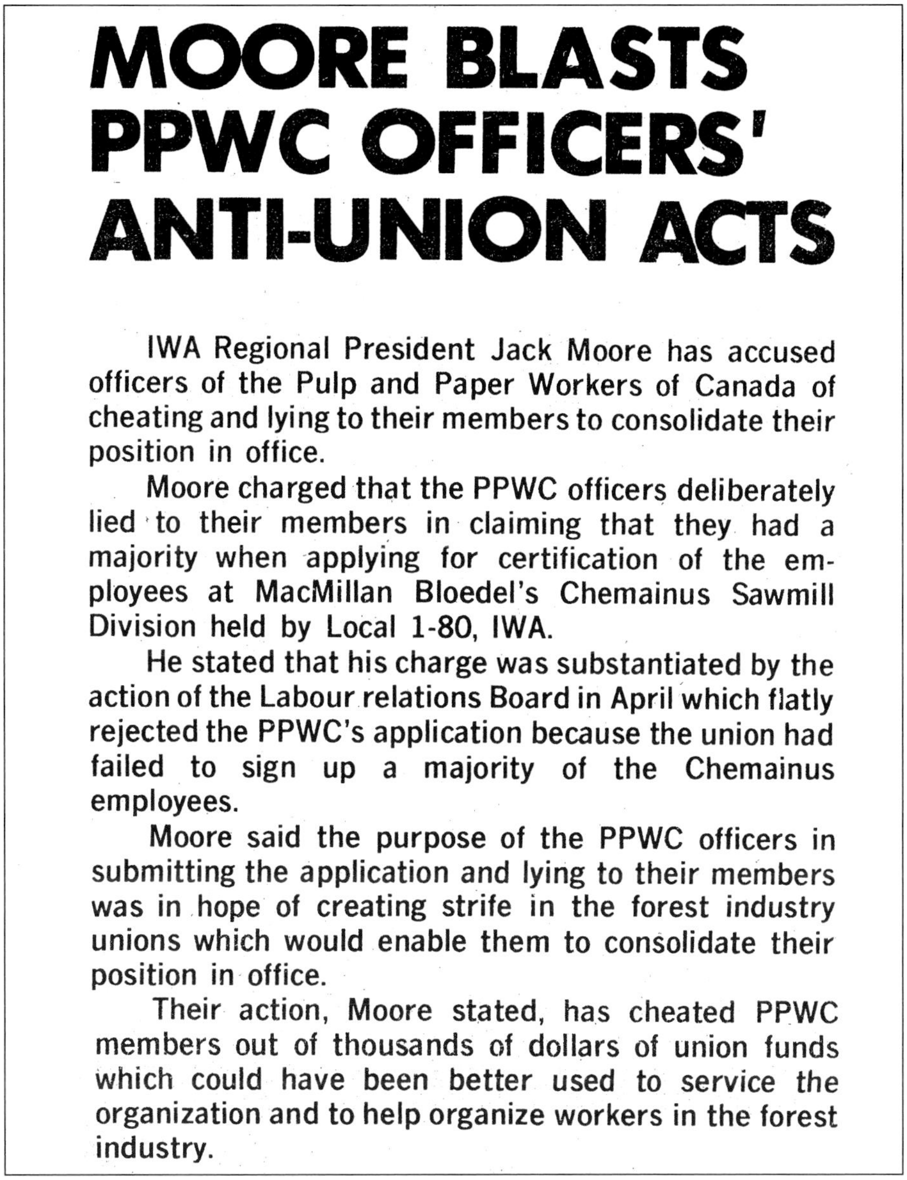

# MOORE BLASTS PPWC OFFICERS' ANTI-UNION ACTS

IWA Regional President Jack Moore has accused officers of the Pulp and Paper Workers of Canada of cheating and lying to their members to consolidate their position in office.

Moore charged that the PPWC officers deliberately lied to their members in claiming that they had a majority when applying for certification of the employees at MacMillan Bloedel's Chemainus Sawmill Division held by Local 1-80, IWA.

He stated that his charge was substantiated by the action of the Labour relations Board in April which flatly rejected the PPWC's application because the union had failed to sign up a majority of the Chemainus employees.

Moore said the purpose of the PPWC officers in submitting the application and lying to their members was in hope of creating strife in the forest industry unions which would enable them to consolidate their position in office.

Their action, Moore stated, has cheated PPWC members out of thousands of dollars of union funds which could have been better used to service the organization and to help organize workers in the forest industry.

STANDING HIS GROUND

In 1971, IWA Region 1 president Jack Moore accused the PPWC of deliberately misleading IWA members during one of its raids on an IWA certification on Vancouver Island.

IWA ARCHIVES

Canadian flag and making sweeping criticisms of international unions, assuming that pro-Canadian sentiment was justification enough for their actions. What the PPWC and CPU refused to recognize was that Canadians within the IWA enjoyed genuine national autonomy within the union's international structure. The IWA had established separate Canadian regions with Canadian officers, who were elected only by Canadian members. Moreover, the Canadian IWA regions had control over union expenditures in Canada, and the Canadian regional conventions dealt with issues of policy affecting Canadian members.

The IWA lost three sawmills on Vancouver Island to PPWC raids in the

**UNCLE SAM GET OUT OF VIETNAM!**

The war in Vietnam fanned the flames of anti-Americanism in Canada in the late 1960s and early 1970s, and these sentiments led many to question the usefulness of US-based international unions north of the border.

PACIFIC TRIBUNE COLLECTION

early 1970s. It was particularly surprised when the PPWC raided the Somass sawmill in Port Alberni. The Somass mill had over a thousand workers and was one of the IWA's most militant strongholds. The IWA defended its turf and soundly defeated the PPWC in an LRB certification vote.

A 1977 PPWC raid on a sawmill organized by Local 1-424 at Williams Lake was another major challenge in this era. The IWA defended its jurisdiction in a legal fight that took three months to settle and cost the union between $75,000 and $100,000. From 1970 to 1977, the PPWC conducted 16 raids against IWA operations, netting a paltry 503 members. Meanwhile, in the same seven-year period, the IWA successfully organized 10,000 previously unorganized workers into the union. In 1978, a truce was reached that greatly reduced this destructive behaviour, and the IWA was able to focus on organizing the unorganized rather than defending its locals.

The raids and jurisdictional disputes of the late 1960s and 1970s illustrated yet again the ultimate folly of organized labour turning in on itself rather than fighting employers. As the inter-union strife took centre stage, some key structural economic changes were beginning to take place in the background. By 1975, working people across Canada came under an attack by capital and government that continues to this day.

## 'All Hell Was Breaking Loose'

Addressing the January 1976 IWA Region 1 conference, Jack Munro read from the IWA Officers' Report: "Negotiations [in] 1975 established, very early, that the complexion of all facets of bargaining were to change drastically." The officers were referring to the immediate issues facing them, and they could not have known how prophetic this observation would be. Although the IWA had won the best settlements in its history in 1975 negotiations, the conditions under which they were achieved marked the onset of an era of serious economic disruption for union members.

By 1975, the economic upheavals that had occurred periodically in the decades since World War II were becoming increasingly frequent and disruptive. Sparked largely by the OPEC oil shocks of 1973, which quadrupled the price of crude oil, runaway inflation walloped the economy in 1973 and 1974. The IWA's difficulties in 1975 were summed up bluntly by Jack Munro: "All hell was breaking loose in the forest industry. We had 30 percent of our membership out of work because of the slumping worldwide lumber markets." Falling lumber prices and a collapsing market for forest products resulted in 14,000 IWA members being laid off. IWA members' problems were complicated when the PPWC and CPU went on strike in July and their secondary

READ OUR LIPS

Activists from Local 1-417 in Kamloops demonstrate against Prime Minister Trudeau's decision to impose wage and price controls in 1975. Trudeau had opposed such controls during the 1974 federal election.

IWA ARCHIVES

UNFAIR TO WORKERS

**Demonstrations against the AIB, like this one at the BC Federation of Labour convention in 1975, were held across the country.**

PACIFIC TRIBUNE COLLECTION
SEAN GRIFFIN PHOTO

picketing resulted in another 10,000 IWA members staying off the job. The IWA was in negotiations with employers, but with so many members out of work, the union felt it was in no position to strike. The summer of 1975 was a season of strikes for other trade unions in BC, however. The pulp unions, retail food industry workers, BC Rail employees, and the Teamsters were among 58,000 workers in BC who were walking picket lines. The entire economy appeared to be in crisis, and the province's NDP government announced it would impose back-to-work legislation. In the economic climate of 1975, the IWA supported the government's position, although most of the labour movement objected strenuously to the NDP legislation.

In late August 1975, NDP labour minister Bill King invited both the IWA and employers to Victoria in order to help facilitate a settlement before the proposed back-to-work legislation became law. Negotiations went on for five weeks, with slow progress being made.

On 9 October 1975, the provincial government introduced its back-to-work legislation, giving unions and employers 48 hours to come up with an agreement or be subjected to the new legislation. Neither the IWA nor forest industry employers wanted a government-mandated settlement, and they reached a last-minute deal on 11 October. The IWA won a 26 percent increase in wages and a 28 percent overall increase over two years in its master agreement. The deal was struck just ahead of the federal government's Thanksgiving day (15 October) announcement that it would create an Anti-Inflation Board (AIB) and bring in wage-and-price controls to curb wage increases for working people.

The IWA and other unions had been warned that wage-and-price controls were coming. In the midst of the IWA's negotiations, federal labour minister John Munro met with officials from the BC Federation of Labour, including the IWA's Munro and Syd Thompson. Without going into details, Minister Munro warned them that wage controls were imminent. "Whoever among you are in negotiations, there's going to be federal legislation, and you aren't going to be happy about it. So if you are getting close to an agreement, you should work at getting an agreement quickly."

The introduction of the AIB and its wage-and-price control guidelines incensed organized labour. The guidelines set a cap of 6 percent for wage gains in the first year of a contract and 4 percent in the second, and it was abundantly clear that one of the unstated goals of the legislation was to rein in the power of organized labour. The AIB was the bluntest example of how the economic crises of the 1970s were portrayed as a problem stemming from workers' salary demands. As labour historian Craig Heron noted:

> By the mid-1970s, instead of wondering how the economy had become so disjointed and chaotic, business people, politicians, civil servants, newspaper editors, and talk-show hosts simply wanted to know what could be done about labour…The crime attributed to organized workers was simply that they were using the structures of collective bargaining as the system had been designed, for maintaining living and working standards in the face of inflation, technological change, and other disruptions. By the mid-1970s these workers' efforts were being painted as motivated by simple greed and selfishness.

The IWA was among many unions denouncing the federal government and AIB for launching an attack on working people across Canada. IWA members were prominent among the more than one million workers who took part in a Canada-wide Day of Protest on 15 October 1976, the first anniversary of the AIB's creation. Sending a clear message to employers and the government, the IWA, like most other unions in Canada, adopted a policy of negotiating all agreements as though the AIB did not exist, although they were well aware they would be under AIB guidelines.

Because the 1975 Coast negotiations were completed just ahead of the fed-

*'By the mid-1970s, instead of wondering how the economy had become so disjointed and chaotic, business people, politicians, civil servants, newspaper editors, and talk-show hosts simply wanted to know what could be done about labour.'*

*Membership in Region 1 was hovering around the 48,000 mark, and members were enjoying a period of prosperity driven by high lumber prices.*

eral government's wage-and-price controls announcement, they escaped the AIB restrictions. In most jurisdictions across the country, IWA locals did experience wage rollbacks on newly negotiated collective agreements during the AIB's existence. Assessments and appeals of AIB rulings that rolled back wage increases began to dominate IWA Research Department activities. By 1978, as the AIB program wound down, wage increases had declined throughout the economy, but prices were soaring. At the end of the 1970s, inflation returned to pre-AIB levels.

When the AIB program concluded in 1978, the forest industry experienced a brief boom. Despite a slowdown in wage increases because of AIB restrictions, the base rate of pay for IWA members in 1978 was $9 per hour – double what it had been five years earlier. Membership in Region 1 was hovering around the 48,000 mark, and the IWA and its members were enjoying a period of prosperity driven by high lumber prices. Nonetheless, there were indications that major changes were about to occur in the forest industry.

## Contracting Out, Round One

In northern Ontario, members of Lumber and Saw locals 2693 and 2995 had prospered along with workers in the IWA throughout the 1960s and early 1970s. A number of smaller locals had merged with 2693 and 2995 in this era, and solid wage and benefit gains were achieved through a combination of union militancy and a scarce labour supply. Because of the area's isolation and lack of job market competition, bushworkers did not hesitate to quit their jobs, comfortable in the knowledge that they could leave one job on Friday and start another on Monday morning. Consequently, despite their heavy investment in new technology, employers were unable to exploit the maximum potential of their mechanical skidders and tree-harvesters as the shortage of bushworkers undermined the higher levels of productivity possible with the new machinery.

Since the mid-1950s, employers in northern Ontario had tried to develop a labour force in which bushworkers owned and operated their own machinery. If enough wood was supplied by owner-operators, the capital and labour costs for employers would be cut dramatically. As an incentive to encourage this shift, employers proposed that owner-operators be paid a special higher rate for piecework. The union recognized the threat such a system posed and successfully stifled it in collective bargaining. Although companies often tried to reintroduce the idea, the union was able to force the companies to back down, occasionally by threatening to strike. By 1958, Lumber and Saw had negotiated agreements that severely restricted the activities of owner-operator

bushworkers throughout most of the region. However, at the Ontario and Minnesota Pulp and Paper Company operations in northwestern Ontario, Lumber and Saw had been unable to eliminate owner-operators.

Ontario and Minnesota Pulp and Paper was the only major timber company in the region and, according to historian Ian Radforth, used its leverage as the major employer to force the union's hand in 1959. Lumber and Saw agreed to allow union members who already owned skidders to continue to operate, but it reached an agreement with the company stating that when these members quit or retired, they would be replaced by workers who used company-owned equipment. Until 1978, this agreement was honoured by the company, which had been taken over in 1965 by Boise Cascade.

Local 2693 president Tulio Mior noted that in 1978, Boise Cascade had a number of new executives at the company helm. Company managers began to encourage employees to purchase company skidders and set up shop as owner-operators. On 15 May 1978, Boise Cascade's Fort Frances operation announced

NO OWNER-OPERATORS HERE

Lumber and Saw's tough stance against contracting out prevented other companies in northern Ontario from pursuing a similar strategy.

IWA LOCAL 2693 ARCHIVES

**Community meetings and fundraising events, many set up by a women's auxiliary, helped maintain morale and boost solidarity during the Boise Cascade strike.**

IWA LOCAL 2693 ARCHIVES

that it was offering its skidders for sale to employees. Lumber and Saw officials made it clear to the company that it was violating the collective agreement and warned members not to trust the company's suggestion that as owner-operators they could make at least $10,000 per year more than they currently earned. When the company persisted in trying to sell its skidders to employees and create an owner-operator workforce, union members walked off the job and shut the company's operations down in July. The Ontario LRB ruled the strike illegal, but Lumber and Saw members set up pickets at the company's pulp mill. Local 2693 vice-president Fred Miron described the incident that led to Lumber and Saw picketing the Fort Frances mill:

> Why we shut the mill down in the first place was, they were bringing the wood across [the Rainy River] from the American side, at International Falls. They would dump American wood in the river and float it across and keep that Fort Frances mill going, even though we had all the wood stopped on our side.
>
> They had a 35-ton big steel tug boat, so our guys would go out and picket with our 15-foot boats. The captain was refusing to ram their boat, so one of the superintendents took it and said, "I'll run this boat." The

picketers had a 15-foot aluminum boat, and this 35-ton tugboat came head on and hit them right on the side, hit our pickets, and went right on top of the boat and sunk them, of course. The captain finally got him [the superintendent] convinced to shut off the motor or our guys would have drowned underneath the boat because they were wearing life jackets and got caught underneath the tug. They damn near drowned. All the mill workers had seen this and that's when we shut the mill down. He damn near killed our people; he just rammed them straight on and went right over. That was the incident that enraged everybody.

The CPU and the Machinists union both honoured the Lumber and Saw picket lines, and production at the mill came to a stop. The company responded by filing contempt charges against Lumber and Saw, and a court order ruled that strikers had to pay fines of $25 per day for every day spent on the picket line. A subsequent court order ruled that workers' bank accounts could be seized, which they were. With the expiration of the contract in early October, the strike spread to the company's Kenora operations as union members' anger at the company escalated.

Lumber and Saw officials were clear that the company was attempting to bust the union. "We knew from experience," said Fred Miron, " that a five-day work week would turn into a seven-day work week with long days." Picket captain Wilf McIntyre remarked:

> Twelve years ago I had the chance to become an owner-operator or an hourly paid worker. I opted for hourly work because I wanted marriage and a family life. The owner-operator has the worry of making massive payments on his equipment and spends two or three hours every night cleaning and fixing the equipment. He has no family life. Once you're an owner-operator with the big worries and big payments, the company has you, because you can't afford to stop work for an argument on price. If you get behind with payments, your house and everything you've worked for is threatened.

The Ontario Provincial Police (OPP) was ordered to Kenora and Fort Frances, and both towns became virtual police states. Tensions often boiled over and company property was vandalized as union members' frustration grew in the wake of the company's and the judicial system's heavy-handed actions. The OPP's lone helicopter was accompanied by as many as 250 officers, who were sent to the towns for the purpose of assisting scabs across the picket line and intimidating strikers. The police presence was augmented by 400 security guards hired by the company.

*'The picketers had a 15-foot aluminum boat, and this 35-ton tugboat came head on and hit them right on the side… went right on top of the boat and sunk them…They damn near drowned.'*

**POLICE STATE**

**The Ontario Provincial Police played a key role in breaking the 1978 Boise Cascade strike.**

IWA LOCAL 2693 ARCHIVES

In February 1979, the company wrote letters to mill workers from other unions who were honouring the Lumber and Saw picket lines, telling them to report to work or be fired. As members of other unions crossed the Lumber and Saw picket line, fights broke out between the strikers and police. Miron, McIntyre, and many other union members were thrown into jail, and strikers were subjected to serious harassment from police on and off the picket line. Union members were routinely pulled over in their vehicles and harassed, and numerous raids and search warrants were executed, often as an excuse to place hidden microphones in members' houses and union offices. Approximately 800 frivolous charges were laid against union members in Kenora and Fort

Frances in order to undermine the union's picket lines. Almost all these charges were later dropped.

With company and government forces aligned against Lumber and Saw, the union was fighting an impossible battle, but nonetheless kept its picket lines up until October 1980. In January 1981, the police charged 12 Lumber and Saw members with conspiracy to commit mischief. By that time, Wilf McIntyre had moved with his family to Hinton, Alberta, to take up a new job.

"I was in my front yard [in Hinton] when I saw this dark car come up the street," remembered McIntyre, "and I recognized the two guys in the car as OPP officers." The OPP had come for McIntyre; he was arrested and taken to the local police station where 25 more charges were laid. "And the cops were telling me I'd get 25 years in jail for each charge," he said. The police then took McIntyre to Edmonton, where he was interrogated at length again. "They were trying to get me to cut a deal – they wanted me to turn on the other guys in the union and testify against them," said McIntyre. From Edmonton, the police took McIntyre to Kenora and then Thunder Bay, where he appeared before the court and was released pending preliminary hearings.

Ultimately, most of the charges were dropped. Tulio Mior and five other defendants were acquitted. McIntyre and four others pled guilty to the mischief charge and were fined $5,000 each. Local 2693 vice-president Fred Miron was fined $10,000 and the legal system's harassment of the "Boise 12," as they were known, came to an end.

Boise Cascade ultimately succeeded at undermining the union, eventually hiring only owner-operators on contract to harvest timber from its land, but it paid a huge price for its attack on Lumber and Saw. Production was shut down for months, and the cost to Ontario taxpayers to provide police and legal support to Boise Cascade and its union-busting efforts was astronomical. As early as February 1979, only seven months into the strike, over $2.1 million had already been spent on policing costs alone.

Although Lumber and Saw lost the strike, it put up a ferocious battle that poisoned Boise Cascade's relations with its workers for years. "The strike served its purpose because it stopped other companies from trying the same thing," said Miron. "They all backed off because we told them at the bargaining table that they would be facing similar strike actions. Every one of our members at Boise Cascade knew during the strike that they were taking the brunt for the whole union." Lumber and Saw's monumental struggle to defend against contracting out would be replicated in British Columbia in 1986, but not before woodworkers were rocked by the recession of the early 1980s.

UNION DUES

As this feature article from *Maclean's* suggests, the confrontation with Boise Cascade attracted media attention across the country.

IWA LOCAL 2693 ARCHIVES

## 'Chiselling and Cheating the Working Man'

In January 1978, MacMillan Bloedel's announcement that it was going to shut down its Vancouver Plywood operation took the union by surprise. The 700 IWA members at the plant faced the prospect of losing their livelihoods, and the union responded quickly to the immediate crisis by protecting its members, as well as examining the state of the industry at large.

The IWA met with the company and suggested a number of remedies, including modernizing the plant's technology. MacMillan Bloedel was not interested in the union's proposals and still intended to shut the plant down. Jack Munro then contacted Social Credit premier Bill Bennett, and Bennett met directly with the company, putting pressure on MacBlo to leave the plant open. After Bennett's intervention, the government and the IWA received assurances the mill would be upgraded and kept open. However, the union was aware that this threat of closure was not necessarily an isolated one.

In the 1970s, the IWA added a number of professionals – including economists and foresters – to its research staff to bolster its understanding of the economic intricacies driving the forest industry. After MacMillan Bloedel threatened to shut down Vancouver Plywood, the IWA's Research Department

BREADLINES (AGAIN)

During the recession, the unemployment rate and cost of living rose dramatically. Economists dubbed this mix of economic stagnation and inflation "stagflation."

PACIFIC TRIBUNE COLLECTION

FACING PAGE

MacMillan Bloedel shut down its plywood plant in Vancouver for the first time in 1978; the plant closed for good in 1980.

PACIFIC TRIBUNE COLLECTION
DAN KEETON PHOTO

THANKS JOE

Celebrating the retirement of Joe Morris (seated, middle) in 1978 are, from left to right, Keith Johnson (International president), Roger Stanyer (Local 1-80 president), Fernie Viala (International second vice-president), and Jack Munro (Region 1 president).

IWA ARCHIVES

launched a study of the potential impact of technological change on union members. The union understood clearly that in order to sell wood products in both domestic and foreign markets, the production costs of western Canadian producers had to be competitive. There was a growing awareness through the 1970s that the forest industry, especially on the BC Coast, was becoming technologically obsolete. The IWA's study recognized that the forest industry's failure to modernize and upgrade could only result in a collapse of the industry. But the researchers also recognized that if technological change was going to cause layoffs and job changes for IWA members, industry and government had an obligation to work with the union and protect the interests and welfare of affected workers. Unfortunately for union members, their well-being was little more than an abstract consideration to the industry and government.

When 1980 arrived, it became apparent that the brief boom at the end of the 1970s was crashing to an end. By February 1980, over 14,000 IWA members had been laid off for varying lengths of time. Despite the IWA's efforts, MacMillan Bloedel shut down Vancouver Plywood in 1980, one of a number of such closures in the industry. And this was only the tip of the iceberg – in the early 1980s, union members suffered through the most serious economic downturn in the IWA's history to that point.

In late 1979, housing construction in Canada and the United States went

LOWER THE
INTEREST RATES!

**IWAers march on the
provincial legislature
in BC in 1981.**

PACIFIC TRIBUNE COLLECTION
SEAN GRIFFIN PHOTO

into a serious decline. Two thirds of BC's lumber was sold in the US, and with the onset of the recession, this market collapsed. The IWA was able to alleviate this situation temporarily when it helped convince the BC government to pass mortgage subsidy legislation that encouraged $200 million in housing construction in the province. As a result, BC had as many housing starts in 1980 as eight other provinces combined, and mounting layoffs in the industry were halted – for a time. However, the continued rise of already high interest rates in 1980 overwhelmed working people throughout the country. Particularly hard hit were resource industry workers, and IWA members suffered unprecedented layoffs and job losses.

The federal government's policy of setting high interest rates through the Bank of Canada was part of a shift away from the Keynesian economic policies that had guided government decisions in the post-war era. Keynesianism recognized that downturns were inevitable in a capitalist system and gave the government an active role in managing the economy in the interest of *all* citizens, including those affected by recession and downturns. Keynesian ideals of full employment, living wages, and a social safety net in the form of programs like unemployment insurance and family allowance drove the federal government's economic policy from 1945 until 1975.

In 1975, the federal government – facing mounting deficits and high inflation – abandoned Keynesianism. Corporate directors and large-scale investors exercised their influence and convinced the federal government to embrace monetarist economic policies designed to control inflation and assure stable returns on their investments.

Monetarism dismissed the ideal of full employment, and its adoption undermined those government policies designed to protect the well-being of workers. Particularly devastating for working people was the government's use of artificially high interest rates to control inflation and slow the economy down. The result was the most severe recession the country had seen since the Great Depression. The IWA was quite aware that the devastating recession was not the result of an "invisible hand" working in the economy, but was the product of conscious decision-making by politicians, bankers, and corporate leaders.

ON THE BRINK

**Members of Local 1-425 gather at their first annual delegated meeting, before the onset of an unforgiving recession.**

UBC SPECIAL COLLECTIONS
1902-255

**LOCAL 1-425**

## A Rock in a Hard Place

"NO PIECE OF CAKE"; "Nothing short of a total bust"; "A pretty tough year." That's how Harvey Arcand of Local 1-425 summed up the local's fortunes in the early 1980s. The local had been carved out of Local 1-424 in 1977 when IWAers in the south Cariboo complained that the Prince George-based local was not addressing some of their concerns, but members soon found life on their own was tough.

After reaching a high of about 1,700 members in the late 1970s, membership declined substantially in the midst of the steep economic downturn of the early 1980s. Exacerbated by technological change at the local's largest employers (including Lignum, Pinette and Therrien Mills, and Weldwood of Canada) and the closure of Canim Lake Sawmills, the local dropped to an all-time low of 800 members in 1982. Without dues coming in, grievances and compensation claims piled up and employers, sensing the union's weakened state, dragged their heels in negotiations. As a result, 1-425 was forced to apply to the regional council for a loan to keep its offices open. But organizers continued pounding the pavement to drum up sup-

The combination of high interest rates and a collapsed market meant that forest companies had to revamp their operations considerably in order to survive the recession. They did this by laying off workers and closing plants in a scramble to cut their losses as quickly as possible. Once again, it was workers who bore the brunt of this transition. In Region 2, for example, the corrugated cardboard plants that had provided work for the bulk of the region's membership began to close. Plants in St. Thomas, Montreal, and Hamilton were all eventually closed and other operations were downsized. Job losses and layoffs quickly mounted, and high interest rates put the squeeze on Region 2 members, as they did on members in Region 1.

At the Region 1 convention of 1981, IWA executive board member Doug Evans expressed the frustration and anger that workers across the country were feeling:

*British Columbia had as many housing starts in 1980 as eight other provinces combined.*

port, the local maintained its educational programs to combat new anti-union tactics, and members from Weldwood of Canada, Merril and Wagner Division, put on the annual "Santa Cruise" bash to boost both solidarity and morale. Strikes, some legal, as in 1981 and 1986, and others not, persisted too. By the late 1980s, as the economy slowly rebounded, this dedication to the IWA started to pay off as membership increased to a respectable 1,200 – with many new members coming from outside the forest industry. But additional challenges lay ahead.

Although the economic recession of the early 1990s hit many IWA locals hard, Local 1-425 escaped without major job losses because the largest mills in its jurisdiction had been completely modernized in the previous decade and thus were able to continue operating. In addition to age-old union questions of wages, working conditions, and collective bargaining, in the 1990s environmental and land-claim issues came to the fore. Both threatened to curtail the number of hectares available for logging – prompting Local 1-425 to form a Save Our

Jobs Committee with industry and community organizations. "We're not saying who's wrong or right, but we believe the government has to get off its butt and resolve these issues," a local IWAer remarked at the time. Resolution, though, often meant deferral; in 1993, for example, large chunks of forest were set aside in and around Deception River, Churn Creek, and the Cariboo Mountains. When the provincial government's Committee on Resources and the Environment (CORE) handed down its decision on the Cariboo region a year later – one that would have limited the annual harvest rate and caused job losses – Local 1-425, the IWA, and community members pushed the ruling NDP to replace the CORE decision with a plan that sought to protect workers and the environment in equal measure. In addition to its pioneering efforts in land-use policy, the local, which prides itself on its proactive and independent character, has pushed ahead in other areas too, running a successful forest worker education program and organizing truckers, service sector workers, and value-added operations. □

When you look at interest rates, if somebody said ten years ago, you're going to be paying 22 percent interest rates, they said, "You're bloody well loan sharking. You should belong to the Mafia." Well, I tell you, the banks and the mortgage companies have nothing on the Mafia. They've got the Federal Government in their back pocket, and they're chiselling and cheating the working man left and right.

This is legalized loan sharking that we're going through, Brother Chairman, and why working men have to put up with this, I'll never know. If that nut next door [Ronald Reagan] started a world war, I'll tell you, they would find money to put into housing to house people to build ships and planes and goddam bombs. They'd find lots of money for that

## Employee and Family Assistance Program

DRAWING ON THE LABOUR movement's heritage of self-help, one that stretches back to workers' benevolent societies in the nineteenth century, the IWA's Employee and Family Assistance Program (EFAP) helps workers and their families deal with a wide range of problems – from alcohol and drug dependency to marital and financial issues.

The plan, which today is co-managed with employers and often operates in conjunction with community-based assessment and resource services (ARS), originated with Local 1-184 in Hudson Bay, Saskatchewan, in the early 1970s. At that time, IWAers Neil Menard and Bob Blanchard recognized that many workers in the small Saskatchewan town needed counselling, advice, and treatment for alcohol addiction and other personal issues. What was more, Menard and Blanchard understood that these problems did not exist in a vacuum: they were often linked to the pressures and hardships of a working life and, when left untreated, had a negative effect on a worker's family, workplace, and

PUTTING PEOPLE FIRST

**EFAP pioneer Neil Menard**

IWA ARCHIVES

community. In 1976 they designed a Troubled Employees Program and took the idea to the IWA's national executive for consideration; three years later in British Columbia, the plan, renamed the Employee Assistance Program and later Employee and Family Assistance Program, was included in a collective agreement between the union and MacMillan Bloedel.

Since that time, several hundred EFAPs, along with 22 ARS agencies, have been set up across the country – spurred on, unfortunately, by corporate downsizing and the withering of the social safety net. On the international stage, similar programs, drawing on the IWA's expertise, have been adopted in several African countries and in Brazil, where the most pressing issue is early intervention and treatment of HIV and AIDS amongst the poor. For his pioneering efforts in this area of union work, Neil Menard, who helped forge these international ties and establish EFAPs in Norway and in Casper, Wyoming, was inducted into the EAP hall of fame by the North American Congress on Employee Assistance Programs in 1990. ❑

then, and it would be cheaper than 22 percent. But when the working man is out of work, and when the economy is floundering, they can't find any money at a decent rate for a working man.

Indeed, interest rates as high as 22 percent meant many IWA members and working people could no longer afford a mortgage on their homes, if they were lucky enough to hang onto their jobs. As many as 20,000 members were out of work in 1981, as the union entered into negotiations with BC's forest industry employers.

The difficulty of negotiating a 1981 agreement was exacerbated when the employers tried foisting the same agreement signed by the pulp unions onto the IWA. (Pulpworkers had settled for a 19 percent increase over two years.) Jack Munro recalled, "We said to the industry, 'Look, do whatever you want with pulp. But we're telling you our settlement is going to be different from the pulp settlement.'" The employers gave the union a "take it or leave it" ultimatum. "The most important problem," commented Munro at the time, "was that [the employer] was presuming, because of a bad market, that they could get away with anything with the IWA." Negotiations collapsed and a provincewide strike began. It lasted for six weeks, until 24 August 1981.

The union ended up winning a fantastic settlement – a 28 percent increase over two years. Munro later noted, "Even our own economist, Doug Smyth, told me it was more than they [the industry] could afford. But it wasn't my fault. I couldn't stop pushing because they had refused to negotiate and had treated us badly. They paid a heavy penalty for it."

JUST ENOUGH

In 1981, the IWA went on strike for six weeks and secured a 28 percent wage hike – a huge increase, but one that just barely kept pace with inflation.

PACIFIC TRIBUNE COLLECTION
SEAN GRIFFIN PHOTO

**ANOTHER MILL DOWN**

Local 1-80's Dan Clements (right, leaning forward) discusses the future of MacMillan Bloedel's Chemainus mill with IWA members in 1983.

PACIFIC TRIBUNE COLLECTION
SEAN GRIFFIN PHOTO

Despite the satisfaction of winning a good collective agreement, the recession continued to batter the forest industry and the IWA. In 1983 negotiations, the union was still reeling from the recession and layoffs its members had endured, and it settled on a three-year contract with marginal gains. While criticized by some, the 1983 contract was largely accepted by the membership as the inevitable product of a devastating recession.

That same year, BC's Social Credit government introduced "restraint" legislation designed to gut organized labour's power and drastically slash social spending. Unions throughout the province joined with social-justice groups to form the Solidarity Coalition. A series of protests took place under the banner of Operation Solidarity, and "Solidarity days" became the biggest labour protest in the history of British Columbia. The government was forced to abandon some of its more extreme proposals in the face of the groundswell of opposition, and as the mass protests gained momentum, the threat of a general strike loomed in November 1983.

But Jack Munro and the IWA were having none of it. With 30 percent of the IWA membership out of work, the union's negotiating committee did not feel it could justify subjecting its members to a general strike. The IWA and other unions in the BC Federation of Labour came to believe that their members would be footing the bill in the event of a general strike. It would be IWA members and their fellow trade unionists who would be losing income on a picket line in the middle of the worst recession since the 1930s. There was a feeling that many of the social-action groups involved in Operation Solidarity did not have nearly as much to lose as did unions like the IWA.

When BC Fed president Art Kube fell ill, Munro agreed to be spokesman for the Fed-affiliated trade unionists, who decided to negotiate a settlement with the government. Many activists accused Munro and the Fed of "selling out" in order to maintain control of the labour movement, and Munro's role as spokesman made him a lightning rod for those angered by what they saw as a premature end to a powerful social coalition. However, Munro later reflected, "If we hadn't stopped Solidarity, it would have set the trade union movement back 20 years. They would have smashed us if we'd have collapsed – and there's little doubt we would have collapsed."

Through the mid-1980s, the number of IWA members in Region 1 hovered steadily around the 37,000 mark. The combination of the recession and technological change had resulted in the loss of thousands of jobs – 4,000 alone from the plywood manufacturing industry when 18 mills shut down.

YOU SAY YOU WANT A REVOLUTION

With the introduction of its "restraint" platform in 1983, BC's Social Credit government continued the neo-conservative assault on working people; organized labour and community groups responded with Operation Solidarity.

PACIFIC TRIBUNE COLLECTION
DAN KEETON PHOTO

219

HERE TODAY, GONE TOMORROW

By the mid-1980s, about 4,000 jobs were lost in the plywood sector in BC alone; given this level of unemployment in the industry, IWA leaders rejected calls for a general strike in 1983.

PACIFIC TRIBUNE COLLECTION
SEAN GRIFFIN PHOTO

FACING PAGE

As tensions mounted during Operation Solidarity, BC Fed leader Art Kube (middle) fell ill and Jack Munro (left) stepped in to take the heat.

PACIFIC TRIBUNE COLLECTION
SEAN GRIFFIN PHOTO

Several thousand more members were still subjected to layoffs of varying lengths. Secondary picketing by pulp mill unions in 1984 threw 15,000 IWA members out of work and angered IWA officials, who felt the pulp mill unions were unfairly exploiting IWA members in their attempt to settle a contract. By 1986, however, a declining Canadian dollar helped make BC products attractive to export markets once again. Moreover, increased productivity as a result of technological change was contributing to a significant degree of employment stability as the industry slowly recovered.

In 1986, the IWA produced an exhaustive study on the impact of technology on production and employment in the forest industry in British Columbia. The IWA study reiterated the point that technological change had always been a factor in the forest industry. Between 1948 and 1960, the number of sawmills in the Coast region dropped from 511 to 147. Similarly, between 1960 and 1980, nearly 75 percent of sawmills in the Interior had gone out of business or amalgamated with larger operations. In the boom market of the late 1970s, marginally efficient sawmills could still survive. But only the most modernized plants and mills were able to minimize the effects of the severe recession of the early 1980s.

While employment in Interior sawmills fell by 12 percent during the recession, production shot up by 18.5 percent. This increase in productivity allowed Interior mills to remain competitive with mills in the southern United States – mills that paid much less to their workers, but which also were much less efficient. While the export-dependent Coast industry was most

## Technology Giveth and Technology Taketh Away

THE CANADIAN FOREST SECTOR has always been export-driven. It sells its products into highly competitive international markets. Consequently, IWA Canada has consistently accepted that technological change is a double-edged sword. The ongoing development of labour-saving technologies changes and eliminates some jobs, but at the same time this process preserves jobs by keeping the industry competitive and efficient.

Since the beginning of logging and sawmilling, a series of new machines and work methods has led to a steady decline in the overall number of workers per unit of output. This was part of the secret behind the success of the CIO unions, even in the depths of the Great Depression: increases in productivity and concentration of capital meant that companies could "sue for peace" with their workers

MULTI-TASKING

In today's sawmills, workers use monitors, joysticks, and sophisticated technology to execute and oversee several tasks at the same time.
IWA ARCHIVES

instead of feeling the need to fight every strike to the death or risk bankruptcy.

The IWA has always been aware of this trend. In March 1956, for instance, CBC television in Vancouver broadcast union-led panel discussions on the topic of technological change and automation. District 1 president Joe Morris explained, "Our union takes the position that we cannot stand in the way of technological progress…Automation is on our doorstep. It will displace some workers and it will displace some industries. It does not follow that it will work undue hardship on the workers. It should, on the contrary, raise our living

**SAWING LOGS WITH RAYS - 1975**

standards, if the enormously increased productivity is utilized for the welfare of people."

The growth of automation led to some colourful flights of fancy about future work processes. The March 1956 *Lumber Worker*, for instance, ran illustrations of logs being sawn with "rays" and graded with X-rays – a scene the paper set in the far-distant year of 1975 – reflecting the attitudes of the day with respect to future technologies.

But while imagining the possibilities of new technologies, there were also concerns about the fate of displaced forest workers. By 1964, technological change had indeed resulted in a smaller workforce, and the IWA identified automation as its most pressing issue. "Increased wages have been justified by the increased output per man hour and the lower costs per unit of production...IWA policy has recognized that the social consequences of automation extend beyond the outer limits of collective bargaining. For this reason the union has joined with the central labour bodies in exerting pressure for the acceptance of public responsibility for the displacement of workers," the *Lumber Worker* commented. Automation during the 1960s most notably reduced the role of unskilled workers in the industry by eliminating repetitive jobs.

The two-sided nature of the process has been identified by some academics. University of British Columbia sociologist Patricia Marchak, for instance, notes in *Falldown: Forest Policy in British Columbia* that prior to the 1980s, technological change was relatively gradual and there was a steady erosion of jobs that was more or less relative to pro-

duction levels. In 1980, for instance, 1963 production levels were achieved with 21 percent fewer workers. But expansion of the industry resulted in more people being employed – there were 17,400 workers in logging in 1963 and 24,200 in 1980, while in sawmills, there were 24,600 in 1961 and 35,800 in 1980.

With the recession of the 1980s, there was a sudden, substantial reduction in these numbers, even though production again increased dramatically. The combination of new technologies and a serious recession affected many workers' views of technological change. IWA members had long been aware that with technology came demands for speedup, higher stress, and for some, lessened job security. They had become more concerned with protecting their jobs from technological change than with challenging its implementation.

To investigate this concern, the IWA research department did a landmark study on the effects and consequences of technological change in 1986. Researchers Phil Legg and Doug Smyth found retraining to be members' main priority with respect to new technologies. In response, the IWA negotiated a series of contract provisions to help insulate members from the effects of technological change.

These included the right to retrain and to advance notice and relocation allowances. By the mid-1990s, the IWA's technological change provisions were among the best won by a Canadian union.

In the "war of words" that attended the "war in the woods," many environmental groups claimed that technology was depleting the forest-sector workforce while increasing the amount of wood being harvested. The evidence does not support this assertion. After the fallout from the recession of the early 1980s, forest-sector employment in Canada remained relatively stable, growing at an average of 2 percent per year from 1985 to 1995, in spite of the recession of the early 1990s. As the 1986 IWA study noted, it is important to distinguish between the effects of the business cycle and the effects of periodic introduction of new processes or machinery.

It's also important to note that failure to introduce new technology can eliminate jobs, too. In the

UP, UP, AND AWAY

**By the 1980s, the advent of helicopter logging increased access to rugged and isolated terrain.**

PHOTO COURTESY GEORGE McKNIGHT

early 1980s, the IWA urged the British Columbia forest industry to upgrade its plywood mills in the face of competition and protectionist moves in the United States. When delegates at the union's 1983 convention ordered a study of the coastal plywood industry, President Jack Munro noted that a similar report had been commissioned in the late 1970s. "They have not modernized, they have not changed their product mix. We have not done anything about tariffs, [the ways] we are making plywood should have been overhauled. And there is little consolence in...the fact that we were right five or six years ago because what we said then is now happening."

affected by currency exchange rate problems during the recession, the mill upgrades that occurred on the Coast were also crucial for the long-term viability of the industry and employment of IWA members. The important conclusion drawn from the study was that if technological change had not occurred, the recession of the 1980s would have resulted in much higher levels of unemployment, and the continued existence of the industry would have been seriously threatened.

As the forest industry stabilized through the mid-1980s, employers attempted to exploit the vulnerability that IWA members were feeling after years of layoffs and job insecurity. The result was the biggest and most costly strike in BC's history.

## Contracting Out, Round Two

In 1983, the IWA had settled for a modest three-year contract with minimal gains. Jack Munro described the 1983 contract as "a lousy deal for us, for sure, but we'd honestly felt that it was our social responsibility to help the industry, the province and the country through the tough times." Unfortunately, employers did not share the same benevolent view when it came to dealing with the workers who created their wealth.

For the IWA, the employers' practice of contracting out work to non-union workers had been a growing problem for years. Beginning in the 1950s, a series of arbitration rulings legitimizing the practice had chipped away at one of the cornerstones of every union's security: the right to maintain a union shop. "From the beginning," said IWA historian Clay Perry, "we have acknowledged that there are instances where contracting out was the only solution to a particular problem. But the past 30 years have proven beyond reasonable doubt that the employer will, if given the opportunity, use those limited practical instances as a foot in the door."

First vice-president Bob Blanchard cited the example of Jack Dale to illustrate how contracting out was affecting IWA members. Dale was a 28-year employee of one company, Blanchard noted, and "he had earned the right to the position of his choosing, tow-boat operator, by virtue of the seniority and job-posting sections of the agreement. One morning his employer approached Jack and said, and I quote, 'We have given your tow-boat job to a contractor but because you have served us so well and loyally, we will not dismiss you. Go run the dozer but it doesn't pay as much.' It's harder work, but at 56 years of age, what choice do you have left?"

By 1986, it was apparent to the IWA that fundamental trade union principles, not to mention the well-being of the union and its members, were at stake. Delegates to that year's Wages and Contract Conference unanimously

*If technological change had not occurred, the recession of the 1980s would have resulted in much higher levels of unemployment, and the continued existence of the industry would have been seriously threatened.*

HIGHBALLIN'
THE WOOD IN

On the BC Coast
and in the Interior,
the use of grapple
yarders put some
loggers out of work;
at the same time,
though, by making
the industry more
competitive, they have
saved many jobs.

IWA ARCHIVES

SHUT 'ER DOWN!

The IWA used a selective strike strategy in the 1986 strike; pictured here are members of Local 1-217 at a BC Forest Products mill.

PACIFIC TRIBUNE COLLECTION
DAN KEETON PHOTO

agreed that pension improvements and protection from contracting out would be the first priorities in negotiations.

The employers badly misjudged the mood of the IWA as negotiations began. Believing they held the upper hand after the upheavals of the recession, the employers came to the bargaining table on 12 May 1986 demanding myriad concessions from IWA members. The session quickly deteriorated as the union rejected the employers' demands in no uncertain terms. Recalled Jack Munro, "When we sat down for the first time with the employers, and they started talking about concessions, I started playing poker. I pulled everything off the table except contracting out and pensions. It had never been done before. I said to them, 'I can tell you today, we've got two issues, pensions and contracting out. Those are what you have to move on and that's it.'"

On 19 June, a provincewide strike vote was called. Over the next three weeks, 31,000 Coast and Interior workers voted 89 percent in favour of strike action in the event negotiations failed. A strike date of 21 July was set, but job action began on 15 July at MacMillan Bloedel's Sproat Lake operation near

NONE SHALL PASS

Members of Local 1-85
stop a load of logs from
arriving at MacMillan
Bloedel's Port Alberni
pulp mill.

IWA LOCAL 1-85 ARCHIVES

Port Alberni, where 130 loggers downed their tools after two IWA drivers were
replaced by independent haulers. Four MacMillan Bloedel logging divisions
were joined by Alberni plywood workers in the walkout and by 21 July, 1,050
workers were off the job.

Two days later, 12,000 IWA members were on strike across the province in
a series of strategic pickets – a selective strike. The union did not want to shut
down the entire province, and occasionally this created frustration as picketing members held the fort at their worksites while other IWA members went
to work. But the importance of the contracting-out issue was well understood
by IWA members – Bill Routley of Duncan Local 1-80 recalled that, in his
local, whatever frustrations existed were insignificant compared to the grassroots sense of solidarity growing among union members.

The selective strike strategy allowed the union to target those major forest
industry firms that were the worst exploiters of the contracting-out system. As
well, it left the union some room to negotiate agreements with companies that
accepted the IWA's stance on the issue. According to Clay Perry, "It became
evident in the course of negotiations that there was a split in the industry. The
major companies were hysterically opposed to us. The small independents,
who didn't have the same contracting-out options, wondered what the problem was. We were able to exploit that conflict of interest within the industry."

By 6 August, 18,000 IWA members had hit the bricks. Several firms on the
Coast were starting to crack, and Doman Industries, a smaller company based

NO LOGGING HERE
Local 1-80 loggers
at BC Forest Products
Caycuse Division
receive moral support
from Reverend Jim
Manly (left) and
Local 1-80
vice-president
Roger Stanyer (right)
during the 1986 strike.
IWA ARCHIVES

in Duncan, agreed to a no-contracting-out deal with the union. A Doman executive said he would rather pull out of Forest Industrial Relations (FIR), the employers' negotiating body, than break his contract with the IWA. Several more firms followed Doman's lead and reached agreements with the union over the next days. When the LRB ruled that the Doman Industries agreement was not valid, both the IWA and Doman announced they would honour their deal in spite of the LRB decision. By the end of August, several firms in the north had also settled with the union.

The new premier of BC, Bill Vander Zalm, was tripping all over himself in an effort to bring the strike to a conclusion. In a naïve gesture that was little more than political grandstanding, Vander Zalm called both sides together for a summit meeting. The premier was under the illusion that his presence would somehow help create a settlement and give him instant credibility, but his efforts failed miserably.

On 2 September, Justice Henry Hutcheon was appointed to sit down with both sides and try to broker a settlement. When Hutcheon's report sided with the IWA on the issue of contracting out, the employers rejected it, and the situation was once again at a stalemate. Worse, the IWA strike fund was running perilously low.

Jack Munro noted, "One Friday we were sitting there with $17 in the bank, and we had cheques out for over $900,000 in strike pay." The union's worries were short-lived. The labour movement across the country rallied to support the IWA – the CLC donated $1 million, as did the British Columbia Government Employees Union. Numerous other unions, pensioners, and working members all made substantial contributions to the strike fund.

At the end of September, 20,000 IWA members were still on strike. The union was paying $800,000 per day in strike pay and negotiations were going nowhere. A three-member commission led by former IWAer Stuart Hodgson was appointed to review the issues and make recommendations. The Hodgson Commission's recommendations were released on 25 November and did little to appease the union. Hodgson's key recommendation was that the industry be allowed to contract out at existing levels. Not surprisingly, his report was met with universal scorn by IWA members. On 3 December, a vote taken by IWA members on whether to settle the strike on the terms of the Hodgson report was rejected by a margin of over 90 percent, higher than the margin of the original strike vote. "The result of that ballot was the high point of the strike. I knew after that we would get a settlement," said Jack Munro.

The strike escalated as more and more union members walked off the job in early December. The BC Fed called for secondary strikes against the businesses of members of the board of directors of FIR companies, even though such action was illegal.

In Ladysmith, Local 1-80 members defied a court injunction and picketed Schon Timber in a powerful show of union solidarity. In order to evade union pickets and keep its operations running, MacMillan Bloedel was using Schon Timber, a non-union operation, to remove logs from the water and then ship them via rail to the company's pulp mill in Port Alberni. IWA members rallied 300 to 800 people to stop this dodge with picket lines that grew bigger by the day, despite court injunctions ordering the picketing to cease. Bob Blanchard referred to the Schon Timber episode as the single most significant event of the strike, which convinced the employers they could not win and helped produce the final settlement shortly thereafter. Indeed, the Schon Timber pickets and the IWA members' overwhelming rejection of the Hodgson report made it clear to employers the IWA would not back down in its fight for union security.

Rather than continue to butt heads with the employers represented by FIR, Roger Stanyer, president of the Duncan local, suggested the union try to reach a contract agreement with employers represented by the Truck Loggers' Association. This association of independent logging contractors was responsible for 50 percent of the logging that occurred on the coast. The IWA and the Truck Loggers reached a tentative agreement, and the IWA asked the Truck Loggers to approach FIR, hoping to extend their settlement. On 5 December,

after 107 days on the picket lines, the strike was settled on the IWA's terms, with a letter of understanding that prohibited the contracting out of IWA members' work. A 40-cent wage increase was won, taking the base rate to $14.08 per hour, and IWA members were now entitled to full pension benefits at age 60. The *Globe and Mail*'s headline on the settlement story read "IWA Wins Big."

The 1986 strike was a historic struggle. Not since the 1953 Interior strike had the union fought such an intense battle to establish a fundamental issue of union rights and security. Prince George Local 1-424 president Frank Everett said, "Job security is something members have been looking for for 30 years. It's what the whole thing was about." The strike also galvanized rank-and-file membership support of the union. "Probably the most important thing we gained or learned was that when the existence of the union is threatened and obvious to the membership, there is no limit to the length the membership will go to save it," said Bill Schumaker, president of Kelowna Local 1-423.

"Collectively, the IWA as an organization emerged from the strike as a fine example of what a trade union should be," commented Gary Kobayashi of

TURNING POINT

Mass picketing at Schon Timber, a non-union log dump in Ladysmith, helped force an end to the lengthy strike.

IWA LOCAL 1-80 ARCHIVES

Local 1-217. "The will of the membership has always been the legitimizing force in the IWA, and in the 1986 strike this will was the difference between resounding victory and humiliating defeat."

More than $2 billion in wages was lost over the course of the strike, and the IWA paid out over $17 million in strike pay. Over $10 million was loaned to the IWA by other trade unions on good faith. In the spring of 1987, IWA members voted 80 percent in favour of a $5 per day assessment to repay the loans. After three and a half months, the entire amount had been repaid.

For all the success of the strike, it was also a hardship for the entire IWA. Many members struggled financially, and many suffered personal and family difficulties from the stress of a prolonged strike. Consistent with its ideals of democratic trade unionism, IWA officers were required to subsist on the same strike pay that the rank and file lived on. Reflecting on the 1986 strike, Jack Munro summed up the feelings of most IWA members when he said, "I hope things never get that bad again."

## On the Prairies

In Alberta, Saskatchewan, and Manitoba, IWA members were affected by the same turbulent economic forces that workers in the rest of the country experienced in this era. IWA members remained militant when necessary to back up their demands, and long, difficult strikes were fought in all three provinces. While new organization took place in this era, it was often done in exceptionally hostile circumstances as employer resistance to an IWA presence remained fierce.

**ALBERTA** In Alberta, numerous small mills that the union had organized in the 1950s and 1960s had gone out of business by the mid-1970s, and North Western Pulp and Power of Hinton was the largest remaining mill. In 1971, 200 Local 1-207 members fought a four-month strike against the company and won the highest wage rate in the Alberta industry. The precedent set by the Hinton strike helped other IWA-organized operations negotiate ever-improving contracts in the 1970s. However, Local 1-206 in southern Alberta struggled with declining membership in the 1970s, and in March 1978 amalgamated into Local 1-207, with headquarters remaining in Edmonton.

While the 1970s were a reasonably prosperous time for Alberta's IWA members, the 1980s proved to be much more difficult. In 1982, Local 1-207 negotiated an agreement with Zeidler Forest Industries in Edmonton and Slave Lake that provided parity with BC wage rates. This agreement turned

*Not since the 1953 Interior strike had the union fought such an intense battle to establish a fundamental issue of union rights and security.*

out to be a high point in the recession of the early 1980s, as negotiations became, according to one IWAer, "an exercise in frustration and despair" at most operations. Local 1-207 members were laid off as production was curtailed in most industries, and several companies closed forever, including Knight Schmidt (trailer manufacturer) in Medicine Hat, Skylark Recreational Vehicles in Lethbridge, and a fibreboard plant in Wabamun.

Layoffs and closures continued to batter Local 1-207 members through the mid-1980s, and membership numbers did not stabilize until 1986. Several mills and plants shut down permanently and a Zeidler operation in Barrhead burnt down in January 1986. On 11 April 1986, Local 1-207 members struck Zeidler's Slave Lake operations when the company attempted to take away established benefits and working condition guarantees. As the already regressive climate of Alberta labour relations worsened, Local 1-207 was on the brink of one of the longest, toughest strikes in IWA history (see sidebar "Hard Times in the Land of Plenty" on pp. 236-237).

GOING STRONG

**Organized by Local 1-207, Nelson Homes in Lloydminster, Alberta, survived the economic downturn of the late 1970s and early 1980s and is still in operation today.**

UBC SPECIAL COLLECTIONS
1903-130

**IN CONTROL**

A mainstay of Saskatchewan's Local 1-184, MacMillan Bloedel's Aspenite plant in Hudson Bay expanded in the early 1970s.

UBC SPECIAL COLLECTIONS
BC 1902-11

**SASKATCHEWAN**    In the 1970s, the IWA continued to grow in Saskatchewan as MacMillan Bloedel and Simpson Timber expanded their operations throughout the province. In Reserve, the local planer mill was shut down in 1971, and the Simpson Timber Company gave employees the opportunity to relocate to the company's new mill in Hudson Bay. Many IWA members from Reserve made the move.

Solid wage and benefit gains were won throughout the decade, although in some cases a lengthy strike was required. An eight-month strike fought at Domtar's Fibre Products division in Saskatoon ended in July 1973 with a good wage-and-benefit package won. In September 1974, Local 1-184 won an excellent contract with MacBlo and Simpson that boosted the base wage from $3.72 per hour to $5.07, an increase of $1.35 over 19 months. MacMillan Bloedel and Simpson Timber workers also won a tremendous benefits package that included the IWA pension plan and cost-of-living clauses that helped address the serious inflation of the 1970s. The agreement was hailed as the finest contract signed on the prairies to that date.

Under the NDP government of Allen Blakeney, Saskatchewan Forest Products or Saskfor (formerly the Saskatchewan Timber Board) continued to develop the timber industry. By the mid-1970s, Saskfor had opened new operations at Meadow Lake, Hudson Bay, Green Lake, and Sturgis. In Carrot River, the IWA represented workers at a peat moss operation. Surrounding land had been cleared of timber but was unsuitable for grain crops, and a peat moss industry was successfully developed.

On the strength of its good contract gains, Local 1-184 had grown to 2,000 members in 1977, but by the end of 1978, large-scale layoffs and plant closures resulted in the membership rolls falling to 1,500 despite ongoing organizing efforts. A strike against Moose Jaw Door and Sash began on 9 May 1978, and by the time the strike ended on 28 May 1982, Local 1-184 members had been pummelled by high interest rates and faced further layoffs. In 1985, Saskfor, by then under the control of Grant Devine's Conservative government, was giving workers another going over as it demanded clawbacks on the hard-won benefits Local 1-184 had established, including the IWA pension plan.

By 1986, a serious confrontation with the employers was inevitable, and it arrived on 1 April 1986. Simpson Timber at Hudson Bay had attempted to terminate the collective agreement prior to its expiry and the 90 IWA members voted overwhelmingly to strike the company. For 15 weeks they maintained an unwavering solidarity in spite of the company's belligerence

## Hard Times in the Land of Plenty

DEFENDING WORKERS' RIGHTS is hard, often dangerous work at the best of times, but in Alberta, a province known in labour circles as "Alabama North" because of its regressive labour laws, it is particularly tough going. Just ask the members of Local 1-207, who participated in the eight-year strike against Zeidler Forest Industries of Slave Lake (veneer) and Edmonton (plywood) from April 1986 to January 1994. At both operations, workers walked off the job after rejecting the company's call for deep wage cuts and reduced benefits – concessions that would have gutted the union's existing collective agreements. In the Alberta capital, workers were also protesting Zeidler's refusal to grant the newly formed IWA-Canada successor rights. "Most of us never knew what a labour strike was before this started," Dorothy Johnson, a striker at Slave Lake, stated. "We do now." Little did she and the rest of the union members know that they would be involved in the longest strike in IWA history.

The company responded quickly to the workers' challenge and fired 23 unionists at its Slave Lake plant in November 1986, a move that the Alberta Labour Relations Board, in a rare moment

of impartiality, ruled unlawful. But the IWA was not just fighting the company, it was fighting the government as well. Provincial labour laws facilitated the use of scab labour, court injunctions severely curtailed the effectiveness of the picket lines, and the police routinely harassed and arrested strikers and assisted the company in bringing in replacement workers. At one point in 1986, 32 RCMP officers were used to escort scab workers past eight IWA pickets protesting half a mile from the Slave Lake operation's gates. Edmonton police officers were no better than their federal counterparts; in addition to helping Zeidler replace striking workers, they routinely scuffled with picketers and monitored union activity with video cameras. "The police kicked us around, they grabbed us, choked us, and threw us in the can and gave us the handcuff treatment," Joe Martha, plant chairman at Slave Lake, told the *Lumber Worker*, summarizing the situation at both Zeidler operations. A provincial government report into police conduct in a variety of Alberta strikes, including the IWA's scrap, agreed, stating: "Police must act within legal authority, even when exceeding legal authority appears morally acceptable and has the support of the general public." The report also noted that in many cases the Edmonton police were not acting with the authority of a court order, but at the behest of the company.

As the length of this battle suggests, however, even in the face of intimidation – at one point the Slave Lake picket camp was shot at – workers, their families, and the union, which paid out about $10

million in strike pay and legal fees, refused to back down. A picket line was maintained at both operations throughout the strike, and local unions from · across the country donated in cash and kind. In July 1987, a caravan from BC, loaded with $125,000 of food, clothes, and school supplies, rolled into Slave Lake to boost solidarity. As well, the labour movement sponsored a nationwide boycott of Zeidler products. In the end, the strike ended in stages. Local 1-207 was decertified at

CARAVAN OF HOPE

**Throughout the lengthy battle, IWA locals sent money, food, clothes, and school supplies to help Zeidler strikers; this "caravan of hope" arrived from BC in the summer of 1987.**

IWA LOCAL 1-207 ARCHIVES

NO MORE SCABS!

**The labour movement in Alberta – and across the country – rallied to support Local 1-207; this gathering was held outside Zeidler's Edmonton plywood plant in 1989.**

IWA ARCHIVES

Zeidler's operation in Edmonton in 1993 after scab workers, permitted to cast a ballot under revisions to Alberta's labour laws prompted by the eight-year stand-off, voted against the IWA. (Significantly, workers who were employed at the plant before the strike voted 60 percent in favour of *keeping* the IWA.) A year later, workers in Slave Lake, fearing a similar move there, withdrew their demands. "I imagine that if the company had not been able to scab out the strikes and had suffered financially, then the government would have intervened in a hurry," Local 1-207 president Mike Pisak remarked at the time. "But when we were suffering because of the use of scabs the government did absolutely nothing. The government would not lift a finger to help us. We can be very proud that our members lasted so long." □

*The RCMP at times outnumbered IWA pickets because of a court injunction limiting the number of IWA members allowed on the picket line.*

and the efforts of the legal system. The company relied heavily on the assistance of the RCMP, who at times outnumbered IWA pickets because of a court injunction limiting the number of IWA members allowed on the picket line. IWA members faced many frivolous charges, but ultimately the chairmen of Simpson Timber and MacMillan Bloedel and the local union president were convicted of contempt of court – each received three-month jail sentences (suspended) and $250 fines for their actions during the strike. After IWA members employed with other companies threatened to strike, the employers caved in and new collective agreements were reached. The difficulties at Simpson Timber in Hudson Bay took on a much more significant dimension a few years later when the mill was closed down (see Local 1-184 sidebar).

**MANITOBA** The forest industry in Manitoba began in 1870, and the first sawmill in the north of the province was constructed on the banks of the Saskatchewan River at The Pas in 1910. By 1916, forest lands in southern Manitoba had largely been harvested, and the focus of the province's forest industry shifted to the region around Pine Falls in the east and The Pas in the north. The mill at The Pas received its supply of wood from Saskatchewan, and Local 2-184 (Saskatchewan) represented workers at the mill until its closure in 1958.

In 1965, IWA Region 1 began its first serious effort to organize woodworkers in Manitoba. The provincial government had been making overtures to forest companies, attempting to entice investment and build the province's timber industry. The area around The Pas was slated for a major forest industry development, and the IWA wanted to ensure it had a foot in the door – largely because while workers in The Pas were being paid as little as 90 cents per hour, 50 miles away in Hudson Bay, Saskatchewan, Local 1-184 members were earning a base rate of $1.82 per hour. Manitoba law required that the union establish a "paper local" before it could actually start operating and organizing in the province, so Local 1-324 was granted a charter in 1965, four years before it began actively organizing.

In 1969, Local 1-324 started signing up woodworkers at the new Churchill Forest Industries (CFI) complex at The Pas. The CFI complex contained a pulp and paper mill, two sawmills, and a planer mill. Local 1-324 achieved a major breakthrough when it signed its first contract in March 1970 with Farmer Erectors, one of the construction companies working at The Pas.

Within two years, Local 1-324 represented all workers at Churchill Forest Industries except those at the pulp mill, who were represented by the Canadian Paperworkers Union. Local 1-324 also inherited members who abandoned the Laborer's International Union for the IWA. As in other regions

of Canada, IWA members established substantial wage-and-benefit packages throughout the 1970s. Local 1-324 came to include virtually all woodworkers in the region around The Pas, furthering the union's ability to make concrete gains during collective bargaining with employers. Local 1-324's organizing efforts also began to spread out from The Pas.

In 1973, the local was certified at Dyck's Containers in Swan River. By July 1974, IWA members at Dyck's had gone on strike to win a first contract. A rabidly anti-union employer, Dyck's dragged out proceedings as long as possible to avoid dealing with the IWA, but the members held firm. The company was ultimately sold in 1976, and the new owner quickly reached a first collective agreement with the IWA. After 27 months on the picket line, the group at Swan River won the day with an impressive show of solidarity. Meanwhile, the union broadened its scope in The Pas and began to represent workers at the Wescana Inn.

Throughout the 1970s, Local 1-324 members had experienced occasional layoffs, but the onset of the recession in the early 1980s saw the IWA's 700 members in Manitoba battered. Layoffs occurred at Manfor (formerly CFI) and throughout IWA operations in Manitoba. The recession made negotiations

SKIDDERS 'N' HARDWOODS

Workers at the Cranberry Portage Halfway Camp in Manitoba were just some of the thousands of workers who joined the IWA in the late 1960s and early 1970s, a period of unprecedented membership growth.

UBC SPECIAL COLLECTIONS
BC 1905-154

extremely difficult, as "the employers have the club and they are really using it to their advantage," commented Region 1 organizer Bob Blanchard. Frustration and hardship were the watchwords used to describe Local 1-324's experience in the early 1980s. "In honesty," stated a 1984 report, "[the Wescana Inn] is the one operation in our Local that has not suffered major lay-offs."

Workers greeted with relief the 1984 announcement that Manfor intended to modernize its facilities at The Pas. Manfor's $40 million investment allowed Local 1-324 members to look to a secure future after the struggles and uncertainty that plagued the industry in the first half of the 1980s.

## Rise and Fall in Region 2

Like its counterpart in the west, Region 2 underwent a cycle of expansion and contraction throughout the 1970s as locals in Ontario, Quebec, and New Brunswick were active on the organizational front. In Hamilton, Etobicoke, Whitby, St. Thomas, and Montreal, for example, 900 IWAers struck Consolidated-Bathurst for 12 weeks in the summer of 1974, gaining new members, higher wages, and protection against rising inflation; at the same time, workers in St. Jean took on InterRoyal Corporation and secured "the best settlement in the furniture industry in Quebec."

In addition to success at the bargaining table, the region expanded its

MANITOBA'S ORIGINAL LOCAL

Seen at their annual delegated meeting in 1978 are, left to right, Local 324 recording secretary Wes Maksymetz, financial secretary James Anderson, and president Bill Benson.
IWA ARCHIVES

### LOCAL 324

## Looking Forward

ORIGINALLY ADMINISTERED out of Prince Albert, Saskatchewan, Local 324, chartered by the IWA in 1965, moved to its current headquarters in The Pas, Manitoba, in 1973.

One of two IWA locals in Manitoba, Local 324 started signing up workers at Churchill Forest Industries, a major employer in the small northern town, and in 1970 negotiated its first contract, which included strong safety and seniority provisions, a clause guaranteeing double time after a 12-hour shift, and a health-and-welfare plan paid for by the employer. Organizers Art Friske and John Smithies played key roles in this pioneering campaign. Since that time, the mill has changed owners

educational services considerably, providing local officers and shop stewards with a wide variety of courses in both English and French, and started to publish a regional newspaper to better communicate with its members. Perhaps the most poignant symbol of Region 2's confidence was an address that Earl R. Patterson, president of the region for a short time after Harvey Ladd stepped down, delivered to the Newfoundland and Labrador Federation of Labour in 1970 – marking the first time an IWA official had returned to Newfoundland since the bitter and bloody campaign of 1959. "When [my talk] was finished, many of the delegates who were aware of the struggle unashamedly wept, including officials on the platform," Patterson reported afterwards, just before talking about the possibility of returning to the island to organize a plant in Stephenville, a small town southwest of Corner Brook.

Between 1968 and 1974, the Ontario-based organization added an additional 3,800 workers to its membership rolls, pushing its total over the 10,000 mark for the first time – a remarkable achievement considering Region 2's enormous geographical size, the diversity of industry within its jurisdiction, and the absence of master agreements. Unlike in BC, where Region 1 negotiated blanket agreements that covered entire sectors of the lumber industry, Region 2 typically bargained on a plant-by-plant basis – even if the operations were owned by a single employer.

"It is our duty to organize," a delegate to Region 2's 1974 convention stated.

*'The Wescana Inn is the one operation in our Local that has not suffered major lay-offs.'*

several times; Churchill Industries gave way to River Sawmills, which in turn was bought out by Manitoba Forestry Resources, or Manfor, a provincial Crown corporation, in the early 1970s. In 1989, as part of a wider move to privatize government-run companies, the provincial government sold its stake to Repap Enterprises, a deal that made the Montreal-based company the second-largest holder of timber lands in Canada. To this day, the company, which is now owned by Tolko Industries, provides the bulk of the local's membership, with about 260 members in the mill and 125 in the woods. These men and women enjoy wage rates and pension benefits that are among the most lucrative in the IWA.

From its base in northern Manitoba, the local has expanded both in size and scope; currently, the 750 members are drawn from its traditional strongholds of sawmilling and logging, as well as from the manufacturing, silvicultural, and service sectors (324 organized the Wescana Inn in The Pas in the mid-1970s and, more recently, a women's shelter). In addition to taking on workplace issues, Local 324 campaigned against wasteful forest practices such as clear-cutting, supported the Manitoba Federation of Labour's Occupational Health Centre – a worker-controlled clinic that specializes in occupational health – and helped to elect the provincial New Democratic Party and Premier Gary Doer in 1999, ending 11 years of anti-labour Tory rule. With this electoral change, and the ongoing commitment of its members and staff, Local 324 is looking forward to new opportunities in the future. □

REVOLT IN REGION 2

Local 2-500, marching in front of Knechtel Furniture Plant in Hanover in 1982, joined the chorus of protest in the 1980s.

IWA LOCAL 500 ARCHIVES

"Having enjoyed the benefits that resulted from collective bargaining, we would be betraying the pioneers, those who made untold sacrifices, those who worked to build this union, if we allow ourselves to slow down in the organiz-ing field." From Local 2-500's expansion amongst furniture makers in and around Hanover to Local 2-306's victory at Chestnut Canoe in Fredericton, New Brunswick, Region 2 helped to fulfill two of the IWA's most cherished objectives: to be truly national in scope and to represent workers at all levels of the industry.

But even amidst this unprecedented success for the IWA in central and eastern Canada, many in Region 2's ranks – Dan Chiasson, Bob Navarretta, Marcel Riopelle, Jean Levesque, Tony Marcantonio, Pierre Collin, and George Bradford among them – sensed that an employer and government counter-offensive, spurred on by the twin threats of economic instability and labour militancy, was in the offing. "Let me tell you that the days that lie ahead will be every bit as much of a challenge to all as those that have gone by," Harvey Ladd told union members in one of his characteristically eloquent speeches. "In the not-too-distant future we once more have got to raise the vision of our movement, dedicate it once again to social justice to even the least amongst us. Labour must lead the way again. We are being much, much too tolerant – of our own deficiency, our own laxity, of governments that have the nerve to bring down [anti-labour] legislation...I am going to tell you now, that the grinding engine of change is on the move. Technological developments in this

electronic era are making plants obsolete that were built just one, two, three years ago. The whole social structure of our society is being sprung into air." Ladd was right.

Between 1974 and the early 1980s, a period defined economically and politically by the Anti-Inflation Board, plant closures and layoffs, and raids by the United Steelworkers, Canadian Paperworkers Union, and the carpenters union, membership in Region 2 started to hemorrhage – dipping as low as 6,000 members. In Hamilton, Local 2-69 lost 170 dues-paying members when Consolidated-Bathurst closed its corrugated box plant in April 1984, a move that was the beginning of a wider industry shakedown prompted by the merger of Consolidated-Bathurst and MacMillan Bloedel.

"One can see the real visage of the two multinationals, stony and livid," an IWAer from Region 2 stated. "It is that of an organization without a soul, whose only motivation is maximum profits." Similar closures, coupled with numerous AIB-ordered wage rollbacks, took place elsewhere in Ontario, Quebec, and New Brunswick as well. "I worked at Knechtel Furniture Factory for 48 years, and I'm 63 years old," Fred Tilker, a member of Hanover's Local 2-500, stated after being laid off in the early 1980s. "They closed the plant down and I am out of a job, nobody wants to hire me any more. I asked all over and they said 'You're too old.'"

There were, of course, some hard-fought victories during this period. In Hawkesbury, Ontario, a small town located east of Ottawa near the Ontario-Quebec border, Local 2-600 took on Amoco Fabrics, a division of industrial giant Standard Oil, in a 20-week confrontation that spanned the summer and

'IT IS OUR DUTY TO ORGANIZE'

**From left to right are Wilf "Chally" Chalmers (first vice-president), Jean-Marie Bédard (president), E.H. Griffith (second vice-president), and Bill Pointon (secretary-treasurer), Region 2 leaders in the early 1980s.**

PHOTO COURTESY CLAUDE LAMBERT

fall of 1980. The local, which demanded a two-year agreement, an increase in the base wage rate, and a cost-of-living clause, was aided by strong community support, especially from the Catholic church. The church called on the company to settle the dispute, raised money and donations, and boosted morale and spirits. It also let the union use the church basement for meetings, asking only that the union help the parish priest give it a new paint job once the strike was over. During the dispute, a number of IWA members tried to stop Amoco from moving equipment into the operation and a riot nearly ensued. Charges were subsequenty laid. "The strike at Amoco Fabrics will no doubt be recorded as one of the major struggles in the history of Region 2," stalwart secretary-treasurer Bill Pointon remarked.

Other strikes – like those waged by Locals 2-167 (Tillsonburg), 2-88 and 2-89 (London), and 2-342 (Hagersville) against Livingston Industries, and by Quebec's 2-78 and 2-96 (St. Jean) against Scanway and Croydon Furniture – were also successful in securing pay hikes and protection against inflation. Overall, though, the region was still losing ground. "Had meetings. Most employees too scared. Could not complete," read a report filed by the region's director of organization in 1982 after several union drives collapsed, underscoring just how bad things had become.

# Région No. 2

*International Woodworkers of America*
*Le Syndicat International des Travailleurs du Bois d'Amérique*

REGION NO. 2 INCLUDES: ONTARIO • QUEBEC • NEW BRUNSWICK • NOVA SCOTIA • PRINCE EDWARD ISLAND • NEWFOUNDLAND

2088 Weston Road, Weston, Ontario  M9N 1X4          Telephone 247-8628

| J.-M. BÉDARD | W. G. CHALMERS | E. H. GRIFFITH | W. J. POINTON |
|---|---|---|---|
| *President* | *First Vice-President* | *Second Vice-President* | *Secretary-Treasurer* |

## LETTER OF INTRODUCTION

On behalf of the many thousands of Members in our Union, the International Woodworkers of America, we would like to take this opportunity to inform you of some of the Plants that are in our Union, and do work much the same as you do. These members have found that the International Woodworkers has done a great job on their behalf by improving their Wages and their weekly earnings by getting benefits when they are sick. Another advantage is obtaining seniority rights and other protective language in a Collective Agreement.

It is common knowledge to the Union that in many of the unorganized plants, that safety and health is not of any great importance to most companies. Their only concern is Production - Production and more Production. However, when the Union is established in the plant and a collective agreement is signed, the Union leaves no stone unturned in seeing to it that the company provide the proper safety and health for all the employees, resulting in a minimum of lost time due to injury or sickness. These matters can only be processed and corrected through grievance procedure and a grievance committee.

Thousands of workers from all walks of life in Canada, such as teachers, nurses, doctors, policemen, firemen and all types of Industrial workers, have realized that they can no longer go it alone and have united in forming a trade union. Some of the Plants in which our Union represents the Employees are in Electrohome, Simmons, Andrew Malcolm, Kenchtel Furniture, Sklar, Elmira, Bogden & Gross, Singer, Hanover Kitchens, Heintzman Piano, Larsen & Shaw, Canada Spool & Bobbin, Consolidated-Bathurst, Abitibi, Spaldings, Diamond National, Allatt Ltd, Livingston Manufacturing, Livingston Transportation, Weyerhaeuser of Canada, Commodore, Mobile Trailers, Lumber, Plywood and Casket operations, and many more, all of whom are proud to be members of our Union the International Woodworkers of America.

The record of the I.W. of A. in negotiating collective agreements in Region No. 2 dealing with and improving wages, vacations, legal Holidays, Life Insurance, Major Medical, Weekly Indemnity, grievance procedure, seniority, safety and health is second to none. The records is available from the Department of Labour.

Why don't you consider the facts and take action now and get yourself organized into a Union, the I.W. of A.

We hope you have found this information worth reading, because we would like you to consider becoming a member of our Union. If you do, you will find it does not cost you money, it pays you to belong to a Union.

JE ME SOUVIENS

Long-time leader of Region 2, Jean-Marie Bédard, pictured here in the early 1960s, was both a socialist and separatist, a political combination common amongst Quebec labour leaders.

IWA ARCHIVES

## LOCAL 400

# Maîtres Chez Nous

UNDER THE DIRECTION of Harvey Ladd, then a leader in Ontario, the IWA made its first substantial gains in Quebec and the Ottawa River Valley in the 1950s and 60s, chartering a clutch of independent locals such as 2-505 at Sterling Furniture in Montreal, 2-78 at Scanway Corporation in St. Jean, and 2-400 at Mercedes Textiles in Kirkland.

At the same time that the IWA was charting new organizational territory, the Quebec labour movement was undergoing a significant realignment of its own as longstanding working-class grievances combined with French Canadian nationalism to produce a new spirit of militancy. Caught up in this political fervour was Jean-Marie Bédard, a young, university-educated socialist and separatist from Quebec City, who joined the IWA as a staff member in the mid-1950s. Bédard, who counted separatist and left-wing heavyweights René Lévesque, leader of the Parti Québécois, and Michel Chartrand, rising star with the militant and

nationalist Confédération des Syndicats Nationaux, amongst his friends, remained as the union's Quebec lieutenant until 1984. "The loyalty that those people [from Quebec] had was remarkable. Not just for the organization, for the IWA, but for [French-speaking people]," IWA national staffer Bob Navarretta recalled, reflecting on the potent mix of separatist and left-wing politics that influenced the Quebec wing of the IWA. "The union was an important component for their cause."

With a membership drawn from Ontario and Quebec, Region 2 spanned Canada's "two solitudes." At no time was this more obvious than in the early to mid 1980s, when the IWA set about merging Regions 1 and 2 in preparation for its eventual secession from the American-based parent organization, a move that brought the political differences between the two sides of the district into sharp relief. The argument in favour of this initiative was straightforward: with the economy in recession, governments and corporations on the offensive, and membership numbers in free fall, it made sense to combine smaller independent locals and sub-locals and pool scarce human and financial resources. Bédard and other local leaders from east of the Ottawa River did not oppose the idea of creating a larger political framework, but they insisted on special terms and conditions – 21 in all – that safeguarded the Quebec organization's autonomy within the IWA. It was a position not unlike those being negotiated by other Quebec-based labour organizations. The Quebec Federation of Labour was granted special status by the Canadian Labour Congress in 1974, and the Quebec wing of the United Auto Workers received similar privileges from its parent organization a decade later.

Following a raucous convention in 1984, Region 2 held its annual election, one that was widely seen by union members as a referendum on the merger proposal and the question of special status for the Quebec locals. Bédard and his allies were shut out by a slate headed by Bill Pointon, a pioneer unionist from Ontario. In the wake of the election, the Quebec locals, already skeptical of IWA president Jack Munro's willingness to work with Quebec – at one point during the merger debate Munro told Bédard that "the best thing he could do [for the IWA] was retire" – started to look for another home. Some locals ended up in the Canadian Paperworkers Union, while others followed Pierre Collin, a service rep under Bédard and a leftist and staunch separatist in his own right, into the newly formed Syndicat des travailleurs et travailleuses des produits manufacturés et du personnel de bureau. "It was disastrous for the IWA as a whole," Claude Lambert, who was president of one of the Quebec locals at the time, remarked years later.

Between the mid-1980s and the early 1990s, Quebec's geographical Local 400 remained inactive. Since 1992, however, things have started to turn around. Buoyed by the work of bilingual organizer Rene Brixhe, a long-time activist with

SITBA SEPARATION

**Prior to the merger of locals and sub-locals in Region 2 and the creation of IWA-Canada, the IWA's Quebec locals left the union in protest.**
IWA ARCHIVES

Lumber and Saw, the IWA secured certifications with Mercedes Textiles in Kirkland and Produits Forestières, a small hardwood and softwood mill in Fort Coulonge. Three more deals have since been signed. "There are many non-union plants in Quebec or plants with independent associations that require strong union organizations," Norm Rivard, national fourth vice-president, observed in 1999, looking to the future. "There are also workers in the eastern part of the province that are potential members." □

LA BELLE PROVINCE

**On the job at Consolidated-Bathurst in St. Laurent in 1960 is Charlie Beaulieu, then president of Local 2-279.**
IWA ARCHIVES

**BACK IN QUEBEC**

After a long absence, the IWA returned to Quebec in 1992; pictured at Produits Forestières in Fort Coulonge are Daniel Dagenais (IWA member) and Mike McCarter (local officer).

IWA ARCHIVES

Indeed, so devastating – and sustained – were the combined effects of high unemployment, high inflation, plant closures, and government labour policy that Patterson's successor as the head of Region 2, Jean-Marie Bédard, a socialist and separatist from Quebec, speculated that what working people were witnessing in this period was not merely an economic downturn, but the "twilight of capitalism" itself. "Capitalism was a necessary phase of history. It developed the means of production and distribution and that was its progressive role. The economy built by capitalism, however, has developed to the point where the material foundations exist on which to build a new social, economic, and political order which we call 'socialism,'" he stated, his language and analysis laying bare his knowledge of history and Marxist economics. "Capitalism has become an obstacle standing in the way of the next phase of historical development, advance, and progress. It is no longer progressive, it is in a state of decay and is profoundly reactionary...The working class of the United States and Canada are being summoned by history to play a significant role, and that is the final elimination of capitalism."

But as inspiring as this analysis might have been, no doubt Bédard and the small army of rank-and-file organizers, fighting in the trenches on a day-to-day basis, understood that despite their best collective efforts, things would likely get worse before they got better. As the region's membership base eroded, so too did its revenue, a financial reality that forced the district to curtail services, shut down its newspaper, lay off office staff and organizers, and hike the per-capita tax levied on local unions, a necessary but unpopular move. "We are getting beat up on and we are getting beat up pretty bloody bad," remarked one union member.

Significantly, by the time of the 1982 convention, local and regional officers had started to debate the possibilities and politics of combining the region's many sub-locals and locals into larger political units and merging the entire structure into Region 1.

Region president Bédard and the Quebec locals asked that a number of conditions be granted to the IWA's Quebec locals to ensure their autonomy in the event of a merger. After Bédard lost the leadership of Region 2 in 1984 to Bill Pointon, those locals, believing their concerns would not be recognized, decided to leave the IWA.

Local autonomy was important to the remaining Region 2 members, but they nevertheless voted overwhelmingly in favour of merger with Region 1. Bill Pointon, who became fourth vice-president of IWA-Canada when the regions joined, spent considerable time and effort co-ordinating a series of smaller mergers involving 28 independent locals and 80 geographic sub-locals in Ontario. These consolidations, based on geographical proximity, took place

*'The working class of the United States and Canada are being summoned by history to play a significant role, and that is the final elimination of capitalism.'*

PROGRESS ON SAFETY

**Verna Ledger (IWA national safety director), Henry Nedergard (Local 1-85), and Robert Sass (University of Saskatchewan) lead a Region 1 safety conference held in Duncan, BC, in 1984.**
IWA ARCHIVES

## 'Assassinated By Their Occupation'

*When we talk about safety, our scope must be broad because evidence shows that fatalities and serious injuries are just as much tied to the economic structure of the industry as they are to specific work site conditions and procedures.*

– Jack Munro, IWA-Canada president, 1991

THROUGH THE 1970s, the IWA expanded its safety program considerably. The various geographic locals developed lines of communication through which they could discuss safety issues, and forest industry workers' exposure to hazardous work environments became an increasingly important issue. Workers who toiled in conditions where there was harmful dust, dangerous chemicals, or excessive noise and vibration received support from the IWA, which slammed employers and the WCB for failing to reduce or eliminate the sources of hazardous exposure.

The IWA had always held employers accountable for workplace conditions and safety, but in the 1950s and early 1960s the union's safety programs raised workers' awareness of the dangers of their work and of their responsibility to look after themselves on the job. By the mid-1970s, however, the focus had shifted squarely to the employers' responsibility and the recognition that health and safety were often dictated by a work environment over which workers had little control. "Each day workers enter a battlefield, but they fight no foreign enemy and conquer no lands. The war they are fighting is against the poisonous chemicals they work with and the working conditions that place serious mental and physical stress upon them," was how Dr. Jeane Stelman described it in the October 1978 *Lumber Worker*.

IWA safety director Verna Ledger was even more blunt when she addressed Region 1's 1978 convention. "Forty-three woodworkers have been 'assassinated' by their occupations in the first eight months of 1978," she commented. "The philosophy that statistics like [these] are inevitable in an industry rated as hazardous as the forest industry is not acceptable nor even believable." Under Ledger's direction, the IWA's safety program aggressively challenged this notion of inevitable casualties.

Of particular concern to the IWA were what Ledger called the "subtle killers and destroyers of health which take months or years to appear." The IWA supported researchers from the University of British Columbia studying "white-finger," also known as Raynaud's Phenomenon – the serious nerve damage that can result from long-term use of vibrating machinery like chain saws. After IWAers attended the first IWA International safety conference in Seattle in 1978, ergonomics (safety and health assessments of the entire workplace environment) became another focal point of IWA safety concerns. The IWA was also one of the first unions to protest the use of PCPs as a wood preservative, and it later attacked the use of formaldehyde as well, demanding that these chemicals be banned.

The IWA found itself continually challenging the WCB for failing to live up to its mandate to address the plight of workers affected by injury and industrial disease. In 1980, the WCB responded by jointly sponsoring a safety conference with employers and the IWA. After an employers' spokesperson made a number of callous remarks blaming "careless workers" for 90 percent of all injuries and criticizing the IWA's safety policy, enraged IWA delegates threatened to walk out of the conference. The interests of profit clearly outstripped any real concern employers had for the well-being of their workers.

Throughout the 1980s, the IWA advanced progressive health and safety initiatives that addressed the concerns of workers. PCPs were banned in the late 1980s, and the right to refuse dangerous work was enshrined in law, although for several years IWA members were routinely disciplined for asserting their rights under the law, necessitating grievance and arbitration hearings. Nonetheless, the union persevered with an attitude to safety that increasingly put the burden of responsibility on employers and work processes. As Verna Ledger commented in 1988, "The IWA will never accept the concept of 'inevitable risk.' Fatalities and injuries in the forest industry are not inevitable."

In 1990, new Ontario labour legislation mandated that all cutter and skidder operators had to take extensive training and become certified by the provincial ministry. The Ontario program was launched with the close collaboration of the IWA. "We insisted that any program that we would develop had to be by people who would do the work," said Local 2693 president Fred Miron.

Regional and national safety conferences were held annually by the early 1990s, and health and safety issues gained increasing prominence during collective bargaining. The IWA launched several comprehensive safety programs in the 1980s and 1990s, often developed at the local or regional level and funded with employer contributions. In 1988, BC IWAers fulfilled a long-term goal when they successfully negotiated an employer-funded safety research program. The Safety Advisory Foundation for Education and Research (SAFER) was put in place for members on the Coast and southern Interior. In the northern Interior, the Safety/ Health Awareness Research Program (SHARP) addressed safety concerns specific to that region.

In 1999, the union began to explore other possibilities for safety programs. National first vice-president Neil Menard, the officer responsible for safety and health issues, led an IWA contingent that met several times with employer and government representatives to explore the possibility of establishing a forest industry safety association. "If there is going to be an association," said Menard, "it has to be jointly run with full participation of our union. It has to be jointly founded, jointly designed, and jointly operated."

In spite of these positive developments, workers continued to be killed and injured on the job. A December 1997 *Lumber Worker* headline read "Struggle for safer workplaces an ongoing battle," and indeed it was as employers continued to demand increased productivity through speedups on the job. Despite decades of union, government, and employer safety initiatives, the casualty toll for woodworkers remains high.

**END OF AN ERA**

Jack Munro (former Region 1 president), Keith Johnson (International president), and Bill Pointon (former Region 2 president) were on hand in September 1986 to attend the first convention of the new unified Canadian Regional Council only months prior to the split from the International.

IWA ARCHIVES

over the next several years, with the end result being a stabilized, streamlined organization in the eastern region.

"Over the years," said Pointon, "one of our basic problems in the East is that we haven't been large enough to direct the attention to organizing. It hasn't been easy – to some extent we've felt isolated…The co-operation from the West has just been excellent in terms of needs…It is time to close the chapter on Region 2 and concentrate on one indivisible union."

## A National Union

On 19-20 June 1986, the IWA held a founding convention in Nanaimo, BC, to formally recognize the merger of Region 1 and Region 2. Nine months later, in March 1987, the 50-year affiliation of Canadian and American woodworkers in the IWA was brought to a close, with the unanimous acceptance of a resolution to divide the International union into two separate entities. The decision to separate from the American woodworkers was amicable on both sides and finalized a process that had begun formally in 1982. (After the split, many of

the Canadian locals dropped the region prefix that had been part of their names previously, though most of the older Region 1 locals kept it.)

Since the early 1970s, Region 1 had been concerned about the International's inability to develop organizational strategies that would help the union grow. The devastating effects of the recession in the early 1980s forced the IWA in Canada to re-evaluate the structure of the union. Western Canada's Region 1 had always been the largest IWA region, and the two Canadian regions accounted for over 60 percent of the IWA's international membership. With American IWA members still reeling from the recession and attacks from employers, the creation of IWA-Canada seemed to be a sound strategic development.

Moreover, the problems experienced by American members as a result of their country's labour legislation were increasingly viewed by Canadian IWAers as a drain on resources. Jack Munro observed that "the problems for US unions were greater than for those in Canada. They faced unfriendly governments at the federal and state levels, governments that were very anti-union…Then the US unions started negotiating concessions, and now they can't get them back." Under American law, permanent replacement workers could be hired in the event of a strike, and indeed, a 1983 strike against Louisiana-Pacific in Oregon and Washington was broken by scab labour. The result was the decertification of the IWA's Louisiana-Pacific locals in 1984.

Louisiana-Pacific's success in attacking the IWA encouraged other employers to launch an assault on woodworkers and their unions in the Pacific

CHARTING A
NEW COURSE

Western Canada's Region 1 local presidents and alternates met at a 1986 convention to discuss the direction of the new national union.

IWA ARCHIVES

# Fighting for the Rights of Injured Workers

IN 1975, LOCAL 1-85 member Sven Frederickson was working at MacMillan Bloedel's Sproat Lake Division as a faller when he was struck by a piece of dead wood that broke his spinal cord. Frederickson, then in his early 50s, instantly became an incomplete quadriplegic.

In 1977, 20-year-old Wolfgang Zimmerman of Local 1-85 had spent only five days doing roadside brushing for MacBlo when a 50-foot alder struck him, fracturing his lower back. Zimmerman became an incomplete paraplegic – after several operations and years of rehabilitation, he regained limited use of his legs.

Frederickson and Zimmerman were subsequently hired as office employees, but MacBlo eliminated both men's jobs in 1982. Frustrated, they

EQUAL ACCESS FOR ALL

In 1994, the Disability Management Committee at Somass Cedar in Port Alberni launched a pilot project designed to reintegrate injured workers into the workplace.

decided to fight back. In 1983, they founded the Disabled Forestry Workers Association, which evolved into the Disabled Forestry Workers Foundation (DFWF) of BC five years later. With assistance from the IWA, other unions, and industry representatives, they produced the critically acclaimed video *Every Twelve Seconds*, which examines how accidents changed the lives of five permanently disabled workers.

Local 1-85 president Earl Foxcroft, an executive director of DFWF, helped raise the profile of

(NIDMAR), the first institution of its kind in Canada, was created at Port Alberni's North Island College.

Opened after years of lobbying by the DFWF, the Institute is an initiative of labour and management designed to help unions and employers get disabled workers returned to the workplace. Institute director Wolfgang Zimmerman noted, "The IWA has always been instrumental in supporting our efforts." The Institute's main functions are developing programs of education, research, and training.

During the 1990s, the reintegration of disabled workers became an increasingly important aspect of labour relations as legally binding "duty to accommodate" provisions spurred employers and unions to help the disabled find meaningful employment. In 1996, national vice-president Harvey Arcand noted that forestry workers were four times more likely than other workers to be injured during their careers and commented that the union "would suffer at the hands of bureaucrats and the courts if we don't get out and develop policies that work and that accommodate the interests of all of our members." The IWA developed its duty-to-accommodate policy through 1996, and the policy was adopted at the 1997 national convention.

disabled workers' issues within the IWA. Following his retirement in 1991, Foxcroft was appointed the IWA's National Injured Workers' Representative and championed the first disabled forestry workers' pilot projects.

In 1990, a joint task force composed of representatives from DFWF, IWA, CPU, MacBlo, and the federal government was struck to develop model plans for the reintegration of disabled workers into the workforce. In the spring of 1994, the first disabled workers pilot project was launched at Port Alberni's Somass mill, with the participation of Local 1-85 and MacBlo.

"It's a program that needs to be looked at, accepted, and done," said IWA-Canada national vice-president Neil Menard. In October 1994, with considerable support from the IWA, local NDP MLA Gerard Janssen, and others, the National Institute of Disability Management and Research

INJURED WORKERS'
ADVOCATE
**Local 1-85 president Earl Foxcroft.**
IWA ARCHIVES

Union business agent Lloyd Szkaley meets with Local 2693 members at a Canadian Pacific Forest Products camp north of Ignace, Ontario, in 1993 to discuss the year's contract talks.

IWA ARCHIVES

Northwest. Weyerhaeuser closed numerous mills in Oregon and Washington in 1985 and 1986, all the while demanding huge concessions from its workers. These actions culminated in a 1986 IWA strike in the two states. When employers threatened to permanently replace workers with scab labour, IWA members backed down and agreed to take wage and benefit cuts of $4.30 per hour.

The settlement in Oregon and Washington took place just as the provincewide strike in BC was heating up. Region 1 officials and members were well aware of how their fellow unionists to the south had been treated, and they knew that FIR would pursue a strategy similar to that of the American employers. As described earlier, FIR's intention to squeeze concessions from the IWA was soundly beaten in BC after a protracted strike. Although the decision to form the IWA-Canada had been made by the time the 1986 Region 1 strike was over, these events at the international level in the 1980s added considerable momentum to the decision to split the union on national lines.

"Our argument for making the union Canadian was that the international union was drifting away from our needs and wants," said Jack Munro. "The American trade union movement was going downhill and was becoming a burden to Canadian trade unions." In the end, the break was made because the IWA in Canada knew it could do better on its own.

## Completing the Circle

Fifty years after woodworkers broke away from the United Brotherhood of Carpenters and Joiners to form the IWA, a historic loop was closed when two Lumber and Saw locals from northern Ontario joined the IWA-Canada in 1987. Local 2995 president Norm Rivard recalled that the UBCJ provided only a minimal level of support when Locals 2693 and 2995 were on strike in the mid-1980s at several mills. "Normal strike pay was supposed to be $50 per week for a single person and $80 if you were married," said Rivard. "Our members were receiving $25 per week, and in some cases received nothing. We asked the UBCJ for assistance on a number of occasions, and Fred Miron and I even flew down to Washington to plead our case. In the end, we got a pittance. That's when we seriously decided to start looking for a new home."

At the same time, the UBCJ and its Lumber and Saw affiliates were kicked out of the Canadian Labour Congress, a situation that did not please the northern Ontario Lumber and Saw officials. Subsequently, the Canadian Paperworkers Union launched a number of raids against Lumber and Saw, and the IWA briefly considered raiding Lumber and Saw as well. However, organizers John Smithies and Lyle Pona convinced the IWA leadership that a raid attempt would likely fail and that negotiations aimed at a merger would provide the best opportunity to bring Lumber and Saw into the IWA.

Preliminary meetings were held in August 1986, and in May 1987, Smithies and Pona met with Local 2693 president Fred Miron in the basement of his home. After five hours of discussion, a merger proposal was developed and taken to both locals 2995 and 2693 for consideration. Before a merger could occur, however, Lumber and Saw members were required to vote for either the IWA or CPU to represent them. The MacMillan Bloedel plywood plant in Nipigon was a pivotal campaign, and the IWA defeated the CPU by a margin of more than two to one. Ultimately, the IWA won election handily over the CPU in every Lumber and Saw-represented plant and logging camp. Lyle Pona recalled that the fact IWA-Canada had recently become an all-Canadian union appealed to the members of Lumber and Saw and was an important factor in their decision to merge with the IWA.

By July 1987, Lumber and Saw Locals 2693 (Thunder Bay) and 2995

*Events at the international level in the 1980s added considerable momentum to the decision to split the union on national lines.*

## LOCAL 2693 AND LOCAL 2995

# Together Again

IN 1987, LOCAL 2693 (Thunder Bay) and Local 2995 (Kapuskasing) voted to leave the Lumber and Sawmill Workers Union, the industrial affiliate of the United Brotherhood of Carpenters and Joiners, and join the IWA. It was a move prompted by two different, but connected, dynamics. For one, the Canadian wing of the IWA, increasingly disenchanted with its American-based parent organization, was recast as a national organization called IWA-Canada — prompting a wave of mergers in Ontario as small, independently chartered IWA locals were reorganized on a geographical basis.

Just as the IWA was starting to place its Ontario operations on a more secure footing, Locals 2693 and 2995 were undergoing some significant changes of their own. In 1980, the two organizations found themselves outside the house of labour after the Canadian Labour Congress expelled the building trades unions, including Lumber and Saw's parent organization, UBCJ, for withholding dues. (The building trades unions were protesting their lack of representation at the CLC.) Shortly thereafter, Locals 2693 and 2995 were caught up in

TAKING THE OATH

**A new executive board and slate of officers are sworn in for Local 2995 in 1996.**

IWA ARCHIVES

a series of raids conducted by the Canadian Paperworkers Union – CPU leaders claimed that since Lumber and Saw was no longer tied to the labour congress, its locals were fair game. The raids, which cost the locals several sawmill and bush operations, were followed by a four-month strike in 1984 to protect seniority rights.

Weakened and financially devastated by both developments, 2693 and 2995 started looking for a new home. In 1987, after failing to reach a merger deal with the CPU, the two Lumber and Saw locals voted to affiliate with the IWA, bringing about 7,000 members into the new national organization. "The IWA fit us like a glove," Fred Miron, former president of Local 2693 and national vice-president, remarked years later. It was a sentiment echoed by Miron's counterpart at Local 2995, Norm Rivard: "To this day I can honestly say that not one of our members have said that we made a bad move in joining."

Although membership in the northern Ontario organizations has dipped as new technology and

258

corporate restructuring have put thousands of people out of work, both locals have won several key battles on the job. Faced with the closure of the Spruce Falls Power and Paper newsprint operation in Kapuskasing, Ontario, and the loss of hundreds of jobs, Local 2995, in co-operation with three other unions, the Ontario government, Kimberly-Clark, and Tembec, worked out a deal to keep the mill operating, albeit with fewer employees, in 1992-93. The local also fought hard against Malette United Sawmill's aggressive push to contract out union work, staging several wildcat strikes to protest the company's violation of the collective agreement. The company responded by accusing 38 workers of taking part in an illegal strike and sued the local for $100,000. The case ended up before the Ontario Labour Relations Board in 1995. Undeterred by the suit, 2995 sent all 38 men to the OLRB hearings in Toronto to have their day in court, a move that shut the mill down for an additional three days. Frustrated by the union's tactics, the company dropped the charges. Recent gains against Columbia Plywood in Hearst in 1999 – including an employer-paid educational fund, built on arrangements made by 2995 a decade earlier – illustrate the continued determination of the Kapuskasing local to improve the lot of woodworkers.

During the 1990s, Local 2995's Thunder Bay counterpart organized Dubreuil Brothers – a saw-milling and logging outfit located about 220 miles east of Thunder Bay in Dubreuilville – after workers there, former members of an employee association, contacted the IWA. Four years later, employees at Industrial Hardwood Products in Thunder Bay, joined 2693. "In Third World countries like El Salvador [where I'm from] there are poor working conditions. Many of us Latinos didn't think we would see the same type of conditions in Canada and even worse," Juan Hernandez, union supporter and veteran of the Industrial Hardwoods plant, remarked after the successful certification drive. "The message to employers in Ontario is that we will go the extra mile to make sure that people's rights are protected," echoed Manny Ranger, an IWA organizer. "Every worker should get dignity and respect in the workplace." Today, Local 2693 represents about 3,300 workers. □

CHOWING DOWN

By 1990, the number of logging camps in northern Ontario was on the decline as employers required workers to commute longer distances to their jobs. These Local 2995 members eat at one of the remaining camps – Abitibi Camp 34 north of Cochrane, Ontario.

IWA ARCHIVES

(Kapuskasing) had openly declared their intention to break away from the UBCJ and merge with the IWA. The UBCJ agreed to a peaceful transition, with one of its conditions for transfer being that the IWA would not raid UBCJ-organized workers in Newfoundland.

The IWA's legacy in Newfoundland from the 1959 strike was powerful. Newfoundland woodworkers remembered the extraordinary efforts the union had undertaken on their behalf 30 years earlier, and they invited IWA-Canada representatives to their meetings. It was not long before the Newfoundlanders were expressing keen interest in becoming IWA members, and they asked the union to organize them. UBCJ officers were infuriated to learn of the IWA's presence in Newfoundland and threatened to scuttle the peaceful transfer of their northern Ontario locals if the IWA did not withdraw from Newfoundland. Reluctantly, the union agreed to withdraw, ultimately gaining 7,000 new members when Locals 2693 and 2995 merged with the union in 1988. (Meanwhile, Newfoundland woodworkers steadily abandoned the UBCJ. Today, it has virtually disappeared from the scene.)

The success of the merger with Lumber and Saw was an early indicator of the wisdom of the Canadian IWA regions' decision to pursue their own union. "We'll be able to share our expertise with brothers in eastern Canada, and we'll

CHAPTER SIX

# Out of the Woods

*'Society is being protected from inflation by a process that repeatedly picks the same people to suffer the same injuries.'*

IN THE FINAL DECADE of the twentieth century, the IWA continued to face many of the same challenges that had held its attention since the union's founding in 1937. Government and employer hostility, economic hard times, questions of sustainability, and fast-paced technological change remained front and centre at union conventions and contract negotiations. The layoffs and exporting of jobs that began in the late 1980s continued as the Conservative federal government under Prime Minister Brian Mulroney heeded the interests of capital while ignoring the welfare of the working class. In common with the majority of Canadians, the IWA had dire concerns about the Canada-US free trade deal, signed in late 1988. In southern Ontario, these fears were quickly realized as over the next few years many of that region's fine furniture factories and plants closed down, unable to compete with American factories that paid their workers a pittance. IWA members were thrown out of work.

In 1990, inflation rose slightly and the federal government reintroduced a policy of high interest rates. High rates and an overvalued Canadian dollar once again led to a drop in housing starts and a collapse in export markets. The made-in-Canada recession of the early 1990s took a horrendous toll on IWA members. By late 1990, 8,000 IWA members had been thrown out of work. Jack Munro commented, "There is something terribly cynical going on here. The whole society is being protected from inflation…by a process that repeatedly picks the same people to suffer the same injuries, to experience time and time again unemployment and desperation…You have to understand that this recession, like the last one, was planned. An intended and deliberate goal of the federal government."

In January 1991, one third of British Columbia's IWA plywood workers had been laid off. By April 1991, 11,000 IWA members were out of work, and communities were being decimated by the extensive layoffs that continued to occur. Blaming the recession, MacMillan Bloedel closed its ALPLY plywood plant and Somass Cedar Mill in Port Alberni, with over 700 IWA jobs lost. "We believe that MacMillan Bloedel has made a corporate decision to shut ALPLY division," said Local 1-85 president Earl Foxcroft. "With nominal investment, we think that the plant would compete with any coastal plywood producer in North America." Indeed, MacMillan Bloedel's failure to seriously consider alternatives that would have kept its facilities open was a slap in the

The signs read:

FISHING CAPITAL? NO UNEMPLOYMENT YES !!

MANUFACTURE LOGS HERE NO MORE "EXPORT"

RICHMOND PROMISED JOBS FOR T.F.L. 44 LOGS

**ENOUGH IS ENOUGH**

In 1991, members of Local 1-85 protested both mill closures and wasteful logging policies; they also called on the provincial government to withdraw MacMillan Bloedel's tree farm licence.

IWA ARCHIVES

265

FIGHTING BACK

Arrayed against the Leyland strikers
were the usual suspects: scabs, goons,
police officers, company officials, and a
hostile Social Credit government.

PACIFIC TRIBUNE COLLECTION
SEAN GRIFFIN PHOTO

## The Leyland Strike

ON 14 SEPTEMBER 1989, 80 workers at Leyland Industries, a plastics manufacturer in Pitt Meadows, BC, went on strike for a first contract. The strike occurred in the wake of the Social Credit government's Bills 19 and 20, draconian anti-labour legislation that made it much easier for employers to maintain lousy working conditions and much more difficult for unions to organize workers. In the Leyland strike, the IWA faced a hostile employer determined to bust the union and an equally hostile justice system that harassed and attempted to intimidate IWA members and officials.

The vast majority of workers at Leyland were women who started at $4.75 per hour with little opportunity for advancement. Working conditions were terrible – poor ventilation resulted in an abundance of toxic fumes, the plant had a terrible safety program, and wage scales hovered around the poverty line.

The Leyland strikers were faced with a barrage of injunctions that limited the number of pickets, and the union faced heavy fines from the provincial

Supreme Court for injunction violations. As the strike continued into the spring of 1989, the strikers remained solid on the picket line. In May 1989, Local 1-357 president David Tones was arrested by the RCMP along with IWA staffers Lyle Olson and Barry King. All three faced trumped-up charges of "intimidation" and were jailed.

Although the charges were later dropped, at the time the arrests and jailings infuriated not only IWA members, but the entire labour movement. A rally held on 10 June 1989 attracted 500 IWA members in defiance of a picketing injunction. Jack Munro lambasted the Crown prosecutor for arresting IWA officials, and Ken Georgetti (then president of the BC Federation of Labour) promised the Leyland strikers they would have the support of the provincial body. This show of strength caused the employer to return to the negotiating table, and on 23 June 1989 a settlement was reached, with Leyland workers receiving wage increases and benefits they had never before enjoyed.

The events at Leyland not only illustrated the importance of union solidarity, but also showed the justice system's willingness to blatantly support the interests of capital, especially in a regressive political climate like that fostered by the Social Credit government in BC. The election of an NDP government in 1991 saw the introduction of progressive labour legislation that redressed much of the damage done to labour relations by Bill Bennett, Bill Vander Zalm, and their Social Credit governments.

face to Port Alberni. The company had changed ownership and restructured after the recession of the 1980s, callously disregarding the community's dependence on forest industry jobs.

IWA members did not sit passively while MacMillan Bloedel was doing its damage. Workers formed numerous committees to explore options that could keep the plants open, but MacMillan Bloedel paid them little heed. On 19 April, IWA members were joined by other unions at a rally outside the provincial legislature to protest the company's actions, as well as the Social Credit government's failure to address the effect of those closures on workers. By the summer of 1991, the lack of response from either party led IWA members to demand that the government withdraw MacMillan Bloedel's tree farm licence.

Local 1-85 member and ALPLY employee Bill Windley commented that the lack of a quality log supply for the mill was a problem – but it was a problem of MacMillan Bloedel's making. "A lot of the problem concerning log supply is that some of the very best old growth is being canted or cut into Japanese squares, then exported. MacMillan Bloedel is exporting large timbers that could be manufactured here to create some jobs in lumber remanufacturing and secondary manufacturing," said Windley.

The export of whole and partially processed logs had long been a grievance for the IWA, which for years had demanded the government restrict the practice and mandate companies to invest more extensively in secondary processing

STOP THE EXPORTS, 1982

IWA members at Berry Point in Vancouver gather to protest the export of raw logs to the United States. At left is Local 1-357 president Terry Smith.

PACIFIC TRIBUNE COLLECTION
DAN KEETON PHOTO

Tree planters at Industrial Timber Mills Caycuse Division Camp 6 on Vancouver Island plant seedlings in the mid-1940s.

IWA LOCAL 1-80 ARCHIVES
W.H. GOLD COLLECTION

in exchange for their right to harvest timber from public lands. The IWA had argued since its inception for such practical measures – measures that would encourage sustainable harvesting in forests and develop the value-added job sector, which had not come close to reaching its potential in British Columbia.

Complicating the recessionary difficulties of the early 1990s further was the presence of environmental groups determined to see huge areas of forest lands protected and left in their natural state. Environmentalists typically focused their efforts directly on politicians and on companies whose logging practices they disapproved of, with little or no thought for the impact their actions had on the workers and communities relying on the forests for their livelihood. Lost in the controversy over preservation and land-use issues was any recognition that the IWA had always been actively concerned about the well-being of forest lands.

## Environmentalism With Its Working Clothes On

In 1939, IWA president Harold Pritchett addressed the union's third annual convention on the topic of "the forest problem." Among Pritchett's observations:

Nature has been exceedingly generous, but indications are that if cutting practices still generally followed are continued, old growth fir will be gone long before new growth is ready for manufacture into lumber of sufficient high quality to compete successfully on world markets.

Although the forestlands of the United States and Canada are of a high-site quality and capable of producing a high rate of forest growth, a large area is at present deforested and standing idle. Whatever reproduction takes place does so, for the most part, in spite of present methods, not as a result of them.

Organized labour must arouse public opinion to a greater degree and weld it to political and community leadership through legislative action to obtain correlation and integration in the use of forest resources, wood products, pure water...wildlife, recreation.

At the IWA's BC Coast District Council meeting that year, a resolution was passed, pointing out: "There has been no effort on the part of the operators or the government to conserve our forest wealth; Therefore, be it resolved: That we urge the government to adopt a practical and suitable conservation and reforestation program."

In 1947, the union made a formal call for mandatory reforestation, a position it reiterated in the 1950s. In 1954, District 1 president Joe Morris spoke eloquently during the debate on a resolution concerned with forest management licences:

> One Local Union has one opinion and another Local Union has another. Some support the big capitalist, another Local Union supports the small capitalist while as far as I am concerned, capitalism in any form has no place in the management of the forests of British Columbia. The forests are the heritage of our people, and should be used for our people, and capitalism, whether it is small or large, has no place in the administration of the natural wealth of this Province...We can't oppose forest management as such, because forest management is good. But we can oppose the management of the forests by the selfish interests of the profit-takers.

The IWA's position on the welfare of the forests remained consistent through the 1960s and 1970s as well, and in a 1978 interview, Jack Munro commented, "Our membership has some of the best environmentalists that exist." Two years later, Region 1 developed an extensive forest policy guide. The preamble noted that IWA forest policy was developed on three basic premises:

1. The nation as a whole is facing both short-term and long-term industrial wood shortages.

*'The forests are the heritage of our people, and should be used for our people, and capitalism, whether it is small or large, has no place in the administration of the natural wealth of this Province.'*

2. A balance in the use of the forest for consumptive and non-consumptive products based upon the economic, social, and recreational needs of society must be established.
3. The concept of multiple use of land must be adopted.

IWA policy called for an extensive inventory of the forest land base and recommended that large areas of forest be classified into four categories of land-use zones: protected forest, recreational forest, multiple-use forest, and commercial forest.

The union supported an aggressive, mandatory reforestation program, with emphasis on sound silviculture practices and on the importance of developing the value-added sector of the industry. Moreover, the union proposed that the federal government establish a Department of Forestry, as well as a forest and forest-product research program.

In September 1988, the IWA adopted a resolution creating the National Committee on Forestry and Environment. The next month, members of Duncan Local 1-80 formed the Woodworkers' Survival Task Force to raise public awareness of wasteful logging practices and job losses. Local 1-80 president Roger Stanyer noted that the Woodworkers' Survival Task Force influenced the provincial government's March 1989 decision to place a 100 percent export tax on log exports from coastal BC.

In a speech at that year's IWA-Canada convention, Jack Munro became the latest in the long line of IWA leaders to advocate sound environmental and conservation practices and also to promote a co-operative effort between woodworkers and environmentalists:

> Let me say, loud and clear, that we are not at war with environmental groups. Only the government wants us to be at war with environmental groups. Governments and corporations know that if we and the environmentalists get together on issues there will be no turning back, so they try to set us against each other. We know that we care about the environment, and we want a process that the people of this country will trust so that we can start making decisions that will protect our jobs and protect the environment.

In 1990, the national office of the IWA released another forest policy statement. Updated in 1996 and entitled *The Forest is the Future*, it set out the union's concerns about long-term sustainability of forests and insisted on the need for a constant, evolving effort to find a balance between environmental, social, and economic concerns. The IWA's forest policy reflected its long experience with changing forest practices and land-use struggles. "We cannot take

*'Governments and corporations know that if we and the environmentalists get together on issues there will be no turning back, so they try to set us against each other.'*

one-sided positions that sacrifice biological diversity, waterways, or forest soil, any more than we can ignore the needs of people, jobs, communities, or the economy," proclaimed the document's preamble. Addressing environmental issues, the IWA's policy statement said:

> While we strive to limit disturbance and minimize impact, we must remember that we are human beings and that we must transform nature to live. There are many historical and international reminders that human beings make poor environmental decisions when they are themselves poor.
>
> We therefore reject as false environmentalism many schemes for the cessation or reduction of commercial forestry.
>
> Many such schemes are wrong, in part because they fail to realize that the world's current demand for forest products will not cease simply because Canadians stop or reduce our harvest of timber. Instead, that timber harvesting will simply be transferred to other nations and regions

**FIGHTING FOR BETTER FOREST PRACTICES**

In November 1988, Local 1-80's Wood-workers' Survival Task Force picketed Fletcher Challenge's Vancouver headquarters to raise public awareness of wasteful logging practices and job losses.

PACIFIC TRIBUNE COLLECTION
DAN KEETON PHOTO

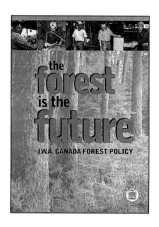

THE WORKING FOREST

During the 1980s
and 1990s, land-use
issues came to
dominate the IWA's
– and the forest
industry's – agenda.
IWA ARCHIVES

where forest practices are not as stringently regulated or as well enforced, are less efficient or require the destruction of tropical rainforest, with resulting deforestation…

Unless they are needed to achieve long-term sustainability, then, reduction of timber harvest levels in Canada would do little to improve the world's environment. It would do much, however, to eliminate job opportunities, disrupt communities and damage or destroy the economy of forest-based towns across Canada…

Sustainable forestry, economic opportunity, community stability, worker and public involvement, environmental protection, reinvestment in our forests: these are elements that make up our vision of a strong, sustainable forest sector. This Forest Policy outlines our goals and presents policies that would allow us to advance toward them.

Throughout the 1980s and 90s, the IWA's extensive analyses and critiques of company forest practices and government forest policy were too often overlooked. Indeed, one of the reasons for the formation of the Woodworkers' Survival Task Force was the provincial government's slashing of forestry department staff. Cutbacks were so severe that the department was no longer capable of monitoring and policing the logging of public lands. Meanwhile, the environmental movement captured the attention of the media with a number of prominent campaigns aimed at setting aside working forests and turning them into parklands.

## Lands For Life – But Not For Workers

In Ontario, the Temagami region was a focal point of environmental protests in 1989 and 1990. Plans to construct a new logging road through a corner of the 6,500-square-kilometre wilderness in northeastern Ontario were disrupted by environmentalists, who demanded old-growth forests in the region be protected. When the environmentalists' court challenge was defeated in the fall of 1989, they mounted blockades of the logging road in an attempt to stop construction. The road was completed in December 1989, and despite delays caused by protesters (among the protesters arrested was the Ontario NDP leader Bob Rae), selective logging began in the area shortly thereafter.

Further complicating the situation was a claim on the land by the Teme-Augama Anishnabai band. In the late 1980s, the IWA had been meeting and consulting with the Teme-Augama Anishnabai, the Ontario Federation of Labour, the Steelworkers union, and the NDP to develop a plan that would provide the band with meaningful input into decisions about resource use in the area. The IWA was optimistic that out of these "stakeholder" meetings

would emerge a workable plan to address the concerns of First Nations, workers, the forest industry, and environmentalists. This optimism was shattered in May 1990 when Ontario's new NDP government under Premier Bob Rae ignored the consultation process initiated by the IWA and other stakeholders and cut a deal directly with the Teme-Augama Anishnabai. The government's deal addressed environmental concerns by protecting the disputed Temagami land, but ignored the decision's effect on workers. The protection of the Temagami came about just as the made-in-Canada recession was battering the economy, and it amplified the difficulties IWA members faced in northern Ontario.

By 1993, the recession in the forest industry had devastated IWA members in northern Ontario, and frustrations over long-term unemployment reached a critical point. The February 1992 closure of the paper machine at Domtar's paper and linerboard mill in Red Rock put 117 IWAers out of work, many of whom ended up on welfare rolls in the forest industry-dependent region. In

CODE OF CONDUCT

In 1993, the Ontario government introduced a new Code of Forest Practices; much of the legislation was repealed by the Conservative government of Mike Harris.

IWA ARCHIVES

273

April 1993, Local 2693 members in the Beardmore area set up information pickets on the Trans-Canada Highway to call the public's attention to their plight.

Despite the union's frustration with the government over the Temagami deal and the hardships faced by the IWA as a result of recession, it pledged to work with the Ontario NDP government to develop a sound forest policy. In April 1993, the Ontario government announced its Code of Forest Practices, new legislation that incorporated many IWA forest policies as a result of consultation with second vice-president Fred Miron. "Less than five years ago we would never have seen a document like this," said Miron. "Not only would we never have seen it, but if they did want to develop one, they [the forest industry] wouldn't have asked for Native, labour, or environmental group participation."

The Ontario Code of Forest Practices was a comprehensive piece of legisla-

### A SPECTACULAR SETTING SAVED

In 1990, Dave Luoma (left), Don Zapp (middle), and Dave Morrison (right), veteran fallers from Local 363, refused to cut a giant stand of old-growth forest on Vancouver Island; the "glorious mix of species" was eventually set aside.

IWA ARCHIVES

## 'Hug a Logger, You'll Never Go Back to Trees'

IN MAY 1990, Dave Luoma, Don Zapp, and Dave Morrison, a three-member falling crew from Local 363 (Courtenay), were working about 100 kilometres north of Campbell River. The three loggers had worked for half a day and were walking through a stand of trees when they came across a spectacular setting of old-growth timber. The 25-acre stand in the White Creek watershed had a glorious mix of all the major softwood timber species on the BC Coast, including Douglas fir,

balsam, hemlock, spruce, red cedar, and cottonwood. Struck by the beauty of this area, the loggers persuaded the company to leave it untouched.

Dave Luoma was a 25-year veteran in the forests and said it was the most incredible group of trees he had ever witnessed. Don Zapp recalled that "as soon as we walked back in and saw the stand, we just couldn't do it, that was it right then and there." One Douglas fir tree in the stand was measured at 285 feet tall.

While the preservation effort of these IWAers was largely lost in the thick fog of environmental politics, it is one of many footnotes to the IWA's legacy as a proponent for sound environmental practices and conservation in the forest industry. □

tion that dealt with all aspects of forest policy, including sustainability issues and environmental concerns. An aspect of the Code that Miron helped develop was its pledge of protection for workers who reported environmental violations. "Say if an employee is building a road and then comes upon an eagle's nest – he can shut the operation down without penalty until a proper solution is found…[Whistle-blower protection] was a major step forward in the 1990s." The Ontario NDP further refined its forest policy in 1995 when it passed the Crown Forest Sustainability Act. However, these progressive approaches were quickly undone with the rise to power of Mike Harris's Conservative government later in 1995.

By June 1996, the Ontario Conservatives had slashed 2,100 jobs from the Ministry of Natural Resources, a loss of 40 percent of the total number of employees. In a complete reversal of NDP forest policy, the Harris government bent over backwards to accommodate the industry. Crucially, the Harris Conservatives left workers and their unions out of the consultation process, which largely consisted of closed-door meetings that involved only corporations and selected environmentalists.

By the spring of 1999, the Conservatives' "Lands for Life" consultation process resulted in over 2.3 million hectares of new parks and park additions, many of which were created from the working forest that supported jobs and

**NO PROTECTION HERE**
During the Ontario government's Lands for Life process, no job protection was offered to IWA members following the creation of new parks and park additions.
IWA ARCHIVES

**LOCAL 830**

# Winnipeg Addition

'WE'RE GLAD TO BE A MEMBER now. We've wanted better representation and have been able to get that with joining the union." That's what Jack Alexander, president of Local 830, told the *Lumber Worker* after the members in his Winnipeg-based local voted to leave the Canadian Paperworkers Union in the early 1990s and hook up with the IWA. One of two IWA locals in Manitoba, Local 830 represents about 250 workers at two corrugated paper operations, Smurfit-MBI and Norampak, and a distribution plant run by Unisource.

All three operations have been fixtures in Winnipeg for decades – the original MBI operation started in 1929 – and, as is often the case in the paper industry, have seen their fair share of mergers and takeovers. The most recent round of corporate restructuring took place in March 1998, when Quebec-based Cascades Inc. bought into the Canadian division of Domtar and formed North American Packaging, or Norampak. Spurred on by a low Canadian dollar, modernized equipment, and, most importantly, a skilled workforce, the corrugated paper plants, which compete with one another, have expanded into the US market; Unisource recently expanded its operations as well. Through all of this, the local has held its own: membership has improved slightly and wages and benefits remain lucrative. "The plant [MBI] has continuously improved its product and maintains its market share," Paul Groleau, a vice-president with Local 830 stated in 1998. "We are busier than ever."

The local has been busy on the political front as well. Along with Local 324 (The Pas) and the Manitoba Federation of Labour, it vigorously opposed changes to the provincial labour code imposed by the Conservative government of Gary Filmon in 1997, which eliminated automatic certification procedures, restricted workers' action on the picket line, and limited the labour movement's abilities to fund political parties. "This is a bullshit law and we'll have no part of it," one IWAer in Manitoba remarked. Two years later, Locals 830 and 324 struck back against the Tories by helping the NDP, under leader Gary Doer, secure a majority government in the provincial election. □

communities. "The result was parks for the preservationists, compensation for companies, and nothing for workers, communities, or First Nations who depend on the forests for their living," said the *Lumber Worker.* "This is a complete sellout of workers," added IWA fourth vice-president Norm Rivard. "To provide compensation for the companies and to provide no protection at all for the people who make their living on the land – that's not acceptable."

## 'Peace in the Woods'

Events in Mike Harris's Ontario were a sobering reminder for IWAers in British Columbia of the difficulties they had experienced with that province's Social Credit government in the 1980s and early 1990s. Land use, lost jobs, and compensation for woodworkers displaced because of land-use decisions had been the major focus of the union there since the mid-1980s.

Most notably, the environmentalists' "Save South Moresby" campaign on the Queen Charlotte Islands attracted nationwide attention from 1985 to 1987. On 11 July 1987, the federal and provincial governments signed an agreement to create a 147,000-hectare national park reserve on the Charlottes. A committee was established to determine compensation for those affected, including Local 1-71 loggers who lost their livelihoods.

**LOSSES AT LYELL ISLAND**
**When the South Moresby Park Reserve was created on the Queen Charlotte Islands, loggers from Local 1-71, like this worker on Lyell Island, lost their jobs.**
IWA ARCHIVES

# Adventures in Social Democracy

CANADIAN SOCIAL DEMOCRATS made headway in the early 1990s when, in quick succession, the New Democrats took power in Ontario in September 1990 and in both British Columbia and Saskatchewan in October 1991. IWA-Canada and its members were strongly supportive of the NDP in all three elections.

**ONTARIO** Commenting on Premier Bob Rae's win in Ontario and on strong NDP showings in Alberta and Manitoba in 1990, IWA president Jack Munro told the 1990 union convention that "those elections stand as declarations, that ordinary working people are no longer talking. They are with those elections coming together, making magnificent statements in Canada that send chills down the spine of the right wingers." Despite Munro's optimism, there were also warnings. "We are ever so aware that the Ontario social democratic experiment is under the microscope," Ontario Federation of Labour president Gord Wilson told the same convention. "There is no quick fix solution—it has taken at least 15 years to drive us into the abyss we currently find ourselves in."

Indeed, the Ontario economy was already in trouble. The effects of the recession of the early 1990s were taking hold, compounded by the shrinking industrial base in the province as a result of the Canada-US Free Trade Agreement. After backing away from an early effort to spend the province out of the recession, the Rae government was forced to cut services and lay off public employees or face fiscal ruin. Rae's decision to cut jobs enraged public sector unions and other groups within the labour movement, who saw it as a monumental betrayal.

By 1995, the Ontario NDP experiment had ended in failure as Mike Harris's "Common Sense Revolution" swept across the province and the Conservative party was elected to power. Harris quickly dismantled the NDP labour code, cut even more severely into public sector spending than Rae had, and undermined much of the social legislation enacted by his predecessor.

"We made a mistake in Ontario when we allowed the NDP to get defeated," IWA president Dave Haggard told the union convention in Thunder Bay two years later. "Not the IWA, because we stood behind them in this province." Haggard warned Ontarians that it had taken 16 years to return the social democrats to power in BC after the fall of Dave Barrett's government in 1975. "And I hope to hell it doesn't take that long because mad as I get at the NDP on any given day…they still give a damn about working people."

**BRITISH COLUMBIA** The 1991 election of Mike Harcourt's NDP government in BC was welcome relief after years of regressive Social Credit party rule. Although Harcourt's government seemed to live in hot water and appeared sure to go down to

LOGGER-POLITICIAN
At Local 1-71's 60th anniversary meeting in
1997, IWA logger and NDP MLA Glenn
Robertson, elected the previous year, talks about
life as a politician in BC.
IWA ARCHIVES

defeat in the mid-90s, a dramatic turnaround
occurred after Harcourt's resignation and the election of Glen Clark as party leader. Clark, whose
leadership bid was strongly supported by the IWA
and many other unions, shocked the opposition
Liberals by winning a narrow election victory in
May 1995. In spite of his own subsequent troubles
and resignation, Clark's campaign gave the NDP
another term in government and a continuation
of the progressive labour laws that have helped
BC's unions increase their membership by over
200,000 members since 1990.

The link between IWA-Canada and the New
Democrats was particularly strong in BC. Before he
became president of the union in 1992, for
instance, Gerry Stoney served as president of the
BC NDP from 1982 to 1988. "Believe me, during
that time I took my lumps from both the right and
the left," he said in his last presidential address to an
IWA convention in November 1996. "But if any
labour union hopes to make any headway in terms
of shaping our economy in ways that respect and
protect workers, we have to start by electing governments that treat our interests and our agenda as
legitimate parts of the political equation."

**SASKATCHEWAN** In Saskatchewan, Roy Romanow's government was faced with a deficit left by
its defeated and disgraced Conservative predecessor. The mess left behind by the Conservatives was
so bad that Romanow even contemplated having

the province declare bankruptcy. The government
made tough choices, which included closing many
rural hospitals and other reductions in government services, and as in Ontario, some public
sector unions were displeased. Nonetheless,
Saskatchewan's labour law reforms improved the
ability of trade unions to organize in the province.

In early 1999 the province announced that it
would greatly expand its forest industry through
a series of joint ventures between First Nations
and the private sector. Romanow called the plan
"the single biggest announcement of private-sector
job creation in the history of the province."
Saskatchewan's New Democrats were re-elected in
1995 and narrowly won a third term of office
in 1999.

**MANITOBA** Manitoba elected an NDP government in September 1999. Premier Gary Doer
quickly moved to rejuvenate health care in the
province after years of neglect by the
Conservatives. Correctly predicting that "this is
the last time I'm coming to the IWA convention as
leader of the opposition," Doer told the 1997
national convention in Thunder Bay that "hard-
working people, we believe, need a government
that will stand with them for a high-wage policy."

Doer's election came during the 1999 IWA convention in Sault Ste. Marie. "The next millennium
we start off with an NDP government," whooped
Local 324 (Winnipeg) president Jim Anderson.
"Come on with us guys, let's go!" ☐

During the negotiations that led to the park's creation, politicians from both levels of government promised that if jobs were lost, there would be fair compensation. MacMillan Bloedel and Western Forest Products were eventually paid $31 million in compensation for the loss of their cutting rights, but with contemptuous disregard for earlier promises, a Compensation Commission ruling in October 1990 refused compensation to the 24 workers laid off as a result of the park's creation.

In May 1989, provincial government plans to ban logging in the Carmanah Valley on the west coast of Vancouver Island led to a demonstration by 2,000 IWA members outside the provincial legislature. Jack Munro told the rally that woodworkers were fed up with being a shock absorber in the ongoing battle over forest management. "The provincial government doesn't have a clue about what it's going to do with our public forests, and the general public has lost confidence in its ability to manage," said Munro. "Now it is wood-

## Trip Wires and Spike Scares

IN THE LATE 1980s and early 1990s, environmental radicals created even more danger in what was already one of the most dangerous jobs in the country. In November 1990 in the Tsitika Valley, loggers discovered that extremists had strung 1.6 kilometres of heavy-gauge fishing line around trees at ankle and neck level. While falling, bucking, or seeking escape routes, a worker could easily

**EXTREME GREENS**
**Local 1-85 faller Mark Spence, pictured here in 1992, displays a 10-inch spike he hit with a chain saw, narrowly escaping serious injury.**
IWA ARCHIVES

hit the invisible fishing line and be at serious risk from a falling tree, a running chain saw, or a line snapped so tight by a falling tree that it would mutilate a bystander.

Radical greens were also spiking trees. This involved drilling a hole into a tree at a right angle, then dropping a spike into the hole. When an unsuspecting faller's chain saw struck the spike, it sent the spike rifling out of the hole at high velocity, putting the faller in grave danger of injury or death. Some spiked trees were taken out of the forest and shipped to sawmills with spikes intact. The potential for flying shrapnel if the spikes collided with massive high-speed band saws was a frightening prospect for workers.

IWAer Ken Nickell struck a spiked tree with his

workers who are paying the price and we resent being pitted against environmentalists, because we are environmentalists too."

While the Social Credit government initially delayed making a decision about the Carmanah Valley, its final choice amounted to little more than sawing the baby in half. On 10 April 1990, the government announced that it would divide the valley between parkland and logging.

"The government is still choosing to make crucial land-use decisions on a valley-to-valley basis without concern for…ecological or economic impacts," said IWA-Canada first vice-president Gerry Stoney. NDP leader Mike Harcourt slammed the Socreds for refusing to deal openly with land-use issues and for pitting environmentalists against workers "so they [the Socreds] can help their corporate friends."

By 1990, the NDP itself was threatened by a labour-environmentalist rift within the party, with the IWA in one corner and the party's green caucus in

*'We resent being pitted against environmentalists, because we are environmentalists too.'*

chain saw in the Walbran Valley in April 1992. In addition to the everyday dangers of falling, Nickell said, "It's just the psychological factor knowing there are spikes and losing concentration and being unable to control the [falling] environment 'cause you're wondering what the hell will happen." Over 90 spiked trees were discovered by loggers in the Walbran in the spring of 1992. Workers began to carry metal detectors and to inspect trees for signs of sawdust or other disturbances around the base that could indicate a spiked tree.

BC forests minister Dan Miller commented in 1992 that "tree-spiking is quite simply an act of violence against people…It is not an attempt to protect trees or encourage co-operation on land use, but instead is a deliberate attempt to cause injury or death to forest workers." The irresponsible actions of eco-terrorists only served to heighten the frustration woodworkers felt towards those environmentalists who acted with flagrant disregard and disrespect not just for their livelihoods, but for their lives.

**DANGEROUS MEASURES**

In 1990, Local 363 faller Dave Stewart discovered heavy-gauge fishing line in the woods strung at ankle and neck height.

PHOTO COURTESY PRODUCTION MAGIC

the other. A compromise land-use resolution introduced by federal NDP MP Bob Skelly temporarily healed the rift. Unveiled at the party's provincial convention that year, the resolution called for a "time limited" planning process for each region of the province. Hailed by all sides as a workable policy, the resolution contained three key proposals: the protection of 12 percent of representative ecosystems; the protection of the land base of the working forest in order to maintain employment and support of forest industry communities; and the settlement of outstanding First Nations land claims to benefit all British Columbians. The resolution became the basis for the NDP's Environment and Jobs Accord, as well as the foundation for a brief period of peace between labour and environmentalists.

With the support of the IWA and organized labour, environmentalists, and First Nations, the Environment and Jobs Accord became a strong plank in the opposition NDP's platform. The Accord proposed the establishment of a regionally based land-use planning framework that would involve all affected parties. Most importantly for the IWA, the Environment and Jobs Accord stated that compensation would be provided to forest workers for job losses. It also included a pledge to stimulate local employment initiatives in new timber trades, intensive silviculture, and labour adjustment programs.

On 10 October 1991, further rapprochement between woodworkers and environmentalists appeared to be at hand when a "Peace in the Woods" accord was signed. The IWA and other resource-worker unions signed an agreement with the Sierra Club, Western Canada Wilderness Committee, Greenpeace, the Valhalla Wilderness Society, Earthlife Canada, and the Canadian Parks and

A SHORT-LIVED ACCORD

In October 1991, the IWA and other labour unions signed a "Peace in the Woods" accord with several environmental organizations. The IWA's Jack Munro and Colleen McCrory of Valhalla Wilderness Society, an unlikely duo, face the press.

IWA ARCHIVES

Wilderness Tourism Council. Both the unions and environmental groups viewed the accord as an important step in establishing dialogue about managing forests in the interests of jobs and the environment. They struck a committee to work towards creating a common front on environmental and job concerns in response to a Social Credit government that both sides agreed had badly mismanaged forest policy. Coming on the heels of two regional accords between IWA-Canada locals and environmental groups, it fostered a spirit of optimism about the prospects for long-term settlements of land-use issues. The election of Mike Harcourt's NDP government in October 1991 bolstered the feeling that change was coming in the woods.

However, the truce was short-lived. By the spring of 1992, protestors were setting up blockades in the Walbran Valley on Vancouver Island, and the radicals among them were spiking trees. The environmental groups' breaking of agreements and failure to consider the welfare of woodworkers evaporated whatever good will had briefly been established. A year later, mass protests at Clayoquot Sound signalled the return of polarized relations between environmentalists and woodworkers.

## 'The Meat in the Sandwich'

In 1988, conflicts over land use and forest industry practices in the Clayoquot Sound area of Vancouver Island caused environmental groups to begin a campaign to have all forest lands in the area protected from timber harvesting. In 1989, the Social Credit government of the day responded by creating the

Clayoquot Sound Sustainable Development Task Force, ostensibly to help resolve conflicts over resource use in Clayoquot Sound. The task force was made up of more than 30 representatives from the area's municipalities and citizens groups, forest companies, government ministries, First Nations, and the IWA.

Local 1-85 president Dave Haggard was the union's representative on the task force, a body designed to operate on the principle of unanimous consensus. But more than a year after it was formed, there had been virtually no progress in developing a comprehensive land-use strategy. "This has been frustrating as

CLAYOQUOT CAST-OFFS

Clive Pemberton (left) and Len Dziama were among a handful of woodworkers left on the west coast of Vancouver Island in 2000.

IWA ARCHIVES

the option of work in the forest as the result of a land-use decision." That broken promise left a devastated group of forest workers desperate for work.

Clive Pemberton, a former camp chairman at the Kennedy Lake division in Clayoquot Sound, commented, "Most people who were here left the area and the people who are still here don't have nearly enough work to keep them going through the year." Forest Renewal BC was viewed by many of the refugees as an employment lifeline, but provided only irregular employment. Nonetheless, IWAer Len Dziama noted, "No matter what anybody says about FRBC, their on-the-ground projects are very worthwhile and provide meaningful and necessary work. They still need to happen."

The displaced forest workers of Clayoquot Sound illustrate all too painfully the human impact of a land-use decision that ignored the fate of woodworkers, and the failure of politicians to keep their promises when it mattered most for those workers. □

## Clayoquot Sound Refugees

BY THE SPRING OF 2000, a small group of woodworkers formerly based in Clayoquot Sound became known as "Clayoquot Refugees." These workers were economic refugees as a result of land-use decisions during the early and mid-1990s that drastically reduced logging in the region. Since 1993, logging in Clayoquot Sound has been reduced to a minuscule level, and over 400 woodworkers have lost their jobs, despite former premier Mike Harcourt's promise in 1994 that "not one forest worker would be left without

hell," said Haggard, "but I still remain optimistic that we are going to accomplish something out of it." Unfortunately, Haggard's optimism was undermined over the next number of years as the welfare of loggers, their families, and their communities took second place to environmentalists' demands for a halt to forest industry activities in the region.

On 13 April 1993, BC's NDP government announced that limited logging would take place in Clayoquot Sound, sparking an environmental protest that garnered international attention. The media portrayed the government's decision almost exclusively as a defeat for environmentalists, who had demanded the government preserve the entire 260,000 hectares of Clayoquot Sound. In the ensuing environmental protests that summer, virtually no attention was paid to the impact of the government's decision on the woodworkers who earned their living in Clayoquot Sound.

The government's ruling meant that the working forest shrank from 81 percent of the region's land to 45 percent. This eliminated 400 direct forest jobs, with another 1,000 due to be lost as a result of reduced timber harvesting. Worse, the government's ruling did not provide for those workers who lost their jobs. In March 1994, Premier Mike Harcourt pledged that "not one forest worker will be left without the option of working in the forest as a result of land-use decisions." A year later, the annual cut rate in Clayoquot Sound was slashed by another 30 percent. The workforce at MacMillan Bloedel's Kennedy Lake logging division was cut from 90 workers to 45. The government's new Forest Renewal BC program was slow out of the starting gate and promised jobs did not materialize for displaced workers. "The government has made some serious decisions which have affected our members and the community," said Dave Haggard. "The very least the government could do is live up to its well-documented commitments to the forest workers who have been thrown out of work by decisions affecting logging in Clayoquot Sound."

Kim Pollock, the director of the IWA's Environment and Land Use Department, commented extensively on the cleavage between workers, industry, and environmental groups. In a 1998 article published in the *Lumber Worker*, Pollock noted:

> "Environmentalism" has turned into a highly codified ideology that originates not with the working class, but largely with the professional middle classes. As such, it is an ideology that often neglects the needs and interests of working people and ignores their key concerns: class unity and solidarity, jobs, and community. Meanwhile, employers are often only too happy to use workers in their ongoing battle to fight off the costs of environmental change.

*'In short, workers all too often are the "meat in the sandwich" in a struggle between industry and green groups.'*

*Despite the NDP's good intentions and policy commitments to protect workers, the woodworkers were the only group that ultimately suffered at Clayoquot Sound.*

In short, workers all too often are the "meat in the sandwich" in a struggle between industry and green groups. This can often mean either that both sides attempt to use and manipulate working people in their struggle for gain and hegemony, or that workers' interests are sacrificed in the struggles and accommodations between these two forces.

The chain of events at Clayoquot Sound in the 1990s bore out Pollock's observations. The fundamental failure of environmentalists to consider the consequences of their actions on workers speaks to the very real class distinctions between the two groups. And despite the NDP's good intentions and policy commitments to protect workers, the woodworkers were the only group that ultimately suffered at Clayoquot Sound.

Nonetheless, IWA members had some success in their response to the green challenge. In 1997, for instance, the outcome was very different when two Greenpeace ships ventured into Vancouver harbour on their way to mount protests farther up the BC Coast. Quick action by IWA Canada union members ensured that the ships were blockaded in port, where they remained stuck for a week. That event, as well as a union-led community blockade at Squamish, helped turn the tide of public opinion against the protesters, who were widely seen as having gone too far in disrupting workplaces and threatening communities.

Since then, the anti-logging crusade has largely moved from blockades to boycotts and marketing campaigns aimed at scaring industry customers into cancelling orders for British Columbian and Canadian products. The IWA has responded, working on the international stage to face down the global scope of capital, environmentalists, and the news media.

## Towards a New Social Contract

With the election of the NDP in British Columbia in October 1991, the Environment and Jobs Accord policy plank was transformed into the Commission on Resources and the Environment (CORE), headed by former ombudsman Stephen Owen. In June 1992, the government directed CORE to begin regional planning processes for Vancouver Island, the Cariboo-Chilcotin region, and the Kootenays. When Owen presented his first recommendations in 1994, it became clear that CORE had not made the protection of forest workers' jobs enough of a priority. In one of the largest rallies in BC history, over 20,000 forest industry workers and community supporters gathered at the provincial legislature in Victoria to denounce the CORE land-use strategy for Vancouver Island.

IWA Canada president Gerry Stoney (who succeeded Jack Munro in 1992)

told the rally, "The price of this CORE is just too high to pay." Stoney criticized CORE's emphasis on the creation of new parklands and the permanent removal of land from working forests. Owen's recommendations also failed to set aside a working forest land base on Vancouver Island. "We will take no more," added Dave Haggard, president of Local 1-85. "We will compromise no more. Stephen Owen has failed in his mandate. He has not done the job that you [Mike Harcourt] have asked him to do…Our communities have suffered enough."

One of the most troubling aspects of the CORE report for the IWA was that it contained only a muted promise that government would commit a specific level of funding to a transition program that would create new jobs. It was becoming clear that a similar failure could occur in the Cariboo-Chilcotin and Kootenays CORE processes.

Ultimately, the government set aside the CORE recommendations in favour of regional land-use plans. On Vancouver Island, the plan proposed to replace CORE was still not to the IWA's liking. "[It] imposes compromise and will mean additional hardship for woodworkers," argued Gerry Stoney. In the Cariboo-Chilcotin region, a new plan was developed, and Premier Harcourt vowed, again, that no jobs would be lost as a result. The IWA was closely involved in drawing up the new arrangements, but remained skeptical about the government's willingness to see it through. IWA Canada fourth vice-president Harvey Arcand predicted, "It's going to take a lot of political will on

ROTTEN TO THE CORE

**In March 1994, 20,000 union members and community supporters showed their opposition to CORE's Vancouver Island land-use plan.**
IWA ARCHIVES

MEDIA FRENZY

IWA president Dave Haggard speaks to the media during the Greenpeace blockade.

IWA ARCHIVES

# David Versus Goliath

AS THE SUMMER "protest season" came around in June 1997, Greenpeace was on a roll. To support its campaign to preserve the "Great Bear Rain Forest" – the whole central Coast of BC – the green group planned protests up and down the Coast.

But Greenpeacers didn't count on the determined opposition of IWA members, their families, and their communities.

Greenpeace was founded in a Vancouver church basement in 1971, but the environmental group had long since moved to its European stronghold of Amsterdam by the time the summer of 1997 began. In the previous decade, Greenpeace had played a key role in the protests, blockades, and boycotts that rocked the coastal forest industry. Although the green group loved to play the role of "David" to the alleged "Goliath" of Coast forest companies, in reality it was itself a multinational lobby group, displaying clear disregard for small groups of working people that stood in its way. Until it met up with a real "David."

In June 1997, Dave Haggard was the newly minted president of IWA Canada. When the union was tipped by old friend Jack Munro that two Greenpeace protest vessels would be docked in Vancouver on their way to blockade loggers in the mid-Coast region, Haggard and other IWA leaders made a quick decision. On 28 June, an information picket line went up around one of the Greenpeace boats, the *Arctic Sunrise*. Four days later, while television cameras rolled, Barry King of Local 1-3567 banged home the boom chain that made sure the *Sunrise* and the smaller *Moby Dick* weren't going anywhere.

Greenpeace howled in vain. The union's 24-hour picket line was honoured by the long-shoremen's, fishermen's and pilots' unions. Haggard, Harvey Arcand, and other IWA representatives took the opportunity to tell the media the union's point of view, and suddenly the tide of public opinion was shifting in favour of working people and forest-based communities on the Coast in a way that it had not turned since before the protests at Clayoquot Sound in 1993.

Haggard told Greenpeace Canada executive director Jean Moffat in a television debate, "The issue is a corporation imposing its will on our members and their families." He suggested Greenpeace should take part in land-use negotiations, not put workers out of their jobs.

"Greenpeace wasn't too goddamn happy about what we did to hold them on the docks in Vancouver," Haggard told reporters. "They're a bunch of hypocrites who blockade our members from going to work and then they scream when we do the same thing…Every time Greenpeace looks over its shoulder, IWA Canada will be there, ready to take action."

And so it was, throughout the summer of 1997. Even though Greenpeace ultimately staged a 4 July illegal getaway, without the benefit of the pilots required to guide them out of port, its troubles were not over.

That same month, IWA members spearheaded a community blockade aimed at keeping protesters out of a contested logging area north of Squamish. After four weeks, Local 2171 third vice-president Ken Bayers claimed victory, noting the union's pride in the people who worked the barricades. "We are a community. This wasn't just loggers, there was everybody from all walks of life."

Greenpeace protesters also received a rude awakening from First Nations groups. When the Greenpeace group arrived on the central Coast, Kitasoo Nation leader Percy Starr first read the riot act to Greenpeace leader Tzeporah Berman and firmly asked her to move her protest. Then several coastal communities declared themselves "Greenpeace-free zones," refusing the protest boats a friendly harbour or services. In August, some Greenpeace members hung a banner on a boom of pulp logs near Duncan, BC. Workers on board sprayed them with water. Finally, Greenpeace and other protest groups were taken to court by Local 2171, which sought lost wages for union members blockaded off the job on Roderick Island.

All in all, a bad year in BC for the greens. Berman didn't know how right she was when she admitted to IWA Canada environment director Kim Pollock in June that it was a mistake not to consult the union before launching the protest season on the Coast. ☐

❋

GOTCHA, GREENPEACE!

The IWA garnered international media attention after it captured two Greenpeace vessels in Vancouver in July 1997.

IWA ARCHIVES

behalf of the politicians in the province to make the bureaucracy hold this deal up." Largely as a result of the efforts of Arcand and Local 1-425 president Wade Fisher, however, the Cariboo-Chilcotin deal turned out to be a workable land-use compromise.

In the west and east Kootenays, new land-use plans were drawn up, but the government would not commit to provide funding for retraining workers who lost their jobs. "Without that assurance," said IWA Canada third vice-president Warren Ulley, "we can't commit to any land-use plan that puts our people out of work." The failure of the process to adequately address workers' needs was a major disappointment after the promise it seemed to hold earlier in the decade.

While the CORE process was stumbling, a new initiative was underway: the development and implementation of a Forest Practices Code. The IWA was consulted during its development, and the Code became law in June 1995. It was intended to rectify the poor logging practices many companies had followed during the years of the Social Credit government's laissez-faire forest management, and it addressed many concerns the IWA had expressed over the

years in its own forest policy statements. Clive Pemberton, an IWA member and camp chairman at Kennedy Lake on Vancouver Island, observed that there had been at least 15 years of bad logging practices and that the Forest Practices Code could not come soon enough.

A 1996 report on the Code's effectiveness found there was over 90 percent compliance by companies licensed to harvest timber, a sound achievement given the size and complexity of the new forest management law embedded in the Code. Nonetheless, the IWA had serious concerns about how the provincial government's environmental policies, including the Code, would affect the jobs of its members. A government report on the Vancouver Forest Region (which covers most of the British Columbia Coast from the Fraser Valley to the Queen Charlotte Islands) showed that as many as 4,000 jobs in the region were threatened by the combination of the Forest Practices Code, Protected Areas Strategy, and Timber Supply Review initiatives. The report warned that due to these programs, numerous plants and mills would face shutdowns because of sharp reductions in timber harvesting.

The IWA's concern about the impact of the government's land-use decisions and forest policy was well-founded. Perhaps the most significant program launched by the NDP government was Forest Renewal BC (FRBC), a Crown corporation with the task of making sure the province's forests were managed in a sustainable fashion, both economically and ecologically. A key aspect of the FRBC plan was to ensure employment for woodworkers, with retraining for those who lost their jobs. When FRBC was set up in April 1994, the recession of the early 1990s had subsided and lumber prices were high. FRBC intended to spend $2 billion on the forest economy over the next five

## When the Going Gets Tough, The Tough Get Countervails

"COUNTERVAILS" SEEMED TO BE the watchword of the US softwood lumber industry throughout the 1980s and 90s. Whenever US firms lost ground in competition for the American domestic market, they demanded countervailing tariffs to offset the advantage Canadian lumber producers allegedly received from government "subsidies."

In 1983, the US Commerce Department found that Canadian policy did not constitute a counter-vailable subsidy to lumber manufacturers in

HEADED FOR THE STATES?

American trade actions against lumber shipments from Canada remain a problem for the forest industry – and for workers who lose their jobs when export markets contract.

IWA ARCHIVES

Canada. But after Canada's share of the US market rose again in the mid-80s, the US coalition sought protection from "unfair" lumber competition once more. The IWA and other Canadian players pointed out that Canadian mills had been made increasingly efficient and the Canadian dollar had been significantly devalued, thus making Canadian lumber cheaper to produce and cheaper for Americans to buy, but this time the Commerce Department ruled in favour of the US industry. It applied a 15 percent duty to all softwood lumber exports from Canada to the US; a later compromise changed the duty to an export tax, which ensured the money collected stayed in Canada.

The IWA was virtually alone in urging the government to negotiate rather than fight an increasingly protectionist American administration, Congress, and industry. "We are still convinced that had we negotiated earlier we could have got off with less of a countervail – perhaps as low as 10 percent," Jack Munro said.

That wasn't the end of the fight, though. In September 1991, Canada notified the US government it would cancel the agreement imposing the export tax. US producers quickly demanded another countervail.

IWA-Canada was involved in lobbying efforts that won a reduction in the countervailing duty from a preliminary ruling that added 14.5 percent to the original 15 percent tariff, down to an additional 6.5 percent. It was only after a series of appeals and legal challenges that two dispute settlement appeal panels set up under the Canada-US Free Trade Agreement ruled that the Canadian industry was not guilty of subsidizing lumber exports to the US.

"Winning the countervailing duty case was an important step in convincing the BC industry it could afford to pay for substantial increases in compensation to IWA members, and that victory has dramatically increased the profitability of prairie and eastern Canadian sawmillers, as well," national officers reported to the 1994 convention.

But the Americans were soon back at it. With Canada's share of the US lumber market rising, the coalition raised another countervail alarm. This time negotiations between industry and governments led to a quota system for Canadian lumber. Under the March 1996 Canada-US Softwood Lumber Quota Agreement, duty-free Canadian exports to the US were capped at 14.7 billion board feet. After that, producers in the four major producing provinces – BC, Alberta, Ontario, and Quebec – were assessed a graduated series of penalty fees.

The agreement was fraught with problems. Canadian exports continued to rise, particularly from provinces not covered by quotas. For a variety of reasons, many firms did not obtain a quota or get enough of a quota. Companies were forced to highball near the end of the "quota year" or lay workers off when a quota was exhausted.

When a sawmill operated by J.S. Jones Timber in Boston Bar, BC, was threatened with closure due to lack of timber in late 1999, IWA president Dave Haggard had had enough. He called on the Canadian government to let the deal lapse when it came due in 2001.

"It's simply not fair," he stated. "The current deal treats producers in various parts of Canada differently, rather than creating a level playing field and allowing free and fair competition. Worse, the system for allocating quota is completely arbitrary."

The Canadian forest industry's struggle to gain access to the American market has been of fundamental importance to the well-being of IWA members across the country. The union has played a prominent role in researching and developing policy positions to ensure that the Canadian forest industry retains its historical importance on world lumber markets and that IWA members continue to benefit from a healthy, vibrant industry. It seems a certainty that the struggle for US access will continue to be a concern for the IWA in the years to come.

years, money that would be raised by doubling the stumpage fees lumber companies paid to the government in return for the timber they harvested from public land. Industry representatives, environmentalists, and the IWA all praised the government for undertaking to ensure the viability of forest lands and jobs in BC. Gerry Stoney commented, "In the past, previous governments talked about special funds and designated spending in the forest sector, but these were only minor items within a budget. They would change each new fiscal year, each new cabinet shuffle, and each new reorganization within a ministry." The FRBC, said Stoney, looked like it would change that pattern and give a new permanence and continuity to guarantee a future for the forest industry. Because FRBC planned to build up funds from increased stumpage rates, it should be able to survive economic downturns in the industry.

However, concerns about FRBC emerged in 1996 when the board of the Crown corporation recommended that it return surplus funds to the provincial treasury. Gerry Stoney assessed the impact of this decision:

> We are disappointed with the Board's decision because we think it doesn't address the real issue of putting our members to work improving our forests.
>
> That's been our priority all the way along; we want to get FRBC projects up and running as quickly as possible and have IWA members preferentially trained and dispatched to do that work. To date, that hasn't happened; forest companies have been far too slow in putting forward projects and government ministries have been just as slow in giving approval to the proposals that have been submitted. Meanwhile, our members are working less.

The IWA was also frustrated with employer indifference to the success of FRBC. Local 1-71 president Darrel Wong bluntly noted that the fundamental problem was employers having too much control over the workings of FRBC. "That's the real problem...the applications are being made and the forest industry isn't working with the IWA," he noted.

FRBC's ability to survive economic downturns was further eroded in 1997 with the collapse of the Asian economy. BC, and particularly the Coast industry, relied heavily on the Asian market, so this was a severe blow to sales. American companies that had previously supplied the Asian markets started oversupplying the American market, driving prices and sales even lower. Insufficient access to the American market as a result of the Canada-US Softwood Lumber Quota Agreement complicated matters further, as did the fact that the BC industry was saddled with high wood costs due to the FRBC "super-stumpage" fees and the increased costs emanating from compliance with the Forest Products Code.

*'It's about time we [said] to forest companies that if you want access to the trees that the people of British Columbia own, then you have an obligation to meet these job targets as well.'*

BIG PLANS

IWA leader Gerry
Stoney endorses Forest
Renewal BC in 1994.
FRBC was set up by the
provincial government
to ensure the viability
of forest lands and jobs
in BC.

IWA ARCHIVES

Among the many casualties of the Asian downturn was another forest industry jobs initiative launched by the government only weeks before the Asian-induced recession struck the economy. The Jobs and Timber Accord was spearheaded by Premier Glen Clark after the NDP won re-election in 1996. Addressing the IWA-Canada convention that November, Clark spoke of the need for a new "social contract" in the woods. "It's about time we started setting targets for jobs," said Clark, "to say to forest companies that if you want access to the trees that the people of British Columbia own, then you have an obligation to meet these job targets as well…The government has to be more socially responsible than they have been in the past. We have to start putting strings attached to public timber, and we have to make sure we don't have a bias in the system towards more revenue, that's as a short-run bias, but a bias that generates more jobs so people can pay more taxes, so that you can work and your families can support each other and communities are healthy, and government will get more money in the long run in any event."

To facilitate secondary and value-added manufacturers, the government required large companies on the Coast to sell 18 percent of the wood they cut to these manufacturers at fair market prices. In the Interior, large companies were mandated to sell 16 percent of their lumber to smaller operations. "One of the major problems that smaller operators face is actually getting a hold of wood they can do something with," commented IWA president Dave Haggard

SO CLOSE, YET SO FAR

**Dave Haggard greeted the NDP's Jobs and Timber Accord, introduced by Premier Glen Clark (left) in 1997, just as markets for forest products, especially in Asia, were starting to collapse.**

PHOTO COURTESY
CHUCK NISBETT

(who succeeded Gerry Stoney in 1996). "They want to make value-added products, and more often than not, the big companies export semi-processed wood and lumber which bypasses them."

The Jobs and Timber Accord set a target of creating 21,000 jobs by the year 2000. By the time it was launched in June 1997, however, two months after the Asian economic collapse, it was basically hamstrung as a result of the forest industry recession. The inability of the Jobs and Timber Accord to become an established working policy was a deep disappointment for the union, as it was a concrete example of the kind of value-added incentives to the industry that the IWA had been calling for since 1937.

Though not as successful as hoped, the FRBC/Jobs and Timber Accord initiatives did create some employment for forest workers. New Forest Opportunities (New Forest) is an FRBC-funded company that started operations in 1998. Without the IWA, it is doubtful that New Forest would exist; its goal of putting workers back to work renewing forest lands has been IWA policy for years. New Forest employed hundreds of woodworkers who had been displaced from the industry over the previous years. It focused on enhanced forestry projects, such as juvenile spacing, pruning, and brushing activities. All its employees are IWA members, and the improvement in wages and working conditions under a union contract was genuinely appreciated by many long-time silviculture workers. "For the first time in 18 seasons [years] of silvicultural work, it felt really good to know that there was a place to address concerns and grievances too, and it was clear that the contractor was behaving accordingly," said new IWA member Ingmar Lee. By late 1999, New Forest had employed more than 1,600 workers on its projects.

NEW UNION JOBS

New Forest
Opportunities
was – and is – one
of FRBC's success
stories. By late 1999
it had got more
than 1,600 workers
back on the job,
mostly in
silviculture.

IWA LOCAL 363 ARCHIVES

New Forest was also responsible for another FRBC employment success story: the Forest Worker Transition Program (FWTP). This was the provincial government's response to unemployment in the forest industry stemming from the recession of the late 1990s. Forest Worker Transition Centres provided services to more than 10,000 displaced forest workers, aiding them in their search for new employment opportunities. "In some cases, these centres are the only meaningful safety net that workers could rely on," observed Dave Haggard. The Forest Worker Transition Program concluded in May 2000.

In September 1999, Haggard stated that the FRBC program had to be reworked to produce better results in terms of creating steady, well-paying jobs both on the Coast and in the Interior. Haggard pointed out that too many of the FRBC jobs were short-term, low-paying "welfare jobs" with little future for workers and their families. But despite FRBC's flaws, the IWA would like to see it continued. The success of New Forest is a success the IWA believes can be built upon. IWA forest policy recognizes that it is crucial for the health of the forest industry to have workers brought back into the forest, even if they have been displaced from their traditional jobs.

## Diversity, Solidarity, and a Proud Legacy

As the IWA moved through the challenges, successes, and upheavals of the 1980s and 1990s, it kept a wary eye on the future. The union had always been mindful of the inevitability and necessity of technological change in the forest industry, and its subsequent impact on the IWA membership rolls. As the forest industry modernized and changed, the union began to pursue new members beyond its traditional jurisdiction. Members adopted an organizing-and-growth strategy at the union's 1997 convention, with the lofty goal of doubling the union's membership. As part of this strategy, 25 percent of the per capita fees paid to the National Office by the various locals were earmarked for organizing purposes. "The IWA is interested in organizing anyone in this country who walks, talks, and looks like a worker," said Dave Haggard.

In 2000, approximately 32 percent of the union's 55,000 members were employed outside the primary forest industry sector. Workers in Canada represented by the IWA include: chocolate makers, civic employees, home care

### RALLY 'ROUND THE FLAG

**In 1995, Local 1-423 became the first IWA local to fly a national union flag on company property. Pictured from left to right are Randy Rudolph, Dave Briscoe, Ed Zilowsky, Troi Caldwell (local president), Gordon Kirby, and Gerry Stoney (national president).**

IWA ARCHIVES

## IWA Canada: A Renowned Name Takes on New Meaning

WHEN THE CANADIAN UNION was formed in 1987, members felt strongly that it should keep the initials "IWA." But "International Woodworkers of America-Canada" did not make sense, so the union remained simply IWA-Canada. The running joke at the time was "The IWA doesn't stand for anything."

However, in 1994, IWA-Canada members voted to keep the old initials but change the union's name. Delegates to the 1994 convention voted unanimously to rechristen the union the

Industrial, Wood, and Allied Workers of Canada (IWA Canada). With a membership employed in increasingly diverse industries and a desire to continue recognizing the union as a Canadian entity, IWA Canada's new name was both mindful of the past and looking to the future.

As part of the International Woodworkers of America from 1937 to 1987, the IWA in Canada had a dynamic history, and the retention of the old union's initials paid homage to that history. While the legacy and symbolic identity of the original IWA lived on in the Canadian union, in 1994 the IWA name disappeared in the United States as it merged with the International Association of Machinists and Aerospace Workers. ☐

❈

## Fifty Years Later: A Truce Between Whites and Reds

AT THE IWA CANADA convention held in September 1998, delegates unanimously endorsed a resolution that abolished the IWA's "errant members" list. "Errant members" were those banned from the union after the 1948 split because of their support of communism – thousands of workers had been banned from membership in the union they had helped build.

National secretary-treasurer Terry Smith noted that it took 50 years to get such a resolution passed because earlier attempts would have resulted in bitter memories being dredged up and irresolvable fights on the convention floor. National president Dave Haggard commented, "I really believe that this resolution is far, far overdue. They were workers and they were IWA members and they helped build this union."

Maurice Rush, a former leader of the Communist Party in British Columbia, was present at the 1998 convention and spoke about the 1948 split. Rush reiterated that the split "was a mistake. Separation did not strengthen the workers. What it did was that it divided the workers and weakened them in their struggle with the employer." Local 363 president Sy Pederson was a former

THE END OF THE ERRANT MEMBERS LIST
At the union's 1998 convention, President Dave Haggard shakes hands with Maurice Rush, former leader of the Communist Party in BC. Rush returned Local 1-85's original charter, missing since the red-white split in 1948.
IWA ARCHIVES

Communist Party member attending the convention. He commented that "the debate was never about whether workers...should have a union or representation. That was given and that was common ground." Pederson suggested that the real debate was concerned with the question of whether or not capitalism could be reformed and whether the working class could prosper under capitalism.

In a brief ceremony, Rush returned the original IWA charter for Port Alberni Local 1-85 to IWA Canada. The original charter had been removed from the union office by red bloc leaders after the 1948 split and had last been cared for by Dave Pritchett, the grandson of Harold Pritchett. Harold Pritchett, who continued to make his living as a sawyer and shingle weaver after the collapse of the WIUC, applied on several occasions for reinstatement as a member of the union, but was never allowed back in to the IWA. □

300

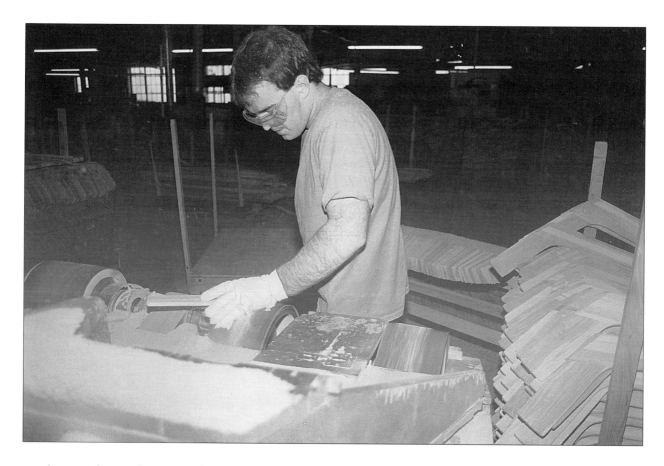

workers, and greenhouse workers in BC; trailer manufacturers in Alberta; civic workers in Saskatchewan; hotel workers in Manitoba; hockey-stick makers (at the only unionized Nike plant in the world) and supermarket workers in Ontario; firehose makers in Quebec; and co-operative dairy workers in New Brunswick.

The union's strong commitment to organize the unorganized bodes well for its success in the future. The IWA's corresponding commitment to the solidarity of all working people has led it to initiate important programs with workers from around the world. Union officers and members have travelled widely to share their ideas and experiences in the interests of international working-class solidarity.

The IWA was founded in 1937 with the awareness that capital knew no borders and that Canadian and American workers had everything to gain by uniting their struggles. IWA members regularly celebrated International Workers Day on May 1 in the union's formative years, and denounced the fascist forces in Europe as a threat to workers around the world. For decades, the union fought on behalf of exploited woodworkers of all races in the American South. District 1's Joe Miyazawa spent six months in 1956 surveying workers'

**JUST UNIONIZE IT!**

A hockey stick plant in Cambridge, Ontario, certified by Local 500, is the only unionized Nike plant in the world.

IWA ARCHIVES

In October 1999, IWA Local 1000 president Joe da Costa (far right) joined Confederación Nacional de Traba-jadores Forestales de Chile members and supporters at a rally in Concepción, Chile.

IWA ARCHIVES

conditions in Japan, and Fijian timber workers interested in setting up a union in their homeland contacted Local 1-85 for advice. Officer Maurice Corbeil responded in detail. District 1 president Joe Morris rose through the ranks of the Canadian labour movement to be appointed head of the International Labor Organization.

IWA conventions regularly dealt with the major foreign policy issues of the day. Members supported calls for nuclear disarmament, denounced the Vietnam War before it became fashionable to do so, denounced American embargoes against Cuba, and pledged support to Third World woodworkers. Trade unionists from Bulgaria and the Soviet Union held exchanges with IWA members. As this chapter of the IWA's history is being written, IWA Canada is actively involved in an international solidarity campaign, providing support, education, and information to the National Confederation of Forest Workers of Chile.

The IWA and its members experienced many ups and downs as they fought to make life better for themselves, their communities, and the world around them throughout the twentieth century. From its earliest days, union members and officials maintained a strong commitment to the basic princi-ples of democratic trade unionism – a union run by and for the rank and file.

The history of the IWA is a powerful testament to the fundamental impor-

tance of working-class solidarity. The capitalist economic system has always provoked working people to challenge the irrational and inhuman qualities of capital's drive for profit. From Blubber Bay to Newfoundland to Slave Lake, the IWA has been a wellspring of communal strength for workers who faced indignities and injustice at the hands of an economic system determined to exploit them. The IWA's historical commitment to the fight for social and economic justice is only the beginning of the story, however. That story continues to be written daily in a wide range of workplaces, by diverse groups of workers from a variety of backgrounds. These people are united by a common dream – a dream that drove the early builders of the union, and a dream that drives IWA members and activists today: the dream that working men and women should be able to hope for a better future and, working together, take steps right now to achieve it.

SOLIDARIDAD INTERNACIONAL

In March 2000, Local 2693 member Rolando Quintul (centre) conducted the IWA's first education course for Chilean unionists at the CTF-IWA Education Centre in Concepción, Chile.
IWA ARCHIVES

# Reflections On Our Past… And Our Future

AGAINST THE ODDS, our union was built at the height of the Great Depression, largely by dedicated organizers who gave selflessly and who were guided by a basic principle: working people deserve better workplaces and a just society.

In the post-World War II world, our union took advantage of good economic times to win better, more secure collective agreements and to work tirelessly for improvements in health, safety, and working conditions.

From the mid-1970s, we faced new challenges: the economic downturn, resulting in the first serious recessions since the 1930s; the challenge of technological change; the growth of the preservationist movement; and the threat of contracting out, culminating in the crucial 1986 strike.

Since 1997, our union has embarked on some new directions. Our national Organizing and Growth Strategy aims to vastly increase our membership, both within and outside the traditional wood sector and in every region of Canada. Our Negotiated Partnership Program aims at developing new relations with companies. Through our International Solidarity Fund program we are forging new links with workers outside Canada. This will help us deal with transnational companies in a globalized economy. We are challenging industry and government to develop new products and reach new markets. More than ever, we need to deal with the effects on our members of forces from outside. To do that, we need to understand change and learn to work proactively, not just in response to events.

Our history, of course, remains unfinished. As a union we have succeeded in negotiating and enforcing excellent collective agreements. We have won benefits and working standards that our grandparents and great-grandparents could only dream about. We have expanded our membership and maintained it in the face of determined opposition from hostile companies and governments. We have overcome grievous internal splits and divisions.

But reading about the past is not enough. We have to learn from it, absorb its lessons, and move on. That's the real challenge of history.

Today, we still face serious obstacles. And as we deal with them, we can learn mightily from our past. We need, for instance, to recover some of the social activism and union pride that motivated our founders and predecessors.

We need to rekindle the sense that the union is "us," that the union is only as strong as its members. Remember: although history is partly about "leaders," it is even more about the hundreds and thousands of working people who, moved by that dream of a better future, walked on picket lines; risked firing, beatings, or jail to face down injustice or ill-treatment; wrote resolutions or signed petitions; called or attended meetings; spoke out in their communities; held rallies; and talked, argued, and reasoned their fellow workers into the union way. These are the real heroes of our history. Generating this sense of activism that dares to dream is one of the biggest challenges we face in the decades to come.

We must, as well, continue the struggle to expand our union. In this, we must think big! We need to identify opportunities and persuade non-unionized workers that they would be better off in a union. And we must demonstrate that our union is a force for positive change in our workplaces and the community.

Similarly, we need to come to terms with the struggle for justice of First Nations within Canada. Land claims and treaty settlements will fundamentally affect many IWA Canada members and we need to ensure that fairness for aboriginal peoples also means fairness for workers.

We also have to think globally. Our world is shrinking in so many ways. Companies now span the globe; capital can move instantaneously from one country to another. Governments have a hard time keeping up. Increasingly, workers need to be global too. We need to expand our contacts with workers in other parts of the world so we can find out what companies are up to and so we can work together. After all, no matter where they live, working people have a lot in common. We need to co-operate more, share ideas, and learn from one another's struggles. Our challenge is to ensure that we are not all levelled down to the lowest conditions, but rather that in elevating our brothers and sisters, we protect and empower ourselves too.

Another global challenge is markets. We face heavy fights to gain and keep market access, whether it's the threat of boycott campaigns by green extremist groups, protectionist laws in the US or Japan, international standards or non-tariff barriers to trade…we can't rest on our laurels when it come to trade. Industry must be challenged to constantly develop new products, find new markets for existing products, and protect and expand existing markets. This is a challenge not just for companies but for workers. After all, without markets for our products, we all go home.

To win these struggles, our members will have to become involved and engaged in their union in new ways. This goes beyond the traditional meaning of "union education" to include full citizenship within our union for the thousands of current and future brothers and sisters who perhaps see the union as an outside force. Again, the union is "us." Working together, we can achieve great, lasting things that will ensure the history of IWA Canada, the beginning of which you hold now in your hands, goes on and on. I have great hope in the future and I hope that having read our history you will want to join in the struggle of carrying that history on.

*Dave Haggard*
*President, IWA Canada*

# Sources and Suggestions for Further Reading

The material for this book is drawn from a wide range of published, unpublished, and archival sources. Most of the books listed below are available through the public library system. The academic texts and journal articles can be found at college and university libraries. If you are unable to access these more specialized collections, local libraries can help by ordering the books and/or articles from other locations.

Craig Heron provides the best general introduction to the history of the Canadian labour movement in *The Canadian Labour Movement: A Short History* (Toronto: Lorimer, 1996); *Working-Class Experience: Rethinking the History of Canadian Labour, 1800-1991* (Toronto: McClelland & Stewart, 1992) by Bryan D. Palmer is a more comprehensive, academic work that examines all areas of the working-class past, including family relations, collective bargaining, union politics, key strikes, and the emergence of a global economy. Both works were instrumental in framing much of our analysis – Palmer in the first half of the book, Heron in the remaining chapters. Other general labour histories include: Paul Phillips, *No Power Greater: A Century of Labour in British Columbia* (Vancouver: BC Federation of Labour, 1967); Black Rose Books Editorial Collective, eds., *Quebec Labour: The Confederation of National Trade Unions Yesterday and Today* (Montreal: Black Rose, 1972); Derek Reimer, ed., *Fighting For Labour: Four Decades of Work in British Columbia, 1910-1950* (Victoria: Provincial Archives, 1978); Irving Abella, ed., *On Strike: Six Key Labour Struggles in Canada, 1919-1949* (Toronto: J. Lewis and Samuel, 1974); *Fifty Years of Labour in Algoma: Essays on Aspects of Algoma's Working-Class History* (Sault Ste. Marie, 1978); Warren Caragata, *Alberta Labour: A Heritage Untold* (Toronto: Lorimer, 1979); Gloria Montero, ed., *We Stood Together: First-Hand Accounts of Dramatic Events in Canada's Labour Past* (Toronto: Lorimer, 1979); Doug Smith, *Let Us Rise: An Illustrated History of the Manitoba Labour Movement* (Vancouver: New Star, 1985); Bill Gillespie, *A Class Act: An Illustrated History of the Labour Movement in Newfoundland and Labrador* (St. John's: Newfoundland and Labrador Federation of Labour, 1986); Laurel Sefton MacDowell and Ian Radforth, eds., *Canadian Working-Class History: Selected Readings* (Toronto: Canadian Scholars' Press, 1992).

The most readable, interesting, and comprehensive history of loggers and logging in Canada is Donald MacKay's *The Lumberjacks* (Toronto: McGraw-

Hill Ryerson, 1978); as noted in the text, MacKay's book was an important resource for us on the early years of logging in Canada. For the West Coast, the best place to start is with Ken Drushka's numerous publications such as *Tie Hackers to Timber Harvesters* (Madeira Park: Harbour, 1998). Other sources that detail the development of the lumber industry in BC include Patricia Marchak, *Green Gold: The Forest Industry in British Columbia* (Vancouver: UBC Press, 1983), Marchak's *Falldown: Forest Policy in BC* (Vancouver: David Suzuki Foundation, 1999), and Ken Bernsohn, *Cutting Up the North: The History of the Forest Industry in the Northern Interior* (North Vancouver: Hancock House, 1981). Most of our analysis of Northern Ontario is drawn from Ian Radforth, *Bushworkers and Bosses: Logging in Northern Ontario, 1900-1980* (Toronto: University of Toronto, 1987). As its title implies, *More Deadly Than War: Pacific Coast Logging, 1827 to 1981* (New York: Garland, 1985) by Andrew Mason Prouty critically examines occupational health and safety issues in the West Coast lumber industry. Richard Rajala tackles the issue of technological change in the forest industry between 1880 and 1930 in "The Forest as Factory: Technological Change and Worker Control in the West Coast Logging Industry, 1880-1930," *Labour/Le Travail* 32 (Fall 1993), pp. 73-104, and "Bill and the Boss: Labor Protest, Technological Change, and the Transformation of the West Coast Logging Camp, 1890-1930," *Journal of Forest History* 33 (October 1989), pp. 168-79.

Not surprisingly, some of the best sources were by workers themselves. Bus Griffiths, a former logger and commercial fisherman, combines his knowledge of the woods with a fondness for storytelling in *Now You're Logging* (Madeira Park: Harbour, 1978), an exceptionally well-drawn comic strip that depicts logging in the "old days." Joe Garner's *Never Chop Your Rope: A Story of British Columbia Logging and the People Who Logged* (Nanaimo: Cinnibar, 1988) is based on interviews with bosses and workers alike. See also volumes 3 and 6 of *Raincoast Chronicles* (Madeira Park: Harbour, 1972, 1976), a popular history magazine edited by Howard White, and an excellent collection of interviews, poetry, and prose about logging entitled *Men of the Forest* (Victoria: Provincial Archives, 1977), edited by David Day. Peter H. Harrison's "Life in a Logging Camp," *BC Studies* 54 (Summer 1982), provides a hands-on look at the day-to-day existence of loggers in the Queen Charlotte Islands.

The IWA has been the focus of many books, articles, and master's and doctoral theses – all of which were consulted in the preparation of this book. Clay Perry's "A History of the IWA," a series of articles that ran in the *Lumber Worker* from November 1995 to June 1998, provides an accessible, even-handed, and comprehensive look at the IWA. Based on interviews conducted by the author with many of the founders of the union, including Arne Johnson, Hjalmar Bergren, Edna Brown, and John McCuish, Myrtle Bergren's *Tough Timber: The Loggers of British Columbia* (Toronto: Progress Books, 1967) is a lively account of the IWA's history in BC to the 1950s; it is also one of the few sources that discusses the role of working women in the formation of the union. Other introductory material includes Jerry Lembcke's and William Tattam's *One Union In Wood: A Political History of the International Woodworkers of America* (Madeira Park/New York: Harbour/International, 1984), one of the few sources that looks at the history of the IWA in both the United States and Canada; this book is sympathetic to the communist founders of the union. In contrast, the pamphlet *The IWA in British Columbia* (Vancouver, 1971) by Grant MacNeil, which was published by the IWA, is written from a decidedly anti-communist bent. Irving Abella dedicates one chapter of his *Nationalism, Communism, and Canadian Labour: The CIO, The Communist Party, and the Canadian Congress of Labour, 1935-1956* (Toronto: University of Toronto, 1973) to the IWA. Several biographies and autobiographies were also important to this study, including Jack Munro with Jane O'Hara, *Union Jack: Labour Leader Jack Munro* (Vancouver: Douglas & McIntyre, 1988), Cyril W. Strong, *My Life as a Newfoundland Union Organizer* (St. John's: Canadian Committee on Labour History, 1987), David Lewis, *The Good Fight: Political Memoirs, 1909-1958* (Toronto: Macmillan, 1981), John Stanton, *Never Say Die: The Life and Times of John Stanton, A Pioneer Labour Lawyer* (Ottawa: Steel Rail, 1987), and Richard Gwyn, *Smallwood: The Unlikely Revolutionary* (Toronto: McClelland & Stewart, 1999).

Several writers have examined the history of the IWA on a local level, usually as part of a wider analysis of the lumber industry in a specific area of British Columbia. Ken Bernsohn's *Slabs, Scabs, and Skidders: A History of the IWA in the Central Interior* (Prince George: IWA Local 1-424, 1978) is a punchy, first-hand account of this history. Richard Rajala analyses the Lake Cowichan district in *The Legacy and the Challenge: A Century of the Forest Industry at Cowichan Lake* (Lake Cowichan: Lake Cowichan Heritage Advisory Committee, 1993). See also Gordon Hak, "On the Fringes: Capital and Labour in Prince George and Port Alberni Forest Districts, British Columbia, 1910-1939" (PhD Thesis, Department of History, Simon Fraser University, 1986); Mary Lillian McRoberts, "The Emergence of a Corporate Structure in the Williams Lake Lumber Industry, 1947-1956" (MA Thesis, Department of History, University of Victoria, 1986); Richard Rajala, "The Rude Science: A Social History of West Coast Logging, 1890-1930" (MA Thesis, Department of History, University of Victoria, 1987); Ann Philomena

Howard, "Working in 'the Central Bank of British Columbia': Workers, Technological Change, and Skill Levels in the Logging Industry of Prince George" (Honours Essay, Department of History, University of Victoria, 1990).

Our analysis of the IWA's "radical roots" is based on the following books and articles. Mark Leier, *Where the Fraser River Flows: The Industrial Workers of the World in British Columbia* (Vancouver: New Star, 1990) and *Rebel Life: The Life and Times of Robert Gosden, Revolutionary, Mystic, Labour Spy* (Vancouver: New Star, 1999) are the best, most accessible books on the Wobblies in British Columbia; the latter is also a valuable guide to writing labour history. J. Peter Campbell looks at the IWW in Ontario in "The Cult of Spontaneity: Finnish-Canadian Bushworkers and the Industrial Workers of the World in Northern Ontario, 1919-1934," *Labour/Le Travail* 41 (Spring 1998), pp. 117-46. *Reformers, Rebels, and Revolutionaries: The Western Canadian Radical Movement, 1899-1919* (Toronto: University of Toronto, 1977) by A. Ross McCormack, *Radical Heritage: Labor, Socialism, and Reform in Washington and British Columbia* (Seattle: University of Washington, 1979) by Carlos Schwantes, and *Fools and Wise Men: The Rise and Fall of the One Big Union* (Toronto: McGraw-Hill Ryerson, 1973) by David J. Bercuson examine other radical organizations such as the Socialist Party of Canada and the One Big Union. Other works that were crucial to our analysis were Gregory S. Kealey, "1919: The Canadian Labour Revolt," *Labour/Le Travail* 13 (Spring 1984), pp. 11-44, and Kealey's "State Repression of Labour and the Left in Canada, 1914-1920: The Impact of the First World War," *Canadian Historical Review* 73:3 (September 1992), pp. 281-314, and Craig Heron, ed., *The Workers' Revolt in Canada, 1917-1925* (Toronto: University of Toronto, 1998).

Gordon Hak's articles "'Line Up or Roll Up: The Lumber Workers Industrial Union in the Prince George District," *BC Studies 86* (Summer 1990), pp. 57-74; "British Columbia Loggers and the Lumber Workers Industrial Union, 1919-1922," *Labour/Le Travail* 23 (Spring 1989), pp. 67-90; and "The Socialist and Labourist Impulse in Small Town British Columbia: Port Alberni and Prince George, 1911-1933," *Canadian Historical Review* 70:4 (December 1989), pp. 519-42 provided the basis for our assessment of the LWIU in BC. Bruce Magnuson's *The Untold Story of Ontario's Bushworkers: A Political Memoir* (Toronto: Progress Books, 1990), a lively account of activism in northern Ontario, and Radforth's more academic *Bushworkers and Bosses* were the key sources for the LWIU and Lumber and Saw in Ontario. *Reesor Siding: A Labour Dispute in Northern Ontario* by Martin Champoux framed our discussion of that terrible event; the pamphlet was translated from its original French by Norm Rivard, president of Local 2995.

The activities of the Communist Party of Canada, discussed at length in Chapters 2, 3, and 4, are detailed in the following books and articles: Heron's and Palmer's general readers; Ian Angus, *Canadian Bolsheviks: The Early Years of the Communist Party of Canada* (Montreal: Vanguard, 1981); Victor Howard, *"We Were the Salt of the Earth!": The On-to-Ottawa Trek and the Regina Riot* (Regina: Canadian Plains Research Centre, 1985); John Kolasky, *Shattered Illusions: The History of Ukrainian Pro-Communist Organizations in Canada* (Toronto: PMA Books, 1979); John Manley, "Canadian Communists, Revolutionary Unionism, and the 'Third Period': The Workers Unity League, 1929-1935," Canadian Historical Association, *Journal* (1994), pp. 167-91; Tom McEwen, *The Forge Glows Red: From Blacksmith to Revolutionary* (Toronto: Progress Books, 1974); Jeanne Myers, "Ethnicity and Class Conflict in Fraser Mills/Maillardville: The Strike of 1931" (MA Thesis, Department of History, Simon Fraser University, 1982); and Gordon Hak, "The Communists and the Unemployed in the Prince George District, 1930-1935," *BC Studies* 68 (Winter 1985-86), pp. 45-61. Lorne Brown's *When Freedom Was Lost* (Montreal: Black Rose, 1987), in particular, informed our take on the Depression, the Communist Party, and the struggle for "work and wages." The chapters on the "emergence of the IWA" and its subsequent "breakthrough" in the post-war period are based on Andrew Parnaby's "'We'll Hang All Policemen From a Sour Apple Tree!': Class, Law, and the Politics of State Power in the Blubber Bay Strike of 1938-1939" (MA Thesis, Department of History, Simon Fraser University, 1995) and Stephen Gray's "Woodworkers and Legitimacy: The IWA in Canada, 1937-1957" (PhD Thesis, Department of History, Simon Fraser University, 1989). *The Canadian Labour Movement* by Heron, *Working-Class Experience* by Palmer, and *Nationalism, Communism and Canadian Labour* by Abella formed the basis of our general understanding of the CIO and the Cold War. The history of this industrial union centre in Canada has yet to be written; those interested in this topic should consult *The CIO, 1935-1955* (Chapel Hill: University of North Carolina, 1995) by Robert H. Zieger, a comprehensive look at the CIO in the United States.

The history of women in the IWA, and in industrial unions more generally, has also been neglected. *Tough Timber* examines the founding of the IWA Ladies' Auxiliary, a development pursued in greater detail in Sara Diamond's "A Union Man's Wife: The Ladies' Auxiliary Movement in the IWA, the Lake Cowichan Experience" in Barbara K. Latham and Roberta J. Pazdro, eds., *Not Just Pin Money: Selected Essays on the History of Women's Work in British Columbia* (Victoria: Camosun College Press, 1984). Our section on working women and World War II is based on Susanne Klausen's article "The Plywood

Girls: Women and Gender Ideology at the Port Alberni Plywood Plant, 1942-1991," *Labour/Le Travail* 41 (Spring 1998), pp. 199-236, and a documentary by the same name. The "Herstory" sidebar is drawn from oral history interviews, convention proceedings, and back issues of the *Lumber Worker*. For more on women in the labour movement consult: Linda Kealey, *Enlisting Women for the Cause: Women, Labour, and the Left in Canada, 1890-1920* (Toronto: University of Toronto, 1998); Joan Sangster *Dreams of Equality: Women on the Canadian Left, 1920-1950* (Toronto: McClelland & Stewart, 1989); Pamela Sugiman, *Labour's Dilemma: The Gender Politics of Auto Workers, 1937-1979* (Toronto: University of Toronto, 1994); and Julie White, *Sisters and Solidarity: Women and Unions in Canada* (Toronto: Thompson Educational, 1993).

Chapters 5 and 6, which cover the period from 1972 to 2000, are based primarily on oral history interviews, convention material, the *Lumber Worker*, and other material accumulated by the IWA in Vancouver. Convention proceedings and union newspapers are available from the University of British Columbia library; those who do not have access to UBC can, of course, order this material through the inter-library loans desk at a local library. Important published sources include the following books and articles. On the CCF/NDP consult Phillips, *No Power Greater;* Walter Young, *Anatomy of a Party: The National CCF, 1932-1961* (Toronto: University of Toronto, 1969); Norman Penner, *The Canadian Left: A Critical Analysis* (Toronto: Prentice-Hall Canada, 1977); David Lewis's memoirs; and Keith Archer, *Political Choices and Electoral Consequences: A Study of Organized Labour and the New Democratic Party* (Kingston and Montreal: McGill/Queen's, 1990). For a critical assessment of the IWA in the failed "Solidarity" movement see Bryan D. Palmer, *Solidarity: The Rise and Fall of An Opposition in British Columbia* (Vancouver: New Star, 1987); readers might want to contrast Palmer's assessment with the discussion provided by Jack Munro in his autobiography. Publications that look at the thorny relationship between logging and the environment could fill a small library; Jeremy Wilson's *Talk and Log: Wilderness Politics in British Columbia, 1965-1996* (Vancouver: UBC Press, 1998), a thorough, comprehensive look at environmental policy-making in BC, and Patricia Marchak's *Logging the Globe* (Montreal-Buffalo: McGill-Queen's, 1995), which examines forestry practices around the world, including BC, are a good place to start. Both books contain extensive bibliographies.

# Index

be able to speak for the IWA with one voice throughout Canada," Jack Munro had proclaimed in June 1987. In the wake of the Lumber and Saw merger, it appeared that this was indeed the case. The creation of IWA-Canada allowed the union to better focus its resources on Canadian workers and issues specific to Canadian jurisdictions. From dealing with made-in-Canada recessions to forest-use policy debates, the IWA carried on as a powerful voice for the rights of workers across Canada.